WAR

WAR

And The After Effects On Those Doing The Dirty Work Of Killing

LEITH LYMAN CUNNINGHAM

ReadersMagnet, LLC

WAR: And The After Effects On Those Doing The Dirty Work Of Killing
Copyright © 2020 by Leith Lyman Cunningham. All rights reserved.

Published in the United States of America
ISBN Paperback: 978-1-951775-44-5
ISBN eBook: 978-1-951775-45-2

All rights reserved. No part of this publication may be reproduced, stored in a retrieval system or transmitted in any way by any means, electronic, mechanical, photocopy, recording or otherwise without the prior permission of the author except as provided by USA copyright law.

The opinions expressed by the author are not necessarily those of ReadersMagnet, LLC.

ReadersMagnet, LLC
10620 Treena Street, Suite 230 | San Diego, California, 92131 USA
1.619.354.2643 | www.readersmagnet.com

Book design copyright © 2020 by ReadersMagnet, LLC. All rights reserved.
Cover design by Ericka Obando
Interior design by Shemaryl Tampus

CONTENTS

Introduction 11
All of mankind to be saved in the grand finale of things to come 14
Get or give 16
My initiation into the real world 17
A father pimps his daughter 18
Close to home grunge 19
Fingers chopped off to keep from going to Korea 21
Shooting off a wife's leg 22
Eastbound and down 24
Things are seldom as the appear on the surface 25
The lessons of life 26
Joining the army 27
Alaska, here we come 27
Troop train experience 28
War breaks out in Korea 29
Bound for Korea 30
Troop ship experience across the Pacific 31
It is always God that fills presidential or leadership positions 33
Destination: Korea 34
My close buddy Billy Magee 34
My other close combat buddy Ernie 34
Posttraumatic stress disorder 35
Weather conditions worse than the Battle of the Bulge 36

Paying the cost for peace and freedom 37
Ordered to throw a grenade 42
A spoiled generation of wimpy brats 43
Having to remove a soldier's leg 45
Put ourselves in these shoes 46
My father in World War I 47
The gut-wrenching plight of Daniel Somers 48
Awaiting me in Korea 54
My turn to fight in battle had come 55
Patriotism suddenly turns sour 55
The goon squad or gestapo enter the picture 56
No friendly faces in this crowd 56
One-way trip into hell 56
Your soul may belong to God, but your hind end belongs to Uncle Sam 57
At least now, I have been given a weapon 58
Misery 101 begins to set in 58
Let the chips fall 59
Angels rush in where fools fear to tread 59
Chocolate didn't do the job 60
I left with a feeling of relief 61
We're getting closer now 62
Securing an ammunition bearer 64
I guess you can't fix dumb 65
General Matthew B. Ridgeway takes over 66
More on the tank guard misery 67
The causes of a damaged mind 67
Love those Marine F-4U Corsair pilots 69
Back to the front 71
"Jesus Christ came to earth to be like us, that we all will be as He is." 74
Piles of dead enemy and empty artillery shells 75
The cowards among us 77
Programmed with a killer instinct 79
Chiseled in stone military rules and regulations 82
This officer had eventually saved my life 82
An effective killing machine 84
The dazzling brilliance of the military leaders 85
Here, try these on for size 86

Opening up Pandora's box 87
A little research reveals something important 89
At the days end 90
Thanking God for simple things 91
While we fight for the rights of others 91
Jim Crow, alive and well in Alabama 91
The care and concern by the Japanese 92
Black feet and legs 93
Doing my own share 93
I am glad I do not have to hang my head, I served 94
A little more here 98
A gruesome but necessary detail 100
Not for the squeamish or faint of heart 100
High-level excitement at Pusan, Korea 102
During war, we learn to expect the unexpected 102
An officer has been humbled 102
An officer, a highlight of my day 103
The routine resumes 103
To immature to be serious 104
We were busy exercising our philosophy 105
I had not considered their firing back 105
Give me a weapon and point me toward the front 106
A happy and enjoyable moment 106
Thoughts of kindness enter my mind 106
My favorite memory of Pusan Korea 107
My adopted Korean daughter 107
Daddy, daddy, daddy 108
A fresh chicken dinner 108
Trust begins to run razor-blade thin 108
Move to Inchon Korea 109
Appointed a security guard at Inchon 109
We were as close to being our own boss as was militarily possible 111
We were doing on the job training 111
Don't do what I do—do as I tell you to do 112
Getting a superior officer's undivided attention 112
I enjoyed this encounter with an officer a little too much 112
The inability to forgive, even in your mind 113

A missed opportunity to openly show any sympathy 113
Careful where you are stepping 114
A government killer that enjoyed his job to much 114
A cry in the night 114
Just another throwaway Korean kid 115
Does the end really justify the means? 115
Too much responsibility for an eighteen-year-old kid..116
Looking forward to the final righteousness of all mankind......................................116
Paying a debt with your life 118
It is impossible to wash some things out of our minds...118
A problem in not understanding their culture..118
You can't fix dumb 119
One of the biggest mistakes of my entire life 119
No one on earth should ever be treated the way this guy was 120
Forgive us, Father—we know not what we do 120
Bury the past, push forward to achieve 121
Horse-face, my Korean soldier friend 121
Power corrupts; absolute power corrupts absolutely 122
An eye for an eye, a tooth for a tooth..122
Jesus Christ is spirit; we must worship Him in spirit 123
A day of surprise learning 123
Fools rush in where angels fear to tread 124
Dumb and Dumber move on down the big hill 124
In for some shock and awe..124
We cannot discuss reality without discussing God in it 125
Getting back to 1951 Inchon, Korea...125
More on the leper colony 126
General Douglas MacArthur (the great one) bites the dust.....................................127
The Word of God is Jesus Christ...128
We accept, believe, and follow either God or Satan 128
The wrath of God has an ending...129
Lead, follow, or get out of the way 129
Believe one or the other 130
God is the same, yesterday, today, and forever 130
Be careful when you think you stand, lest you fall 130
Being sent as a replacement into hell on earth 131
Back in Inchon 132

"Old men start wars; young men have to fight and die in them"	138
Back again to 1950 Pusan, Korea	139
Holding the life of another in your hands	141
A mother waiting for the son	142
Dealing with war demons	142
No one to trust	142
Langley, an all-mouth redneck from Kentucky	143
I was a glutton for punishment	144
A heart of stone	148
My early years	148
Seeking a pass to go home	149
What rules?	149
Fond memories of yesteryear	150
I became a happy camper	150
God puts my feet to the fire	151
I am no different than anyone else	152
Then God steps in big time	153
I began to feel His presence in my life	154
The amazing grace of God	154
A reward for our earthly toil	156
Thank God for His forgiveness	157
My own future foretold	157
Plan A is put into effect	158
A will and a reason to prevail	159
My spiritual awakening	159
Fast forward	160
Rewards at the end of the tunnel	161
To all veterans of the forgotten Korean War	163
This is the way to treat the dockworkers	164
It soon became worse!	166
50 Years Later, the Battle of Chosen Ends	168
The war didn't stop at the Chosin Reservoir	169
No greater love than this	173
The MacArthur blunder that caused many lost lives	174
Thank God for whistling death	174
We all learned the new meaning of the word cold	174
The combat medic who saw too much	175

Being lonely in a crowd	175
Learning when to speak, and when not too	176
A sincere man speaks out about self	176
Lingering memories that live on	176
Reaching one's limits	177
Promises given by our nation, then reneged upon	177
Everyone wants peace; a few at the top want to dictate the terms	178
Some had gone insane	178
Warehoused and forgotten veterans	179
Being spit upon and called baby killers	179
Leaving Korea was the happiest day of my life	179
I thought I had finally gotten rid of the snow and the cold	180
All were now going home	180
Where is he now?	181
Hunt down and kill the mad dogs	182
Beware of drunken cousins	182
Thanks for the signal	182
Causing folks to run scared	183
Ironheaded gangsters	183
Not wanting to be live cowards, they became dead ones	183
Oops, wrong one hits the deck	184
All the talking is done	184
The game is on	184
God is in control of all things, and all the time	185
I thank God every day that they didn't come	185
The master plan of God	201
Cross References	203
"Christ came here to be like us, that we all will be as He is"	208
All of mankind to be saved	216
A Shot Across The Bows, To All Unpatriotic Cowards	217

INTRODUCTION

I would first like to introduce myself. My name is Leith Lyman Cunningham. I am eighty-six years old and am a survivor of the Korean War where I served as a machine gunner in frontline combat with the Second Infantry Division. I had been wounded in action on March 7, 1951, and spent the most part of the next year in an army hospital, recovering from frostbitten feet, and had been evacuated off the frontlines weighing barely over one hundred pounds because of the huge blunder of General Douglas MacArthur in failing to accept his own intelligence reports of the Chinese Communists forces massing in huge numbers at the far north Yalu river area, preparing for their surprise attack on our own uninformed, short in numbers of military fighting men that MacArthur was keeping the truth from because of his own unbelief. Telling everyone, "I'll have the boys home by Christmas." Then because of the inability to trust anyone other than himself. It eventually caused the death and dismemberment of multiple thousands of military personnel, and over fifty-three hundred cases of frostbite that caused untold misery and suffering of men losing their feet and legs and even years later having to deal with a host of external and internal damage being done by the severe below zero weather and the men not having decent food, sleep, foot wear or clothing.

MacArthur had not ordered any cold-weather clothing or gear while we were coming into the coldest winter in Korea in a hundred years. Because of this huge blunder, our frontline troops suffered unnecessary and unbelievable misery and pain caused by the highhanded, overbearing mentality of the so-called military genius that viewed himself as some sort of a god. That first winter in Korea, our troops suffered fifty-three hundred cases of often severe and debilitating frostbite especially the men fighting and dying there on the frontlines. I had been evacuated and sent home to Michigan to be lodged in Percy Jones Army Hospital in Battle Creek, Michigan, where I was taken care of for several months, having several operations to clamp off nerves on my feet to help me tolerate being in a cold climate. I was finally sent to a warm climate at Camp Rucker, Alabama, to finish out my enlistment.

My goal in this book is twofold. First, I am writing about some of my own actions and experiences in the United States Army. Being both in a war zone and then to be in actual frontline battle against our North Korean and Chinese enemy. I will be trying to help the reader to get a feel for themselves some of the things that are prone to happen when nations go to war against other nations. Normal laws in the nature of war need to be modified or suspended altogether simply because there are too many other immediate things to be concerned about rather than worrying about the local existing laws of the land. Very quickly, the law of the fittest becomes the law of the land. The guy that is holding the deadliest weapon will, all too often, be the one that rules the day. Or the group that is holding the upper hand by outnumbering the other one.

I try to mix it up a little in adding interesting material to grab the attention of folks enough to keep one from becoming bored to death by reading it. At the end of reading about what war and being in a war zone is all about, it is my desire that everyone might have get truer reality of it in their heart and mind. Being able to put themselves into another person's shoes. Having empathy and a differing perspective on what others have had to go through so that the rest of us would be able to live in peace and freedom. I secondly add a spiritual side on the aftereffects that all of this would have impact on different individuals as well, later on in life. That there be no atheists in a foxhole might be true after all. I have never found or come across a military person serving in deadly combat and having survived it that didn't give God all the credit for getting them through it.

I use the word of God throughout in an easy-to-understand way in reaching out to the heart and mind and inner being of some who might be looking for truth apart from the custom, ritual, and traditions of men, accepted believed and taught by the present-day deceiving so-called Christian religion. I do not mean to be talking down to anyone. I only accept, believe,, and teach what Jesus Christ, in His word, is teaching to me as I understand it that the Christian religion will not acknowledge or teach to their own converts. They—most one and all forty-one thousand and growing number around the world identifying themselves as Christian—are getting heavy into the accepting, believing, and teaching the custom, ritual, and traditions of man while being in denial of the truth of God.

After well over a half century of being called by God and studying His true Word, it has left me with a great big question mark on how the supposed followers of God can be so far off in misunderstanding His Word. But it doesn't surprise me at all if we pause a moment and think about it, and it shouldn't surprise you either. When Jesus Christ came teaching His people the truth two thousand years ago, how did they, *the people of God*, respond to His teaching? They didn't believe Him then either. Instead, they crucified and killed him in the most inhumane and painful way possible for bringing them the actual truth of God by driving a spike through his hands into a stake to hold and restrain him, then to make Him suffer in the most cruel, evil, and demented way they could come up with. So, no, I do not expect all of the people of God to accept and to believe this Godly truth I am writing about here either.

Those talked about in the past were the people of God in their own time and day. Today, I am addressing you, the present-day people of God, that there is not even a shadow of doubt because that is exactly how God addresses us, His people today in Revelation where I will show you at the bottom of this paragraph. But I am writing it to you, a person of God now who might be at a place in life now to receive, accept, believe, and to follow after the Word and way of God and His Son Jesus Christ, as opposed to this worlds counterfeit Christianity known as the Babylon of confusion that God commands us all to come out of in *Revelation 18:4*: "And I heard another voice from heaven, saying, come out of her, *my people*, that ye be not partakers of her sins, and that ye receive not of her plagues."

In plain and simple language, this is talking to those claiming Christian status while instead of following after and believing God, they instead are accepting and believing as truth, the customs, rituals, and traditions of men or the ungodly deception being palate-fed them each week by the false anti-God message of hocus-pocus religion identified as the Babylon of confusion. Where in Revelation 18:4 God commands us "to come out of her *my people*" *(the false teaching so called Christian church all around the world)*

Instead of doing away with idolatry and paganism, they have adopted their false and anti-God practices. All the while turning their deceived backs upon the truth of God and making up strange-sounding names not seen anywhere in the Bible to worship and bow down to. They jump right in knee-deep in celebrating pagan times, days, seasons, customs, rituals, and traditions of a satanic deceived group of forty-one thousand so-called Christian churches that God has sent them all to believe a lie because they received not the love of the truth. And for this cause, God shall send them *strong delusion,* that they should believe a lie (2 Thessalonians 2:11–12). That they all might be damned who believed not the truth, but had pleasure in unrighteousness. Such as all of the following paganism and idolatry that has become so dear and holy to them (never mind what the Word and the way of God has to say about it all):

Easter, Christmas, Lent, Ash Wednesday, Saint Patrick's Day, Valentine's Day, Halloween, Maundy Thursday, the rapture lies, the triune god lie, making God out to be a closed Trinity instead of the open to all of the family of God that He is. The immortal soul lie. The Christian hell hoax, the dying and going to heaven hoax that has no truth at all to it. Calling upon Mary a dead woman to answer prayers, making Mary superior to her immortal, spirit Son Jesus Christ. Until recently, eating fish on Fridays in honor of the half-man, half-fish god Dagon, a string of beads to chant over, the infallibility of the pope and to many more to list down here. Taught and preached about as being something as God ordained that so-called Christians are supposed to be doing. Where God tells us, it is all an abomination to Him.

ALL OF MANKIND TO BE SAVED IN THE GRAND FINALE OF THINGS TO COME

However, to me, it will be well worth every single penny, all the effort, energy, time, and resources that I spent to get this book published. Even if it never sells a book to one person, I will be as happy as a woodpecker in a lumberyard. The reason I can truthfully say that is because all the time I am spending in exercising my God-given mind in seeking and searching out His word and the way He has purposed and planned out all of our salvation from before the world began, I am at the same time filling my time, my head, and my life, and my whole being with what the wishes, desires; and the long-range purpose and plan of God has always been and continues to be for all of *His people*. That, my brothers and sisters, is you and me that I am talking about here.

I have traded in my machine gun, all of my hand grenades, my M1 rifle and all ammunition, C rations and TS card, along with a burning desire to kill, maim, and destroy others made in the image and likeness of God. I now belong in a new and different kind of army, an army that will not and cannot ever fail. Mine eyes have seen the glory of the coming of the Lord. He is sifting out the vintage where His grapes of wrath are stored. He has loosed the faithful lightning of His terrible swift sword. His truth goes marching on. I traded in all of my old weapons for new and different ones that cannot ever fail to work. The double-edged sword I use now has razor-sharp edges on both sides to cut in deep and be able to penetrate some of the most obstinate, stubborn, tough, and resistant bone and body parts known to God and man. Notice what the Word of God has to say about it below in Hebrews.

"For the word of God is living and active, sharper than any two-edged sword, piercing to the division of soul and of spirit, of joints and of marrow, and discerning the thoughts and intentions of the heart. And no creature is hidden from his sight, but all are naked and exposed to the eyes of him to whom we must give account" (*Hebrews 4:12*, ESV). I have willingly placed myself under the authority of God and His Son Jesus Christ. I fall short of the mark more often than I like to admit or remember; still, I do not walk around all humped over in guilt because I believe Christ is who He claims to be: the Savior of all of mankind and, in fact and truth, the Savior of all creation. I accept His great sacrifice in taking upon Himself all of our past, present, and future sins, that we all be assured of eternal life. I spend hours every day on my computer in sharpening up my sword for battle, as I read the Word of God, study His truth, put it in print in my own words, and give it away—or in sharpening and honing my spiritual skills to be of use to God and my fellowman, woman, and child. Wherever God wants to use me, I will be available. I have nothing at all to sell. Any royalties paid to me by the publisher I will use to buy back more books to give away.

I hope you will stick with me as I document a portion of my military life and duty in the United States Army during the Korean War, and along with it to also recount some of the aftereffects of other personal civilian life happenings and experiences related to being programmed and trained to kill. I will tell you how my military service actually became a big part of my finally believing, accepting, and now even teaching the awesome truth of God to others, that is so lacking in this perverted world in which we live. As sad as it is to say, and something that I have had to learn to accept and deal with, you will never, in trillion times a trillion years, learn the truth of God from any of the mainstream Christian churches on earth unless or until God first reveals it to them. At this time, God is not doing that.

My aim in this book will be to help everyone reading it to identify with things I write about that may equal some of the things that have happened in your own life that has driven or steered yourself into a certain direction, whether good, bad, or indifferent. Many of us are now or have been following things that are harmful to ourselves and others. Maybe we need to take a fresh look on things we could or should change. We have all sinned and have fallen short of the mark of being righteous as Christ was, is, and always will be. Whether we believe it or not, whether we like it or not. No matter what we accept and believe as the truth of God during our physical lives here on earth, He is going to save all of mankind without one exception, because Christ has already paid the full and complete cost of sin by willingly taking upon Himself the penalty of sin for all of mankind. That, my brothers, sisters, and friends is the absolute truth of God. There is nothing at all that we need to do about our salvation; that price or cost has already been paid in full by the sacrifice our Lord and Savior Jesus Christ.

To even suppose we have a part in our own salvation is to show doubt on the great and willing sacrifice that Jesus Christ accepted upon Himself to pay in full, in our stead—all past, present and future sins ever committed by every single carnal human being ever to be born and taken in the breath of life on this earth. Thinking that somehow, we have to do this or that or the next thing to make ourselves righteous and acceptable to our Father God is the height of misunderstanding and a completely false belief system adhered to and taught by the Babylon of confusion that God commands us, *His people*, to come out of in Revelation 18:4 *(the anti-god, Christian religion around the world)*. The greatest efforts possible that mankind, in any way, would ever be able to come up with in comparison to what Christ has already done in saving themselves is by far and away an impossible task of make-believe that will never exist. There is nothing at all physically that any person can do to make themselves spiritual.

GET OR GIVE

WE DO HAVE A CHOICE TO MAKE TO make it easier to follow the Word of God after we recognize the need for a change to take place in our lives. We can narrow it down to just two basic things. One is the way of God and the other way is the way of Satan. Another way to state it is the way of truth and the other is the way of lies and deception. It is called the *get* or the *give* principle. The more that we learn to exercise the *give* principle, the closer we become to our Father God. Because God is the giver of all good things, and his gifts are irrevocable (see *Romans 11:29*). The more we follow after the get principle, the more we are following after the god of this world, Satan (see *2 Corinthians 4:4*). I would like you all to see God the way He actually is. Your church is not teaching you that. They one and all are too busy following after the customs, rituals, and traditions of idolatry and paganism brought into the church by folks from the past that had one foot in idolatry and paganism and the other foot in the so-called Christian church, following after (Satan) the god of this world, while thinking they were following God.

In this writing, I will try and keep things interesting for you while revealing some personal frontline combat and war zone atrocities and other things of life that are nearly unbelievable, and in fact many will not believe it because it seems too far-fetched at times. But I hope that I will be getting your attention on things that are of a life-and-death nature that in due time will have an effect on every person born on this earth. Your own salvation is safe and secure; it is a done deal. Jesus Christ has paid the cost required for all sin, past, present, and future for all time. But if you would like to know more about life on this earth after Christ returns here to begin His thousand-year rule and reign, read on because your church will not tell you because they do not know themselves. They are the *blind* leading the *blind*. Not a single one of them is apt to believe what I am writing here as the truth of God. Nevertheless, it is all true!

MY INITIATION INTO THE REAL WORLD

This book is about my earlier life as just another naïve young farm boy being born and raised up in the outback, in the boondocks of northern lower Michigan. My only philosophy was, "If it feels good, do it," unaware of the things going on out in the world at large. But too soon that would all change when at age seventeen, I had joined the United States Army. The culture shock began to hit me right between the eyes, as the real world was being exposed to me. I had not even the slightest or faintest glimmer of such things happening around me or in the lives of my new army brothers, but I was soon to find out. For some odd reason that I am still trying to figure out, a young seventeen-year-old boy in my platoon that I had just become slightly acquainted with felt the need to get things off his chest one day. It surprised me because he was not a buddy or friend at all; he evidently just needed to have some relief by revealing his problem to another person.

He had gone on in a matter-of-fact way and told me how his mother had, throughout his young life and especially so during his teen years, had sexually molested him. He didn't use that terminology in explaining it, he just told me what she had done. She would spread-eagle him on her bed, make him lie still and tie him down on it prior to the molestation. He was telling me things beyond that as well, things that I no longer specifically remember. He had gone on and gotten it off his chest with seemingly little or no emotion, as if it had become a routine that he had become accustomed to. But now, after eighty-six years of living life on this sin-sick orb we call earth and the experiences of my own life, I now realize that young boy was attempting to get some relief from reality that he wasn't quite able to understand or cope with on his own. I had let him down because I was just too young and uninformed myself; it had required him to just go on alone and gut it out.

On the outside, I may have appeared to be calm and collected as I listened to him, wondering how I might be of a help to him. But on the inside, there was a boiling hot turmoil going on; it had really rattled me. I was learning too much too soon about the world that we live in and what goes on in it when the lights go out behind closed doors, hidden from any eyes that might possibly be of some help. Along with it, I was learning a steady truth about how man and woman kind really operate behind those closed doors. I learned early on that life behind closed doors and out of sight and hearing were nothing at all like life out in the open under the light of day. They were two completely different things. I will have more to say about some of these things as we go along.

A FATHER PIMPS HIS DAUGHTER

I BEGAN TO WONDER HOW MANY YOUNG BOYS were in the same boat and had joined the army to get away from it. After coming home from Korea, I continued on with life and had learned things in my own neighborhood that had been going on and had been exposed, at least some of them had been, while others never did get caught, even though it was common knowledge in the neighborhood. There was a family that lived in our vicinity where the seemingly worthless father was a drunk and was molesting his own daughter. She was a beautiful young girl about fourteen or fifteen years old. At home, with the mother in the home too, her father required that she dress about like Daisy Mae in the Little Abner comic strip in the Sunday paper. Scantily clad in short shorts and clothing that didn't leave too much for the imagination. Young men, old men and boys were beating a path to her door to be welcomed in with open arms by the drunkard father, as long as they brought along a little booze of some kind to the party.

They one and all, under those circumstances, were welcome to take little Daisy Mae upstairs and do a little roll in the hay with her. During the winter months and living in a home where no one was working and any extra money was being spent on the old man staying in a fall down slobbery drunken stupor, the house was always freezing cold. But no problem; they would just break up a chair or another piece of furniture to burn in their old woodstove. Sometimes they would just remove a partition from another room that they reasoned they could do without and use it to keep from freezing. I never heard about what happened to that family, but what chance does a young girl stand in becoming normal after such abuse by her whole family? Back in those days, she couldn't even have joined the military to escape it all. They would not have allowed her to leave the nest and kill the goose that continued laying those golden eggs.

CLOSE TO HOME GRUNGE

So, it is not just war and the ungodly things that happen when foreign soldiers are occupying other nations that can cause severe, untold, undocumented abuses of life beyond what the mind is able to continue on and stay sane. Another family that lived near us had a mother and father and a lot of kids. I had gone to school with all the older ones. After staying pregnant most all the time between kids being born into the family, as well as losing some in childbirth, they ended up with ten kids when the mother just got sick and tired of having kids. She moved out and left the old man alone with the kids and moved back to the state she had come from. The four oldest kids were boys and were all grown up and had left home too. The next four in the family were all girls from about twelve to seventeen years old. They were bound to stay and take care of their younger siblings, the youngest two being boys.

The father had always worked hard and made a reasonably decent living for all of them and was not a drunkard that spent money he didn't have on booze. He got along well with his neighbors and was thought to be a pretty decent person, but without a mate now in which to have an intimate relationship with, he began to have sexual relations with his young daughters. All the kids were likable and would give you the shirt off their own backs, but every single one of them including the girls were notorious liars and thieves. You would not have been able to hire and pay them to tell the truth; it is something evidently, they couldn't get out through their teeth. The girls and some of the older boys were always trying to skin someone out of their money.

The old man had always been fairly strict with them all in making them toe the mark or suffer the consequences, and now that they had something on him, it seemed only the right thing to do and get even along the way. They began to close him down when he would get to feeling his oats and the need for one of his daughter's presence in the bedroom. They suddenly had found the goose that was to continue laying those golden eggs. They were getting treated a lot better now, more special attention being shown them as he loosened his grip on them and allowed them to have things a little better. But the day soon came when the old man who had been dancing to his own music, suddenly found himself having to pay the fiddler. They sent him to Jackson prison for twelve years.

The family, as I have always understood it, more or less must have just come apart, and everyone went their own way paying the cost for what the old man had laid upon the backs of them all. I don't know what happened to all of them, but I do know what happened to four of them, and none of it surprises me at all. The oldest girl, the one with the biggest target on her back by the old man, the one that most likely suffered more at his hands than any of the other ones—being the oldest girl, she was probably trying to keep from feeling guilty in what she was being required to do by telling herself it was all keeping the family together, they were getting fed and had a home to live in, and in time it would all be over—she had stopped in at our home to see our family and say hi one day many years after her father had gone to prison. And it was obvious she was teetering on the edge, all googly-eyed, flighty, and an emotional basket case. Soon afterward, I had learned she had gone insane and had been placed into an institution to be cared for.

The next-to-the-youngest boy had always seemed a little brighter and more alert than the others. I remember when I came home from the Korean War and had bought me the sharpest '46 aqua-blue color Ford convertible that money could buy. It had blue dot taillights, white sidewall tires, twin glass pack mufflers, and I had to carry a stick with me to beat the girls away from it and from wanting a ride in it. I specifically remember this little boy stepping up on the running board with a great big ear-to-ear smile on his beaming, happy face as I was talking with him. It was the last time I ever saw him. I got word later on that he had gotten run over and crushed to death by a freight train. I can close my eyes and see him still in my mind's eye. Another tragedy before one's time. On the other hand, who knows, maybe a blessing in disguise in the long run for him.

The next-to-the-oldest boy was a couple years older and a lot bigger then I was. He was a piece of work; there is no other way to describe him. The whole family was a pack of thieves, but he had claimed to be the chief thief of the family, claiming he could walk out of the local grocery store with twenty-five pounds of flour under his father's overcoat; he would wear it for that purpose. When he would be getting ready to go into town on Saturday nights, he was worse than a woman. He had hair crimpers that he would hold over an old coal oil lamp to get it hot and then crimp his hair with it. To top himself off, he would pour about a tablespoon of a greasy product called "Brilliantine" into his hands and rub it all through his hair where it would be running down the back of his neck. His jacket would be covered with carnival ribbons and pins of every nature. At that point, he was ready to go.

This guy had talent and natural ability oozing out of himself in many different areas. He could charm a rattlesnake with his gift of gab, and if any Major League baseball player had ever seen him throw a stone, apple, or anything else as fast, as high, and as far as he could, he no doubt would have been scouted to play professional baseball in the Major Leagues. He seemed to know every individual and business person in our area that had money and wasn't shy about asking them to release some of it to him. He would come at you from ten feet away with extended hand to greet folks with; he would have made a great politician. He would approach the pigeon that he intended to pluck for the day and give them a hard-luck sob story about his poor little siblings being at home in the cold house without anything to eat. And before he knew it, they would almost be begging him to accept a little something from them to help out. He would refuse at first, and then when the right moment arrived, he would tearfully cave in and humbly accept their generosity.

My older brother had come home on a furlough from the Army Air Corps, and we were anticipating what we could do while he was home, and none of us had any money. My unnamed friend never missed a beat as he instantly came up with the solution. The old man that owned and operated the hardware store in town was known to be fairly wealthy, and he had gone to him earlier and gotten money to help the family. We were all dressed up already, and he didn't think that would work out too good, so he borrowed an old dirty pair of coveralls, mussed his hair up, and buttoned the coveralls all the way up to hide his clean clothing underneath. We sat in the car around the corner while waiting for him to go see the old man and return. It didn't take him no time at all, and he was back with big smile on his face and a hundred dollar bill in his hand.

We had gone straight to the bank, and he had gotten it all broken down in one-dollar bills. He really enjoyed pulling the big wad of cash out in front of waitresses in a restaurant; he was definitely the man about town. We proceeded on with doing the best that we could in helping him spend it all. The exploits of this guy and the way he lived his life could very well fill a book all by itself, but the point I would like to make is, this guy had all of the potential to be whatever he wanted to be, but by being born in the environment and into the extremely poor and abusive family atmosphere that he grew up in, without any decent training and proper leadership from his parents, he didn't stand much of a chance of reaching even close to his potential. But get this in our mind: none of us holier-than-thou so-called Christians have the right to judge, condemn, or look down on folks that fall short of the mark. Because every single one of us have the same carnal nature in our own DNA too. There but for the grace of God go all of us.

FINGERS CHOPPED OFF TO KEEP FROM GOING TO KOREA

THE KOREAN WAR CAME ALONG, AND HE WAS drafted into the army. I had already quit school and joined the army myself a few months earlier. I had been wounded in action on March 7, 1951, and evacuated off the front line where I had served as a machine gunner in the *Second Infantry Division*. Within a few weeks, I had been evacuated back home to Percy Jones Army Hospital in Battle Creek, Michigan, where I spent the most part of a year recovering from being frostbitten in Korea and putting weight back on that I lost in the severe and brutal Korean winter. I had weighed in at a little over a hundred pound the day I was evacuated out of Korea. I was on my way to the dining hall at Percy Jones Hospital one day, and as I looked over to my left, I saw my old friend sitting, talking with other comrades. He had his arm in a sling with a hand all bandaged up, and I assumed he has just gotten back from Korea also.

It was really good to see him, an old buddy from back home. We got right into reminiscing about all the good times and asking about each other's families and how they are all doing, where they were all at now. I knew all of his family and he knew all of mine; we both knew most all of the same people really good, so we had a lot to catch up on. During the course of talking until we were blue in the face, I had asked about his wounded arm and hand, assuming he had also just returned from action in the Korean War. He didn't hesitate to fill me in on all the shocking details that had caused him to be there in Percy Jones Army Hospital. He had finished his basic training and was being sent home on a delay en route to Korea.

While at home and not wanting to be cannon fodder for the war effort, he and his oldest brother cooked up a scheme to avoid it all. He put his hand on a block of wood and had his brother chop off three of the fingers on his right hand, making certain he would get the trigger finger. Not wanting to be a dead hero, he settled for being a live coward; still, it was good to see him. The last time I saw him, he had gotten married to a really nice-appearing lady and had a nearly grown-up son with her, and they seemed to be doing well. A good part of the reason why I suppose is because he had learned well how to milk the system. He was drawing his VA compensation check for being a wounded Korean War veteran.

SHOOTING OFF A WIFE'S LEG

We go now to his next to the oldest sister and how things had been working out for her. Being the second girl, she had also been a victim of her father's sexual molestation and abuse beyond what anyone would ever know. She had been the quiet one, not one to be an up-front, prominent-type person; she stayed back in the shadows as much as she could. I had heard through her brothers that she had married a black man and had children with him. But ended up divorcing him because in a heated family battle, he had shot one of her legs off. I never knew when any of them was telling the truth because they were all such liars. One day, she had driven in our yard and wanted to stop in and say hello.

We invited her and a grown son in to visit. In the course of the conversation, I told her what I had heard and asked her if it was true, had her husband really shot her leg off? She, in a heartbeat said, "It sure is," as she pulled up her pant leg and showed us her artificial leg. I continued on and asked her questions about it. I asked her why he had shot her leg off. She said, "He did it because I called him a nigger." I then asked her, "Was he?" And she said, "Yes, he was." That was the last time I saw her and feel really bad that so many unfortunate human beings made in the image and likeness of God must continue on having to suffer the negative effects of a society steeped in such ungodly practices that will never end until Jesus Christ returns to earth to rule and reign in the kingdom of God here on earth.

I will list one more episode of my life after the Korean War to help others to see and maybe try and understand what happens to a mind and a heart of a person who has been trained and programmed to kill and destroy others of their own kind. The infantry has been called *"the backbone of the military."* There has to be people that do the up-close and personal, on-the-ground, in-the-trenches, in-their-face, hand-to-hand combat when necessary. Plain and simply the kill-or-be killed, *"the infantryman."* That is what I was trained and programmed to do. Like anything else a person does, the more you do it, the easier and more natural it becomes and the better you get at it. Those you kill today will not be the ones that kill you or your comrades and buddies tomorrow. The Korean War was finally over for me, but I came home with blood on my hands.

And but for the grace of God, I no doubt had been spared a life locked behind bars in some prison for shedding even more blood after returning home because of the threat against myself and family by two drunken, know-nothing brothers that thrived on evil, hate, and on the get-even principle. Since I was not long out of the being programmed and trained to kill and destroy others that I had nothing at all against, but my superiors had given the order to do so, but now these two a—holes that were spending all of their time planning on how to stir up trouble and find a reason to get into a knock down drag out fist fight. They both more or less stayed in a drunken stupor and didn't care who they hurt or how bad they had beaten them. Nor the bloody condition` they were in when they got through with them. They had become a present and possible deadly threat against myself along with my wife and kids. I was prepared to drop them both stone-cold dead in their tracks. There came a day and a time that I had expected these two, to come looking for me, to get even with me by ganging up on me and knocking hell out of me, or to even kill me. I had taken my double barrel 12 gage shot gun, some buck shot and a couple slugs and left an easy trail for them to follow, in the fresh snow, from our house to a secluded place where we all used to hunt. I waited for them to show up, but thank God they never came. If they had, my life would have been a totally different story. They would have found their bodies when the snow melted off in the spring.

There are many other sinister examples of people and their evil, ungodly practices that I have known well throughout my eighty-six years of life on this corrupted earth on which we live, and though I try to bury some of it so deep that it can never be dug up again, while still I know that it is never going to happen that way, we just have to learn to live with it. I reveal these things as I do that others, hopefully, will be able to see and understand by tapping into the power, strength, and might of God, we can and all will rise eventually above our carnal nature as we emulate and imitate, to the best of our ability, God our Father and the righteousness given to us within His words of truth to obey and to follow, that He has been putting in front of our eyes in the Bible.

EASTBOUND AND DOWN

As a long-distance steel hauling truck driver, I was headed to the East Coast with a load of something and had stopped into a truck stop to eat in Pennsylvania. As I was heading out the door to get back on the road, two young boys about fifteen or sixteen years old approached me in the midst of a full-blown panic attack they had going on. In great fear for their very lives, they kept looking over their shoulder, expecting to be attacked any moment. They asked me which way I was going and I had told them east, to New York City. They begged and pleaded for me to let them ride along because they had claimed someone was trying to kill them. They were almost out of their minds in fear, but I wasn't authorized to take anybody with me, and I didn't know but what if they were trying to con me for some reason? They kept at me and wore me down with their close encounter with death at the hands of other young guys that had given them a ride and was now trying to kill them.

The guys that had given them a ride had driven them out into the woods, turned them loose, and had been coming after them, shooting at them while they were running as fast as they could through the woods to get away from them; they showed all the signs of being exhausted, out of breath, and in an unkempt way of dress. It sounded like something bogus and made up to me, but they kept begging for a ride. I finally told them I would take them along on one condition. I had asked them if they had any family at home that knew they were traveling across country, and the one kid said he had a sister he could call. I told him to call his sister and not to even say hi to her, but to hand the phone directly to me, which he did do. After talking with her I was convinced that they really were half scared to death and I agreed to take them with me.

A couple hundred mile farther east, they were still scoping out everyone on the road, thinking they were sure to be caught and killed at any moment. I had to stop for the night finally because I had run out of driving time in my logbook. They begged me to keep going, but I told them I couldn't. I told them to catch another ride to the state they lived in, but they were really reluctant to approach any stranger again. I told them if they were still there in the morning when I got back on the road, that I would take them with me.

When I woke up and got out of my truck in the morning, both of them had their faces pressed up against the glass in the entryway of the truck stop door, zeroing in on me, anxiously waiting and completely focused on me as I was getting out of the truck. They were sure glad to be on the road again after I had breakfast. I took them to the nearest drop-off location to their hometown and dropped them off. Realizing that they had just gone through such a traumatic event in their young lives to no doubt now still forty years or so later have to suffer from the effects of it for the rest of their lives. I really did feel sorry for them, but like all the rest of us have had to learn, it was an initiation into hidden and often evil woes of life.

THINGS ARE SELDOM AS THE APPEAR ON THE SURFACE

After our kids had grown up and left home, my wife, Nancy, and I had bought a couple of bicycles to ride around the country roads in our area to stay in a little better shape and just for something different to do. A neighborhood family with a couple kids six or eight years old began riding with us with their kids as they were growing up. A few years had gone by and we had not stayed in touch very much, and one day, I was home alone when the girl, now grown up to about sixteen or seventeen years, old saw me outside sitting on my patio. She was riding her bike and had stopped in to say hi and visit a while. In the course of our conversation, she became melancholy and evidently needed to get some things off her chest. She then began telling me of a family problem that was causing her grief.

She had gone on and told me how a boy in her school had sexually molested her and went on telling me how he had raped her against her will and the problems it was causing her at home with her parents. She was falling to pieces fast as she recounted the painful experience in graphic detail. Being in tears now, she needed some comfort, but I thank God that I knew at the time it shouldn't be coming from me as I would have dealt with it if it had been my own daughter or granddaughters. I would have held them and have given them assurance and warmth and would have hugged and kissed them to try and comfort them. Instead, I felt it unwise to be here alone with her at my place in the emotional condition she was in. Should the wrong person come along and misread the situation, I could find myself in a precarious position to be able to explain the reality to someone who had already had different thoughts going through their mind.

At that point, I had given her a kind listening ear and sympathy but told her I needed to get some exercise and was going for a bike ride, that she could come along if she wanted to. I didn't know of what else I might be able to do to make her feel better. She jumped at the chance, and within a few minutes, she had dried up all her tears, and we were enjoying biking down the road that I live on. After having told me of the traumatic and mind-boggling hurt and pain the boy had inflicted upon her, I was feeling really sorry for her as I wondered what more I might do, maybe talk to her folks or something—I didn't really know. We had not gone far down the road when we saw a bike coming toward us. When it got closer, she excitedly exclaimed, *"He's the one!"* The one that had raped her.

They both began immediately talking and joking around with each other, and I wanted to get her away from him. I said, "Come on, let's finish our ride." She took one look at him and told me, "I am going to go for a ride with him." So, I left as fast as I could get out of there with more understanding of life on this earth and a determination inside to be careful of being taken in by anyone claiming themselves to being a rape victim. This girl had gone on to become married to a decent man that works hard and provides very well for her. They never could have any kids of their own but seem to be happy with life as it is and living in a nice home they have acquired for themselves. You live, you look, you watch, you stay alert, you pay attention, you become aware of things happening around you and do not bury your head in the sand. God will bring things into our lives of great value, but we must do our own part in recognizing the lesson He is sending us.

THE LESSONS OF LIFE

Later on, in my life I began to recognize that God was calling me into His service and revealing things I needed to know. It wasn't enough that I just knew the good in the world, to really know the problems of humanity, I also had to know the dark side of all of us too. God it seems may have been preparing me for a way to be a specific servant in His kingdom. I began to believe and to somewhat accept that He might be teaching and mentoring me to be a part of the thousand-year rule and reign of Jesus Christ here on earth. If so, I was being initiated into the most important position of life possible for a human being made in the image and like ness of God, and just thinking about being a part of it, causes the hair on the back of my neck to stand up, as the cold chills run down my backbone.

I had to anticipate the possibility that God **was** calling me into the future and even now in His present work in His kingdom. To possibly be an integral and needed part to actually be spending time during the thousand-year rule and reign of Jesus Christ here on earth as one of His elects. In a nut shell, if this be true, God has been using all of my experiences of life to draw me closer to His Word and way of life that He has given us all instructions on through the pages of His Word, the Bible. It is the reason that I intertwine my physical nature and mind set in this book with the spiritual side that He continues to show me. God is causing our worst nightmares of life to work out for our own eventual good. That is if we believe Romans 8:28 And we know that all things work together for good to them that love God, to them who are the called according to his purpose.

JOINING THE ARMY

I had quit school as soon as I turned seventeen in 1949 and joined the United States Army. I took my basic training at Fort Riley, Kansas, with my good friend Billy Magee, a kid from the Fife Lake, Michigan, area, as too was myself. Within a year of finishing our basic infantry training, we were both in Korea, fighting in frontline combat against the brutal North Koreans and the CCF, the Chinese Communist Forces. In May of 1950, prior to shipping out to Korea, I was stationed at Fort Eustis, Virginia, with three stevedore, longshoreman companies. The 113th, the 114th, and the 115th Transportation Port Companies. We were in the process of moving all three companies to operate our vocation out of Alaska when the Korean War broke out.

ALASKA, HERE WE COME

We as a group boarded a troop train at Newport News, Virginia, bound for Fort Lawton, Washington, on our way to Alaska. This is where I probably really began my life of trial-and-error education. It is where I really put the statement, "You can't do that!" to a test. By offsetting it with my own developing philosophy that kept telling me, "Well, maybe not, but let's give it a good try anyhow." It was a most fun and exciting thing to be doing for someone who had never had the chance to travel around anywhere before joining the army. I believe it was about three thousand miles from the East Coast where we had been stationed, to the West Coast where we were to ship out to Alaska. I still have many vivid fun and happy images floating around in my memory bank that brings a big smile to my face when I remember back to those days.

TROOP TRAIN EXPERIENCE

Riding that troop train hooked together with a civilian passenger train full of people of all sizes and shapes, all across the United States, was one of the most exciting and neat things that I had ever done or even dreamed about doing. Like I have already said before, even looking back upon it today brings a smile upon my face and a glad heart to have experienced it all, and especially so if one didn't mind breaking a few chiseled-in-granite military rules, and that is one thing that I was never accused of. I actually spent quite a bit of effort and time in learning the rules and regulations of the location I was serving in. We were all supposed to stay together within the confines of the troop train only; we were not supposed to mingle with any of the civilians. We didn't want to miss out on all of the fun we imagined we could get into among the civilians. So, plans were being put in motion to skip past the rules and regulations.

Rules that only made breaking them more fun and exciting to try and figure out how to get around the rules whenever the train would stop. We would hop off and sneak up to a civilian lounge car, where we didn't know what we would find there, but it seemed at the time to be worth scoping out. We did have to be concerned about the civilian lounge cars being sidetracked at some point and being disconnected from the troop train. But in that case, if it did stop, we would still be able and have the time to get back to the troop train. At least, that is what we reasoned, and how it always worked out to be true.

It was a most fun, enjoyable, and memorable occasion to have taken part in. I recall at the time of being in the Union train station in Chicago, Illinois and having a chance to see Clark Gable on his way passing through to somewhere. Then us six hundred plus soldiers leisurely crossing back and forth around the station and taking in all the new sights and sounds of the exciting time away from home and out from under the parental control of my straitlaced father. Just too many things of high-level excitement of that which was happening all around me, for an eighteen-year-old farm boy whose longest trip prior to joining the army was once in a blue moon, having the chance to ride along with someone down to Cadillac, Michigan, about twenty miles from where we lived.

Now, here I am in the midst of six hundred and some army brothers, all dressed alike in khaki uniforms and milling around and gawking at all of the sights, sounds, smells, and feelings of togetherness of belonging to such an important part of what we all stood for. It made us all feel like we belonged to something bigger than ourselves, and of course, we really did. I thank the Almighty God of all heaven and earth that I have learned to love and to appreciate, for working it all out for my own good, seen here in Romans 8:28: "*And we know that in* all things *God works for the good of those who love him, who have been called according to his purpose."* If we love Him, God even makes our sins and mistakes to eventually work out for our own good.

By the time we had gotten to Fort Lawton, Washington, and were just getting settled in and waiting to continue our trip to Alaska, all hell broke loose in Korea, as the North Koreans attacked the South with a brutal, savagery of killing and destroying their southern neighbor, brothers and sisters, and a people just like themselves. The unprepared and ragtag South Koreans were being overrun and slaughtered at every turn. They needed our help, and they needed it immediately. Our whole plan for Alaska was put aside as we geared up now to head for Korea. It was an exciting time in my life that I look back on, appreciate, and enjoy reminiscing about. Many of those fun- and joy-filled memories cause me to lie in bed at times, reflecting upon them in my mind to the point I sometimes have to laugh right out loud. Anybody overhearing me would likely think I had gone nuts.

WAR BREAKS OUT IN KOREA

ON *JUNE 25, 1950*, THE KOREAN WAR BEGAN when some seventy-five thousand brutal and highly battle-trained soldiers from the North Korean People's Army poured across the 38th parallel, the boundary between the Soviet-backed Democratic People's Republic of Korea to the north and the pro-Western Republic of Korea to the south. The USA went to war in Korea for three reasons. The first reason was the "Domino theory." Salami tactics in Eastern Europe was not the only place where Communists were coming to power. In the Far East too they were getting powerful. China turned Communist in 1949. Just barely over seventeen years old at the time, I wasn't yet smart or wise enough to feel any fear of the enemy. I was just extremely thankful for the opportunity to be among those being selected to go to Korea and looked forward to whatever awaited us when we got there.

Truman believed that if one country fell to Communism, then others would follow, like a line of dominoes. He was worried that if Korea fell, the next "domino" would be Japan, which was very important for American trade. This was probably the most important reason for America's involvement in the war. The second reason was just to try to undermine Communism. President Truman believed that capitalism, freedom, and the American way of life were in danger of being overrun by Communism. President Truman eventually became my hero for his firing MacArthur for insubordination. MacArthur was a god in the mind of the Japanese, so much so he must have believed that he was too. He had gotten too big for his own britches in going against President Truman.

The Truman Doctrine had been one of "containment," stopping the Communists gaining any more territory. In April 1950, the American National Security Council issued a report (NSC 68) recommending that America abandon "containment" and start "rolling back" Communism. This led Truman to consider driving the Communists out of North Korea. Finally, Truman realized the USA was in a competition for world domination with the USSR. By supporting South Korea, America was able to fight Communism without directly attacking Russia. Russia immediately began supplying the North Koreans with jet planes and other war machinery superior to what we had. Their new Soviet Mig Jet was faster than anything we had at the time, but our pilots were more skilled and able to outperform them in the air battles.

BOUND FOR KOREA

Consequently then, back at Fort Lawton, the plans had to be changed from going to Alaska, where we had been waiting in limbo. We were immediately redirected to go down to Camp Stoneman in California and ship out directly to Pusan, Korea, where we would be receiving war material and supplies to fight the war that had now begun, which President Truman had committed our country to be all in. Where troops and supplies of every description were now being routed to Korea. We landed at Pusan, Korea, after a sixteen-day journey on a troop ship across the Pacific Ocean to begin our longshoreman operation in July 1950. Every single day now became a unique and special experience in seeing and being a part of how quick and effectively a military operation or maneuver can be implemented and put into motion to reach a desired goal.

TROOP SHIP EXPERIENCE ACROSS THE PACIFIC

The troop ship voyage across the sparkling blue waters of the Pacific was a wonder to behold. As the ship sliced through the pristine blue water, it would part and throw out tons of crystal clear white foamy water on either side. I would sit or lie on my belly for hours at the bow of the ship with a good buddy, looking down though a round or oblong hole in the center of the bow of the ship, watching the white foam as it came boiling out on each side of the ship, reminding me of a snow plow on the Michigan roads during the wintertime. It was mesmerizing, it had a calming effect, and it was easy to get caught up in its spell.

The water looked as if it was coming at full speed ahead up at our face when the bow of the ship would dip down into the water as we lay there watching it and looking through the oblong hole; then as the bow of the ship rose up out of the water, it receded at the same speed down and away from us. It was a memorable occasion to be long enjoyed and much remembered. A unique experience to take part in with a lot of other young soldiers getting their feet wet for the first time. We would gather at select locations on deck, smoking, talking, and joking around like young kids our age do. We would entertain each other by playing cards, telling stories, and reminiscing and talking about our girlfriends at home and such. No one seemed the slightest bit anxious or worried about heading into a war zone situation that none of us was remotely prepared for but would too soon be in it up to our necks.

I remember one guy named Clark, a big good-looking kid from one of the Southern states who had a really neat Southern drawl. I just liked to hear him talk. He would always let everybody that wanted to, to read the letters from his girlfriend that would be plastered up with her lipstick. Some guys played guitars, and a lot of singing country music was going on, especially so after dark during the night. It was too hot and stuffy down in the sleeping areas where bunks hung from chains fastened to the deck above; we were stacked about six men deep. A canvas was stretched inside of a steel frame big enough to hold one person. You were almost touching the guy above you and the one below. We would go up on deck and look over the sides of the ship and watch what looked like big balls of fire a foot or two in diameter rubbing along the sides of the ship and finally disappearing off the fantail. The sailors told us that they were phosphorous balls.

After doing a little research on the matter, I was surprised to learn I could not find a single thing to deny or to add light on the subject. It's as if there is no such thing at all, and yet I along with a lot of other guys did see them clearly. So, we may have been at the right place at the right time to have experienced an unusual phenomenon, in which case, it makes it that much more meaningful for having had the opportunity to witness it. In any event, it added to our excitement and the joy of discovery as we headed on across the Pacific for our rendezvous with fate at the end of our journey in Pusan, Korea. I will always be grateful and thankful that God has given us all an eye in the memory of our mind to bring back such awesome, enjoyable, and pleasant things to review, see again, and then lock them back up until they surface and come to mind again.

At times, we would have a school of flying fish or dolphins or both together following alongside the ship, waiting for scraps that the ship would release at certain times. When the ship would dip down while the ocean would rise up, we would be able to look straight out and get a good panoramic view of them streaking along underwater, passing the ship. Then at times just playing around and chasing one another up and out of the water, doing flips and all sorts of fun-to-watch actions. To make it all even better, we had good, pleasant, warm and sunny sailing weather all the way across to Pusan, Korea. An all-paid-for ocean voyage by our Uncle Sam whose watchful care we all served under. I always liked the sailors both onshore and at sea; we got along well with them except for the times we would spend making fun of them as they in turn made fun of us. We called them "swab jockeys," and they called us "ground pounders."

I was proud to be an American back then and remember seeing President Truman one time in Washington DC. He was a one-of-a kind president that I did appreciate. I recall he had a plaque on his desk that read, "The buck stops here." I am glad we now have a president in Donald J. Trump that is keeping his campaign promises to once again "make America great." He is the reason I am finally proud of being an American again, because he is doing all he can to restore the power, strength, positive influence, and prestige to our great country in spite of the unhinged left-wing Democratic party and news media that know nothing but obstruction and throwing up roadblocks to prevent the President Trump from doing even greater things than he already has accomplished.

Having already done more now than the Obama administration did in eight years, still I do appreciate and am thankful that Obama was the one that God had placed as the leader of our country during his term in office, and he needed to be supported too, as God commands of us all. It takes a certain type of an individual to take all of the negative heat that any president has to put up with and still lead the people. Having to get up every morning and listen to one more day stacked upon another of being attacked by half the people of his own country. No matter how extremely well he is doing, never having to be acknowledged, appreciated, or reported as a positive by the fake news and the unhinged ugly maggot-mouthed Maxine Watters–type that believes only in being an obstructionist.

IT IS ALWAYS GOD THAT FILLS PRESIDENTIAL OR LEADERSHIP POSITIONS

I especially thank the Almighty God of all heaven and earth for placing a president at the helm of our government today that we once more can feel proud of his "peace through strength" policy of not allowing third world dictators and tyrants to dictate the terms of how we govern ourselves. Milk-and-pablum-fed liberals don't much like his bold approach of governing, but to me, it is exactly what is needed in this wishy-washy, namby-pamby world of the appeasement movement that Obama led by. Now I know how Michelle Obama felt when she said she was never proud of her country until they elected her husband POTUS. Clarke charged *on Twitter*, "I've never been prouder since we got rid of him." Now I am proud of our country again. None of us should grumble, gripe, and be involved in obstructionism or express hate against one that God has placed in a position to lead our nation.

The sixteen-day ocean voyage to Korea was a fun time and makes for good, fond, and enjoyable memories yet today. Even though the smoking lamp was out *(no light at all allowed on deck)*, we always found a way to get our relaxing smoking done in out of the way areas. At one point, several of us were up topside in an area a couple floors higher than the main deck on one side and only one floor down to the lower main deck, on the other side. We had scoped it out good to decide a plan of action should anyone come up the steps that we had come up, looking for soldiers violating their strict rules and regulations. We were smoking up a storm, having fun and telling jokes on each other, when suddenly, we heard someone coming up the steps; and assuming it to be the night watchman, we all headed for the escape route we had picked out earlier. All of us but one got away clean, but one guy misjudged the area he should have jumped in and completely missed the first deck.

The rest of us jumped over the rail where it was only one floor down to the deck, and we ended up in good shape and hit the deck without any problem and not being detected. The other guy had gone over the rail where it was two floors down to the deck, and he had hit it like a ton of bricks and was still lame and limping when we had gotten to Pusan, Korea. We ribbed the daylights out of him and never let him forget it. We were too young and immature to be worried or concerned that we are now going full steam ahead heading into a war zone. It was all too exciting to witness all the different things going on around us, that was all new to us. But in Korea, things had taken a turn for the worst.

DESTINATION: KOREA

The going was tough for our troops on the front line that had been doing occupation duty in Japan after WWII. They were soft and out of condition, without much, if any, recent training to bring them up to fighting ready conditions. They just sent them in against the brutal, battle-hardened North Korean meat grinder to slow their advance and keep them from running us out of Korea. Our backs were against the wall at the Pusan port where we had docked off the Sea of Japan. My good friend and buddy from back home, that I had joined the army with, Billy Magee, was one of the first in his outfit to be shot down and killed in battle while serving on the front line there in Korea, in the Twenty-fifth Infantry Division. He was a really great kid that I liked and ran around with while we were both stationed at Fort Riley, Kansas. I can close my eyes and still see him just as he was back then.

MY CLOSE BUDDY BILLY MAGEE

His serial number was one digit before mine. He never really got the chance to live. However, I didn't know about it until a year or so later after I had been wounded and evacuated back home. I was home and driving out of town one day and met a car going the opposite way and noticed it was Billy's sisters. I turned around and caught up with them in town. I wanted to find out how Billy was and how he was doing. I thought he might even be with them and I was really looking forward to seeing him as I had asked them about him. I still remember how bad I had felt when they told me he had been killed in action. My folks had known it but had held it from me, thinking it wasn't something I needed to hear at the time.

MY OTHER CLOSE COMBAT BUDDY ERNIE

I have erected a monument at my home in memory and in honor of both Billy and my other best friend Ernie Lee, whom I had seen for the last time as the medic was attending to him after being ripped apart by burp gun fire in the hands of a Chinese soldier. I don't know if he lived or died. After that, it was just put your head down shift gears into automatically putting one foot in front of the other and go forward without any emotion left to show, surrounded by a bunch of other zombie-like half-starved and gaunt creatures like myself with eyes sunken back in our heads with the hope of seeing another tomorrow. I didn't have any buddies left in my outfit to talk with. They had all either been wounded in action and evacuated to army hospitals in Japan or had been killed. For this reason, I didn't have any great urge to stay and fight with my friends and buddies because they were all gone.

March 9, 1950, consequently was the happiest day of my life. I was carried onto a C-47 plane and flown out of the rottenest godforsaken cesspool of blood, gore, and filth beyond the imaginations of men. I do have to say that the South Koreans did not squander the shed blood of my military brothers and sisters. Look how far they have come since those days. So much for the lie that someone got started years ago, telling us we lost the war.

We sent those North Korean and CCF troops packing and drove their sorry hind ends right back from whence they came and have kept them there for over sixty-five years now. My comrades did not have to die in vain or for a tie; plain and simply we won that war. South Korea is to be praised, recognized, and given much credit. Their bulldog tenacity and work ethic to rise above their master/slave position under the Japanese occupation of their country being removed, they flourish and have not squandered the freedom that myself and our military forces fought for and many died for. It is a tribute to those who died that others may be free.

POSTTRAUMATIC STRESS DISORDER

As I sit in the midst of WWII, Korean, and Vietnam War combat veterans every two weeks, to hear their stories of lengthy and bloody combat experiences at our VA group meetings in Traverse City, Michigan, where we are being treated for posttraumatic stress disorder, I marvel at what many of my Army, Marine, Navy, Coast Guard and Seabee comrades had to endure to survive and go through during a seemingly endless time frame and yet survive it all. We are all in agreement: war is hell! Sometimes, it overwhelms us as we follow along with an experience being revealed by a comrade and imagine ourselves going through the same things that the other guy has had to endure.

While some of my comrades had been required to spend longer and more lengthy combat tours of duty, with seemingly no end in sight, in comparison to the relative short time I spent on frontline combat service, I wonder how they ever made it through and lived to come home to anything but a normal life. I was involved for the most part in one major battle, a continuous sixty-day-and-night defense of Wonju, Korea. Never out of the unfit weather, even for an animal to live in, for over two months. In the brutal below-zero weather, without any decent cold-weather clothing to wear. No such thing as a bath or a change of clothing, except for socks. Mountain sleeping bags taken away from us, not even an army horse blanket to cover me, only the clothing I had on that never got cleaned, just getting worse and more rank and ragged by the day, tattered and torn with holes being burned in them when we finally got near enough to a fire to soak in a little warmth for a moment. Never a hot meal and on the move either toward or away from the enemy. Either walking to keep from freezing or my teeth chattering so loud and wondering if the enemy could hear it. Weak and emaciated to the point it became a struggle to get one foot in front of the other. Either attacking, killing, and destroying the enemy or being attacked and destroyed by the enemy. Yet what I lacked in length of time on the battlefield, I feel I more than made up for it in the intensity and conditions we were required to fight and try to survive in.

WEATHER CONDITIONS WORSE THAN THE BATTLE OF THE BULGE

A TANKER FROM THE THIRTY-EIGHTH TANK COMPANY, a veteran who survived the German World War II Ardennes winter offensive known as the Battle of the Bulge recalled how he had thought the German cold was the worst cold in the world, but Korea eventually was worse than the Ardennes, lasting longer and dominating your life as the Ardennes cold never did. In the Ardennes, you always believed that the cold would break in a day or so; in Korea, you never did. Because of the never-ending spending of energy without receiving any decent cold-weather clothing, along with prolonged night and day exposure of wallowing around in the same clothing day after day in the ice and knee-deep snow, never being inside or under any protection at all. Those of us that made it home alive were extremely fortunate, for which I thank God.

For the past several years now, I have belonged to a group of combat veterans at the Traverse City, Michigan, VA, where the VA is helping us deal with posttraumatic stress disorder that still remains a problem inside of those having spent time experiencing too much of the blood and gore, having to dealt with in their mind and psyche. You come home and learn really quick, no one gives a damn about your sob stories in an attempt at getting it off your chest, so, you just shut-up and keep your mouth closed because it only tends to close off any productive conversation between yourself and our society, because it cuts others out of the conversation, that know nothing about that which is being discussed, and it becomes an embarrassment to them. The lack of bringing it out in the open and dealing with it just drove it down deeper inside.

We found out really quick that nobody wants to hear anything about what you have to say about your job of being the programmed and trained killing machine that Uncle Sam has brought you to execute death against enemies of our country. Going after other nations and destroying other human beings, you learn to keep it to yourself—it's not fashionable in a crowd to bring up combat and killing. The war on the battlefields are over and done with, the killings have stopped, but the war in the mind and heart continue on still. You leave home one sort of a person without ever having developed much of any kind of opinion. You come back home an altogether different person. Sometimes, you find yourself doing odd things that you cannot explain why you did it yourself, no reason to expect that anyone else can explain either.

It manifests itself in many different ways: having a short fuse, being overly sensitive at the drop of a hat, self-medicating themselves into oblivion, being jumpy and irritated at sudden noises, hard to get along with at home and many other things that make a normal life completely out of their reach. I would like to take some time here to reveal some different experiences from others I have known and spent time with and listened to a varied set of actions and circumstances they had gone through in combat to bring about that which they have had to suffer through and gut it out and try to be normal. I will be using fictitious names for the most part to protect their own privacy. They have told me it is okay to do that.

PAYING THE COST FOR PEACE AND FREEDOM

KENNY IS A GOOD EXAMPLE TO BEGIN WITH. He has seen way more than his share of unrelenting, unending, and brutal, bloody combat than some of us. Kenny is a Korean War veteran that knows well how it feels to be swarmed over by never-ending, overwhelming numbers of Chinese soldiers in their wildlike Indian attacks, in their highly planned frenzied, bloodcurdling yelling, screaming, and bugle-blowing bonsai attacks against the Third Infantry Division that he belonged to in Korea. Bringing cold chills up the spine of those in their path. His outfit bore the brunt of some of the most devastating, cruel, sustained, and seemingly endless bonsai attacks against them during the Korean War. He has, over time, talked about some of his life as a combat infantryman. Telling us of some of the horror episodes and experiences on the frontlines of the Korean War.

He talked about "Outpost Harry," and how overwhelming hordes of Chinese soldiers were in the process of swarming over them in attack after attack as his outfit held their ground and repulsed them again and again. Telling us his BAR (Browning Automatic Rifle) or M1 rifle would become smoking hot as he fired clip after clip into the close-in attacking Chinese soldiers that piled up all around them at their outpost. He had told us that he had prayed to God that they would quit coming so he wouldn't have to shoot and kill any more of them, but still, they continued to come against them. Until they finally had sacrificed all of the men they could stand to lose. Kenny and his comrades had held their ground, having lost many lives themselves. His outfit had received a commendation, a recognition for valor, bravery, and courage

Kenny told us about the day they were being under another bonsai attack as he was sitting on the edge of his foxhole with another buddy close by. His rifle had either jammed or had quit firing right, and he was in the process of fixing it. He had not noticed a Chinese soldier that had crept up close to his hole and evidently wanted to save his country money on spending a bullet. He made a stab at him with his bayonet to get the job done, but fortunately for Kenny, his buddy on the other end of the foxhole had been alert and shot over Kenny's head and killed the Chinese soldier before the bayonet had struck its mark. Kenny had somehow fallen backward, and the dead Chinese soldier with blood gushing out all over himself fell right on top of him. Now lying back in the hole with the enemy soldier right on top of him, with being soaked with enemy blood now, mixed with the buildup of dirt on his clothing, the fighting just continued on as another day in the life of Kenny.

Kenny came home to his sweetheart that he had married and was trying to settle down and make a life and raise a family with, still carrying a burden too big to have to deal with alone. But he couldn't keep a job. He claimed he held the record for being fired; he told us he had been fired three times in one day. His new wife was working at the time, and she had a talk with him and told him what she wanted to happen, what she would be willing to do for him and their marriage. She told Kenny she wanted him to take a whole year off and try to get readjusted to a normal life, and maybe help him deal with his war demons. So that is exactly what he did; he took a whole year off.

He spent a good portion of his time out in the woods and along a stream in the area in which they lived. He talked about not ever being able to get his hands clean and free from blood, no matter how long or how much he washed them; he would look down as he sat beside the stream and see blood dripping off them. He continued on in his time off and the time he was spending being alone to think and to contemplate how to get this buildup of all this nasty blood and gore in the past out in the open and to be able to deal with it. He talked about sitting by the water's edge now on a regular basis, letting his hands hang in the water as he would move them around, washing them off again and again, until one day he wasn't able to see blood dripping off them anymore. Kenny is not all the way back yet, and neither are any of the rest of us, but thank God, the VA is helping us deal with it now.

Larry Lelito has given me permission to tell of experiences he has published in his book titled *True Hard*. As I have had to go by memory over the years as Larry has talked about them, I have tried to get things as accurate as I can recall of Larry relating them to us in our posttraumatic stress disorder group meetings at the VA facility in Traverse City, Michigan.

My friend and comrade at arms Larry Lelito served as a Marine sniper in the Vietnam War. Larry had seen more up close and personal combat than some others; because of being a sniper he had witnessed his victims drop dead in their tracks by his own eyes, the bullet coming from his own sniper rifle. Unless one finds themselves in hand to hand combat, much of combat is knowing when and where to concentrate your fire power against the enemy to be most effective. If a listening post at night for example suspects enemy by sight, sound and in Korea, even by smell, and it is reported in and affirmed, all of the unit's fire power will be aimed toward the suspected direction from whence came what ever it was that alerted them. If there is return fire it will be met with even more fire power if possible. There may be a sporadic heated battle going on throughout the night, where both our forces and the enemy are losing men either by their death or from being wounded and sent to the rear to have their wounds taken care of. In the morning you can expect to find dead enemy bodies that you faced during the night. No one can claim to have personally killed a certain number, not knowing where your bullets were going. As a machine gunner myself, I should be able to expect that I was responsible for my share of the dead and wounded enemy soldiers that came at us at times in waves or even from ambush and not being seen at all. A Machine gun puts out a lot of deadly fire into the area from the direction which the enemy attacks from.

It was different with Larry, unless he was operating as just an infantry Marine in combat. He has told the group many hair-raising episodes that he had been involved in as a sniper, many teetering on total exhaustion, near-death experiences. I will try and remember this one he had talked about in the jungle area of Vietnam. Somehow in the midst of a heated battle, Larry and a squad of Marines had been separated from the main group and found themselves fending for themselves, avoiding the enemy patrols and just trying to survive.

The jungles' never-ending stifling heat and humidity taking its toll as they burned energy attempting to escape the enemy. Before long and too soon, it had caused them to be running out of water, food, and gun power. Until there wasn't any water left, no food in a long while but still having to go forward operating on the guts and glory the Marine Corps had trained and beaten into them for survival, and now everyone was on the edge of collapse. One Marine had already passed out, and they all figured he must have cashed in his chips and was done for, or soon would be. Yet they must still try and muster up enough strength and find a way to survive. Where there is a will, there is a way; sometimes we surprise ourselves in all that God can do through us to help others after getting a second breath.

As Larry was lying by the stream's edge, sucking in all of the hot and humid air he was able to in attempting to regain some energy and strength to move on. He noticed some snails on the creek bed and, thinking about his downed Marine comrade, he began to formulate a possible plan. He had reached down in the water and brought up some of those snails. He cracked some of them open and begin chewing and mushing them around in his mouth until they had become partially liquefied.

Then taking the incapacitated Marine on the ground, getting him in a position that allowed for it to happen, Larry spit the mushed-up snails into his mouth. With this last-ditch effort, the fallen Marine finally regained consciousness and in time was able to survive the whole ordeal, while eventually they too had all finally gotten themselves back to where they belonged to within a couple more days. Just one more day stacked upon another one in their relentless pursuit of trying to achieve the goal their government and military commanders required of them. All this and much more as their neighbors back home were accusing them of being baby killers and were spitting on them when they did return home, all shot to hell after securing freedom for others to live and prosper in.

Thanks in part to such Lilly-livered activist cowards and celebrities like Hanoi Jane Fonda that conspired with the enemy in Vietnam. Had Eisenhower been president at the time. she would no doubt have been executed in the same way Julius and Ethel Rosenberg, who were spies that had given the Soviet Union atom bomb secrets during the Korean War. Hanoi Jane had worked for it, had earned it, and some think she had it coming to her. After all, it is unknown the number of our military prisoners that had to suffer unbelievable torture and torment and die on account of her actions.

I personally know Vietnam veterans that still hold Hanoi Jane in contempt, and in my opinion, they have every right to do so. I am a Korean War veteran, and her globe-trotting as an activist that caused so many American service men so much pain and suffering caused me to view her as an enemy of our country that doesn't deserve to be a citizen. War to keep from being enslaved by some other country is bad enough by itself, without having a—holes like Hanoi Jane add to the misery. War is the most horrible, evil, corrupt, miserable, hateful, demeaning insanity that mankind has ever come up with. I get that! But I prefer it to slavery and would still be willing to fight for freedom if I was able to.

Things like this that are experienced in combat or in a war zone are not isolated incidences that happen once in a blue moon. In a combat zone and especially so in actual battle with the enemy, such unusual things of this nature happen on a regular daily basis where armed forces from one country are on alert to catch the armed forces from another country asleep, unaware or letting their guard down to where they become vulnerable for surprise attack and quite often the annihilation and demise of many of their own military personnel. Nothing at all should be considered normal in a day of kill or be killed if one expects to stay alive. Sometimes, it is just a matter of who is able to react or to respond first to surprise encounters with the enemy. It pays to have your senses about you at all times.

Larry was telling us the other day at our PTSD group meeting about an encounter he had experienced with an enemy soldier one night sitting in a forward position called a listening post out in front of the main group of Marines. To hopefully be able to detect any enemy that might be sneaking in on them to surprise attack the main group during the night. Larry, along with his squad leader, waited quietly in anticipation of hearing or feeling the unusual or sensing things that often happen that you become accustomed to on the battlefield that wake up your thinking and reasoning ability.

The squad leader had dozed off, and Larry was to be on the alert for possible enemy infiltration; and if anything of question concerned him, then he was to wake up the squad leader. In the pitch-black dark after midnight and on into the night, Larry thought from time to time he could hear something moving out in front of them. He woke the squad leader up and told him about it and the direction it was coming from. The squad leader suggested then that he was going to send up a flare to illuminate the whole area and to be ready for it. Larry was making himself ready for what was about to take place.

As the flare had gone off and lit everything up like daylight, they were both momentarily thunder struck by what they were looking at—there was an enemy soldier just beyond arm's reach, looking them right in the eye. Just imagine yourselves being there and the feeling that must have gone over and through them in that moment. And not only in that moment, but the endless number of times since then that it has again and again played out in their tortured and tormented minds and heart of taking the lives of others made in the image and likeness of God, same as themselves. Larry and the squad leader had killed the soldier and had sprayed the whole area of enemy soldiers coming in close behind them with their automatic weapons.

As the enemy continued moving in with the now-dead one and on in pursuit of two marines going full steam ahead back into their own line of defense, Larry and his squad leader had turned and ran just as fast as they could to get out of the area back to their own lines as the enemy gave chase, coming after them full bore now. Unbeknownst to the enemy, the whole Marine outfit was waiting for them to all come into firing range, where a wholesale slaughter of dead enemy soldiers began piling up in the area with the main body of Marines mowing them down now with the overwhelming odds having been turned against the attacking enemy.

I hope we can recognize these experiences I write about, to reflect upon the high cost of freedom that so many have stepped up and done their share that the rest of us can enjoy the freedom that many have paid the ultimate price required with their own lives.

ORDERED TO THROW A GRENADE

Not yet spending much time on the battlefield I suppose, and not yet being acquainted with things that were going on around him and the required procedures they were being ordered to apply. Or just knowing inside himself that some things he just would not do, no matter what! Larry's squad came upon a hole in the ground being used as enemy safety areas from which to sneak attack an unsuspecting American military unit by catching them off guard. In order to combat better-supplied American and South Vietnamese forces during the Vietnam War, Communist guerrilla troops known as Vietcong (VC) dug tens of thousands of miles of tunnels, including an extensive network running underneath the Cu Chi district northwest of Saigon, called spider holes.

An old Vietnamese man had poked his head out from within as the squad leader ordered Larry to throw a fragmentation grenade into the hole. Which would have ripped everything in its path to shreds, including the old man. The old man, finding himself way to close in meeting his maker, was using hand gestures and—with worried, pleading eyes—was begging the best way that he knew how for any empathy, sympathy, or compassion that might be shown him by these strange foreign soldiers that held his own life in their hands.

Larry refused to throw the grenade, knowing the possible consequences he would have to face for insubordination and refusing to follow the orders of the one in authority. It is a most serious and possibly even a deadly military sin to refuse an order during combat, and probably even more so in the Marine Corps. Soldiers have been shot for doing so. The senior one in charge ordered him once more to throw the grenade into the hole. Larry refused again and told him flat out that he would not do it.

Some little time had passed as the old man was waiting anxiously to find out what his fate was going to. He came up out of the hole, and following behind him was several women and some little kids. Larry was ready to accept whatever awaited him and was totally prepared to pay the cost, knowing that the lives of innocent Vietnamese civilians had been saved and that he had had a part in it. It had not taken the one in command long to agree with how Larry had refused to throw the grenade. He had by this time now agreed that Larry had done the right thing in this certain set of circumstances, and no further action would need to be taken. No doubt, somewhere in Vietnam today, there is children having grown up now and as old people are still thanking their god for a Marine like Larry.

One more experience of Larry that he told us about while carrying out his duties for the day. On another seek-and-destroy Marine Corps mission in the Vietnam jungles, like many they had gone on before. They had found themselves isolated from the main group and were attempting to stay away and out of sight of the Vietcong enemy patrols that had pushed them past what a human being is able to withstand and endure to stay on their feet. They had run out of water long ago, and putting one foot in front of the other was nearly impossible. Things were looking pretty bleak. Larry had reached his own limits and needed assistance in going on. As things were getting worse by the minute without any hope in sight, they had stumbled onto a bomb crater filled with water in it.

Since water is a valuable asset anywhere on earth for survival, the other jungle inhabitants were all using it as their own watering hole too. Larry was able to drag himself up to the edge of the water-filled crater, and he began to swirl away the water buffalo dung floating all over the surface before he was able to drink what he had agreed to be his fill of the best-tasting water on earth at that moment in time.

A SPOILED GENERATION OF WIMPY BRATS

WHENEVER I SIT IN A RESTAURANT AND FOLKS bring their spoiled rotten kids in for a treat for the family to all enjoy and be thankful for and the kids begin their tantrums and fits of rage, demanding to please themselves at all costs. "I don't like this, I don't like that, I want this, I don't want that," unable to please or comfort them out of a "gimme, gimme, gimme," selfish tirade, I have a hidden desire inside of myself in wondering and finding out how they might look at things differently if they had to go a couple days without food or water in the sweltering jungle heat, then lead them all down to a bomb crater filled with water and buffalo poop and then hand out *Dixie Cups* to see what their response would be. I bet they would all be a tad less squeamish in learning a valuable lesson of life.

Nancy and I were sitting in the Sugar Bowl restaurant in Fife Lake, Michigan, about twenty years ago, and a big giant of a man walked in; and since the place was filled up, I asked him to sit with us, and he did. He was probably about six foot three or four feet tall, weighed around 250 pounds or so. He was all tanned up and had a ponytail that hung down halfway down to his waist, about two and a half feet across the shoulders. He looked tough enough to go bear hunting with a switch.

I was wearing something that had identified me as being a Korean War veteran. He was a combat Marine out of the Vietnam War. He had received seven purple hearts for wounds received in Vietnam, along with other commendations too. In the middle of telling us a combat experience, he suddenly began crying and fell all to pieces to the point that he had to get up immediately and leave the restaurant. We never saw him again. If he is still alive on this earth and has never received any help in dealing with his war demons, I hate to think about where he might be now in his mental, emotional, physical, and spiritual journey through life after war experiences.

A longtime friend that I have known for most all of his life, that I will call Carl, had been a combat soldier in Vietnam and was at a country vegetable farm market in our area one day when I had run into him and had had a good conversation with him. I had not seen him for quite a while, and we got to discussing the different aspects of being in combat. Carl had confided among many other things that he needed to get off his chest, something that no one else in any branch of the military I have ever talked to has ever admitted doing.

As the enemy Vietcong had moved in on them in overwhelming numbers, dropping his comrades in every direction, Carl had thought it was the end of the line for him; it would soon be over with. He had been so scared and paralyzed with fear that he had had a full-blown bowel movement in his pants. I know how hard it must have been for him to tell me about it, but I am glad he did that others may get a true picture of what exactly life on the front lines in war is all about. I have seen such fear many different times in the eyes of those having to meet an overwhelming enemy force, expecting that it might very well be their last day of life on this earth. But who have continued on keeping up the fire and turning the tide of battle and putting the enemy to rout with their tails between their legs.

I remember reading a quote from a well-known military person whose name I cannot remember. He said something to the effect, "When two forces meet in battle and both of them are ready to throw in the towel and quit, the one that keeps on fighting will always win."

My friend and comrade at arms Ted, a Korean War survivor, was with a frontline infantry outfit fighting against the overwhelming CCF forces that had quietly sneaked multiple thousands of battle-hardened combat troops in during the nighttime cover of darkness. They were all anxiously waiting and licking their chops for the command to attack the outfit that Ted had been assigned to, along with the other combat divisions in North Korea. Ted was wounded in action on the last day of November 1950, for which he later received the Purple Heart for. On December 1, 1950, Ted was captured and taken prisoner by the Chinese army. His Chinese captors immediately began marching all the American military personnel they had captured north, to be lodged in a Chinese prisoner of war camp. Where he remained for the next thirty-three months.

They weren't given any other option, either keep up or die wherever they dropped. Ted told us that South Koreans along the way would try and catch up and give them a little something to eat or drink whenever they could. But it was a very difficult journey from being wounded and without any decent food of any kind. Because our Air Force was involved in interdiction flights during the daylight hours to bomb and strafe the Chinese supply line to inhibit there being able to mount a major battle and keep from running out of ammunition and necessary supplies. For this reason, the CCF prisoners were being marched at night to avoid being under attack. At one point during the night, the prisoners were crossing over a river that the Chinese had made a narrow one-lane makeshift bridge that only allowed a single file to cross.

Right in the middle of the bridge, they came face-to-face with a supply line of Chinese soldiers guiding mules loaded down with supplies for their men fighting on the front lines. Since the supplies were of greater importance than the prisoners were, the prisoners were halted and made to give way and stand still on the rickety bridge until the mule train had passed on through. He talked about the fear that continued to build up inside as the mules would bump and jostle them around as they went by loaded down heavy with their war materials, wondering as he could look down and see the water below, swirling around beneath them, how long before he would lose his grip and be in even worse shape than he was already in.

HAVING TO REMOVE A SOLDIER'S LEG

THEY ALL FINALLY HAD MADE IT TO A permanent prison of war camp in the far north near the Yalu river, where treatment was varied—some not so good, some not so bad. The Chinese in command wouldn't take care of the wounded; they just let them gut it out and do the best that they could for themselves. Ted said they were being fed a diet of rotten fish and spoiled sorghum. A wounded soldier with a leg on the edge of gangrene needed to have it removed, or life would be over for him. Since the Chinese wouldn't give them any help in these things, they were left with only one option; somehow, they would have to remove it themselves. Talk about having to make tough decisions. Still, someone had to step up, and they did.

They secured all the necessary supplies that they anticipated they would be needing. Along with any medication that they could get from the Chinese that might be needed or could help the healing process—bandages and a lot of sterile-type cloth material as they could possibly find in a prisoner of war camp and then a saw to do the job with. With several men holding the man down and keeping him as still as possible, the operation began as the one picked to do the sawing went to work on his leg. After much expected grief, pain and suffering, the trouble spot wound and the leg had been removed, leaving him with a stub now; and to their relief, the man remained alive. But to their own horror, they had not allowed for enough skin to lap over and cover the end.

With no other option, they had to begin all over again to cut a couple more inches off the leg to allow for enough skin to seal it up and cover the end of his leg. None of this was being done with any painkiller at all. The man survived the ordeal, but I can't imagine how any human being could stand that much torturous, unending pain in the amount of time it must have taken to complete the job. But it does show that the urge to live on can be a powerful motivator to allow it to happen. I hope after all of that, the individual had gone on and been able to have a family and live a decent and normal life after he returned home.

PUT OURSELVES IN THESE SHOES

I WILL BORROW THIS HEARTRENDING INCIDENT FROM THE Vietnam War that I read about many years ago in the *Readers Digest*. This seek-and-destroy recon patrol mission in the jungle areas of Vietnam were hot on the trail of some enemy Vietcong soldiers. When they suddenly became alert and aware of some small flickers of sunlight that were reflecting and coming from a location up ahead in the direction they were pursuing the enemy soldiers in.

Not wanting to walk into a possible trap the Vietcong had set for them, they laid down a heavy volley of automatic machine gun fire into the area where the reflections were coming from. Cautiously approaching the area to check it out, they were shocked almost beyond belief as a young Vietnamese girl lay on the thicket, bleeding badly and almost dead. This had an instant mind-boggling effect on the whole recon squad as they tried to give comfort to the little girl.

The little girl was able to communicate with them and told them what had happened. The Vietcong had captured her and was using her to help them escape from the recon patrol. She somehow had been able to communicate how the Vietcong had chained her to a tree with a machine gun and ammunition to use on the pursuing patrol. They had told her that the American soldiers would eat her if they found her, unless she would shoot them down first.

The squad leader had held her in his arms, attempting to comfort and to ease her fears as he had watched her little heart continue beating through a gaping hole in her chest and heart cavity. She had died then in his arms. There was nothing else that they could do. I include this here that we all might wonder if any of those men made it home alive; we can only begin to guess what they all have had to suffer and endure on that just one evil action of war while appearing to be living a normal life.

MY FATHER IN WORLD WAR I

My own father served on the front lines in three major battles against the German army, in trench warfare in France in 1918. He was wounded in action when an artillery round sent shards of steel into his legs, and later on the Germans had used mustard gas against them, and it had damaged him in different ways. He was never able to smell or taste anything for the rest of his life. It had also had a negative effect on his mind somehow, and it restricted how he was unable, later in life, dealing with certain things.

He couldn't deal with killing a hog or doctoring an animal on the farm we were raised up on; my mother had to learn to do all that sort of stuff. He could never stand the sight of blood. I suppose because he been assigned as a litter bearer that was called upon to bring the wounded and dead soldiers off the battlefield. He never did talk much about his service with the exception of one thing that had an obvious impact on his mind and being.

Himself and his litter bearer comrade had been called out to an area on a hillside where a dead comrade had fallen. They got there and only a half of a body lay there on the ground. Continuing on bringing in others in that area, either wounded or dead, they had worked their way up and over the hill to the other side where other causalities were being taken in. There on the opposite side of the hill they had found the other half of the man from the other side of the hill. That war was hell, there is no doubt, but there will be an end to all wars when God decides enough is enough. I will have more to say about that as we go along.

Men, and now women too, go to war and do whatever is being required of them—be it killing another person that has been identified as an enemy, sitting at a computer, fixing roads, building bridges, doing mechanic work, running a bulldozer, driving a vehicle, or anything under the sun that those above you commanded you to do. Your own set of values, likes, or dislikes have nothing at all to do with it. Violating the order has consequences; you go forward at your own risk. In a combat area where everybody becomes dependent on the guy next to you, the one on your left and on your right that fails to do his assigned job could easily cause others to die. One who deserts his commanded position on the battlefield is subject to immediate death by a superior officer and possibly by the regular soldier standing behind him that was watching him run and leaving himself vulnerable and at risk of death by the enemy.

It may not be mentioned for all to spread it around to demoralize or to deceive the public, but the truth is, I believe it may be more prevalent than any of us would like to think about. Considering this aspect of military life alone that no one is exempt from is one more reason that the Veterans Administration, in my opinion, should be run by people in authority that actually have the veterans' best interests and well-being at a very high place in their administrative responsibility instead of finding it easier to fall back on the well-exercised excuse of admitting, "Yes, we have an occasional one that falls through the cracks."

It is not an occasional one, my friends. I live in a sparsely populated, rural area in Michigan. I personally know of several veterans that have suffered endlessly for years in attempting to apply for compensation that they have worked for, have earned, and have coming to them; then after filing again and again just to receive another rubber stamped "Claim denied" message from the VA with some hocus-pocus language that no one else besides themselves can understand. While a couple of my Korean War combat friends have never received their worked for and earned compensation for the wounds and severe-weather conditions that cut their lives short, they both died waiting for the VA and our government to act as promised. Keep reading below.

THE GUT-WRENCHING PLIGHT OF DANIEL SOMERS

Daniel Somers was a veteran of Operation Iraqi Freedom. He was part of Task Force Lightning, an intelligence unit. In 2004–2005, he was mainly assigned to a Tactical Human-Intelligence Team (THT) in Baghdad, Iraq, where he ran more than four hundred combat missions as a machine gunner in the turret of a Humvee, interviewed countless

WAR: And The After Effects On Those Doing The Dirty Work Of Killing

Iraqis ranging from concerned citizens to community leaders and government officials, and interrogated dozens of insurgents and terrorist suspects.

In 2006–2007, Daniel worked with Joint Special Operations Command (JSOC) through his former unit in Mosul where he ran the Northern Iraq Intelligence Center. His official role was as a senior analyst for the Levant (Lebanon, Syria, Jordan, Israel, and part of Turkey). Daniel suffered greatly from PTSD and had been diagnosed with traumatic brain injury and several other war-related conditions. On June 10, 2013, Daniel wrote the following letter to his family before taking his life. Daniel was thirty years old. His wife and family have given permission to publish it.

I am sorry that it has come to this.

The fact is, for as long as I can remember my motivation for getting up every day has been so that you would not have to bury me. As things have continued to get worse, it has become clear that this alone is not a sufficient reason to carry on. The fact is, I am not getting better, I am not going to get better, and I will most certainly deteriorate further as time goes on. From a logical standpoint, it is better to simply end things quickly and let any repercussions from that play out in the short term than to drag things out into the long term.

You will perhaps be sad for a time, but over time you will forget and begin to carry on. Far better that than to inflict my growing misery upon you for years and decades to come, dragging you down with me. It is because I love you that I cannot do this to you. You will come to see that it is a far better thing as one day after another passes during which you do not have to worry about me or even give me a second thought. You will find that your world is better without me in it.

I really have been trying to hang on, for more than a decade now. Each day has been a testament to the extent to which I cared, suffering unspeakable horror as quietly as possible so that you could feel as though I was still here for you. In truth, I was nothing more than a prop, filling space so that my absence would not be noted. In truth, I have already been absent for a long, long time.

My body has become nothing but a cage, a source of pain and constant problems. The illness I have has caused me pain that not even the strongest medicines could dull, and there is no cure. All day, every day a screaming agony in every nerve ending in my body. It is nothing short of torture. My mind is a wasteland, filled with visions of incredible horror, unceasing depression, and crippling anxiety, even with all of the medications the doctors dare give. Simple things that everyone else takes for granted are nearly impossible for me. I cannot laugh or cry. I can barely leave the house. I derive no pleasure from any activity. Everything simply comes down to passing time until I can sleep again. Now, to sleep forever seems to be the most merciful thing.

You must not blame yourself. The simple truth is this: During my first deployment, I was made to participate in things, the enormity of which is hard to describe. War crimes, crimes against humanity. Though I did not participate willingly and made what I thought was my best effort to stop these events, there are some things that a person simply cannot come back from. I take some pride in that, actually, as to move on in life after being part of such a thing would be the mark of a sociopath in my mind. These things go far beyond what most are even aware of.

To force me to do these things and then participate in the ensuing coverup is more than any government has the right to demand. Then, the same government has turned around and abandoned me. They offer no help, and actively block the pursuit of gaining outside help via their corrupt agents at the DEA. Any blame rests with them.

Beyond that, there are the host of physical illnesses that have struck me down again and again, for which they also offer no help. There might be some progress by now if they had not spent nearly twenty years denying the illness that I and so many others were exposed to. Further complicating matters is the repeated and severe brain injuries to which I was subjected, which they also seem to be expending no effort into understanding. What is known is that each of these should have been cause enough for immediate medical attention, which was not rendered.

Lastly, the DEA enters the picture again as they have now managed to create such a culture of fear in the medical community that doctors are too scared to even take the necessary steps to control the symptoms. All under the guise of a completely manufactured "overprescribing epidemic," which stands in stark relief to all of the legitimate research, which shows the opposite to be true. Perhaps, with the right medication at the right doses, I could have bought a couple of decent years, but even that is too much to ask from a regime built upon the idea that suffering is noble and relief is just for the weak.

However, when the challenges facing a person are already so great that all but the weakest would give up, these extra factors are enough to push a person over the edge.

Is it any wonder then that the latest figures show 22 veterans killing themselves each day? That is more veterans than children killed at Sandy Hook, *every single day*. Where are the huge policy initiatives? Why isn't the president standing with *those* families at the state of the union? Perhaps because we were not killed by a single lunatic, but rather by his own system of dehumanization, neglect, and indifference.

It leaves us to where all we have to look forward to is constant pain, misery, poverty, and dishonor. I assure you that, when the numbers do finally drop, it will merely be because those who were pushed the farthest are all already dead.

WAR: And The After Effects On Those Doing The Dirty Work Of Killing

And for what? Bush's religious lunacy? Cheney's ever-growing fortune and that of his corporate friends? Is this what we destroy lives for?

Since then, I have tried everything to fill the void. I tried to move into a position of greater power and influence to try and right some of the wrongs. I deployed again, where I put a huge emphasis on saving lives. The fact of the matter, though, is that any new lives saved do not replace those who were murdered. It is an exercise in futility.

Then, I pursued replacing destruction with creation. For a time this provided a distraction, but it could not last. The fact is that any kind of ordinary life is an insult to those who died at my hand. How can I possibly go around like everyone else while the widows and orphans I created continue to struggle? If they could see me sitting here in suburbia, in my comfortable home working on some music project they would be outraged, and rightfully so.

I thought perhaps I could make some headway with this film project, maybe even directly appealing to those I had wronged and exposing a greater truth, but that is also now being taken away from me. I fear that, just as with everything else that requires the involvement of people who cannot understand by virtue of never having been there, it is going to fall apart as careers get in the way.

The last thought that has occurred to me is one of some kind of final mission. It is true that I have found that I am capable of finding some kind of reprieve by doing things that are worthwhile on the scale of life and death. While it is a nice thought to consider doing some good with my skills, experience, and killer instinct, the truth is that it isn't realistic. First, there are the logistics of financing and equipping my own operation, then there is the near certainty of a grisly death, international incidents, and being branded a terrorist in the media that would follow. What is really stopping me, though, is that I simply am too sick to be effective in the field anymore. That, too, has been taken from me.

Thus, I am left with basically nothing. Too trapped in a war to be at peace, too damaged to be at war. Abandoned by those who would take the easy route, and a liability to those who stick it out and thus deserve better. So you see, not only am I better off dead, but the world is better without me in it

This is what brought me to my actual final mission. Not suicide, but a mercy killing. I know how to kill, and I know how to do it so that there is no pain whatsoever. It was quick, and I did not suffer. And above all, now I am free. I feel no more pain. I have no more nightmares or flashbacks or hallucinations. I am no longer constantly depressed or afraid or worried

I am free.

I ask that you be happy for me for that. It is perhaps the best break I could have hoped for. Please accept this and be glad for me.

Daniel Somers

"Wars that kill, where a man drops stone cold dead on the spot, may at times be the best option." General George S Patton has been quoted as saying, "Every good soldier should die in the last battle."

These are things that I write about here that are going on every single day in wars and in war zones that so many have to suffer so much for, for so long, and it should cause every thinking, reasoning human being on our planet to pray and ask God to return Jesus Christ to earth to establish His kingdom here to put a final and total stop to man's inhumanity toward and against all of humanity and to usher in His righteous kingdom. It is going to happen, God has promised us that it will, and He cannot lie.

God knows that mankind left to himself would eventually destroy our planet and everything on it unless He stops it from happening. "And except those days should be shortened, there should no flesh be saved: but for the elect's sake those days shall be shortened" (*Matthew 24:22*). And to drive the message home for some who may doubt it, God leaves it recorded again here in *Mark 13:20*: "And except that the Lord had shortened those days, no flesh should be saved: but for the elect's sake, whom he hath chosen, he hath shortened the days."

We are all different and react and respond to certain situations and experiences of life in different ways as well. What might be fun for one, the same thing might be emotionally painful for another to experience. Like the two little boys standing at the water's edge and splashing their feet in the water and having fun and laughing about it all. Then along comes a big wave that really splashes them both good.

One little boy throws a big tantrum and runs crying to his mother while the other little boy laughs and claps his hand like it was the best thing that has ever happened to him. I had taken my two grandkids to Busch Gardens in Florida where we got on a ride called *Rapid River Ride*. A big raft that would hold ten or twelve people. It was possible to do the whole ride and not get a drop of water on you, but as it spun around and around as it went down this swift creek-like waterway, if you got in the wrong spot on the raft, you would be drenched to the gills.

We were having a blast laughing, joking, and having fun while watching people as they lined up and loaded on with us for the ride. There were two really attractive black reasonably young women dressed to kill without a hair out of place that were sitting right across from where we were sitting. They were having a ball like everyone else on the raft as it began its wild ride down the fast-flowing water like a white-water river raft ride.

About halfway through the ride, it came about just right that it completely drenched both of those beautiful young women. One was laughing and enjoying it all and having a barrel of fun, as if she had just won the lottery. The other one was madder than a wet hen and was swearing and cursing like a drunken sailor; it had ruined her day, and she was hell-bent on seeing to it that everyone else was going to suffer too. Some say perception is reality; how we individually perceive something to be, that is the way it is for us. This lady gone mad must have perceived it to have been one absolute and total disaster beyond the imaginations of man.

So, in a nutshell, everything that happens in our lives has the potential to steer us either into one direction or another. What might steer and motivate one person to do good, the exact same thing might well send another person on a trip over the edge. One might throw a party, the other one might commit suicide or end up doing something in between. That's the way it is with life in general and maybe especially so in having to do the dirty work of killing, maiming, and destroying others like us made in the image and likeness of God.

Many have been known to volunteer to go back again and again to the war zone to exercise that which they have been programmed and trained to do. To go right back into the bloody combat of kill or be killed, their minds and psyche seemingly not allowing them to do otherwise in fulfilling that which they have been trained to do. I am writing about this to let you know how life in general and the military experience of myself and others like me have gone through and how it has affected some of our lives after combat and all that it entails. Leaving the miserable battle zone in Korea was by far the happiest day of my life, and I have no desire at all to go back.

The whole thing, the good, bad and the ugly of it all, has changed my life around 180 degrees. I still feel the symbolic, not literal, smashing me down by my God and the thumping me on my back with the symbolic two-by-four God uses on stubborn people like me as He grabs me by the nape of my neck and slams me down hard again and again as long and as many times that it will take Him to deal with me on His potter's wheel. God is never going to give up or quit on even one individual made in His own image, after His own likeness. We are all of the God family, that is why we refer to Him as Father. God is reproducing Himself in mankind; we are all to become as He is.

Where His intentions are to make certain when He is finished with me and you and all of mankind, He will have an exquisite model of perfection like His firstborn Son, Jesus Christ, where He can then exclaim to us at the proper time. His Lord said to him, "Well *done,* good and faithful servant; you have been faithful over a few things, I will make you ruler over many things. Enter into the joy of your Lord" (*Matthew 25:23*). And not for me alone; what God can do for one, He can and will do for all.

AWAITING ME IN KOREA

I came into the Second Infantry Division right after they had been trapped in a pass south of Kunri, North Korea. The Chinese army had them cut off and surrounded and was waiting in ambush on them and opened up with artillery, machine gun, burp gun, tommy gun, hand grenade, small arms, and mortar crossfire. Clogging the pass and filling it with blown-up vehicles of every nature, being a target of their artillery and mortar rounds, making it impossible to go in either direction. For the Chinese enemy, it was like a shooting gallery where they didn't have to worry much about any return fire.

In one afternoon, the Chinese enemy had inflicted over three thousand causalities upon the Second Infantry Division that day. Leaving it severely lacking in up-to-strength manpower to defend themselves. That is the reason that I ended up serving in frontline combat as a machine gunner in the Second Infantry Division. The powers that be rounded up as many rear echelon troops from different outfits as could possibly be spared and shipped as soon as possible to frontline duty. I was in the group that had been earmarked for the Second Indianhead Infantry Division. Others had been sent as replacements for other outfits overwhelmed and massacred at the chosen reservoir.

But it wouldn't happen just yet; it takes a great amount of planning, strategy, and the exercising of a caution in going off half-cocked in moving men and weapons into a position to be able and ready to fight and win. During January 1951, everything was in place, and it was all systems go. I would be getting my wish of fighting those animalistic North Koreans and Chinese Communist Forces to make them pay in their own blood, guts, and gore to be poured out and soak those godforsaken frozen mountains and stinking rice paddies that were being fertilized with "gook poop." Like the General George S. Patton's quote about war, "The object of war is not to die for your country but to make the other bastard die for his."

MY TURN TO FIGHT IN BATTLE HAD COME

I had gone overseas and had been with a longshoreman outfit in Pusan, Korea. We were stevedores that had been trained in every aspect of transportation, either by plane, ship, rail, truck, donkey, pack horse, or by hand. One day, I was living the life of relative ease, in comparison to the combat troops. The next day, I, along with other rear echelon soldiers in other outfits, were being pulled from our rear echelon duty and transported north to the battlefield. The military didn't have time to bring replacements in from the United States; hence, we all became the goat. It was the logical thing to do because we had been trained to do it. But we were soft, out of condition, and had not been issued any decent cold-weather clothing. Still, I didn't balk at the chance because it was exactly what I had been wanting to do.

PATRIOTISM SUDDENLY TURNS SOUR

I was ready to go and do all the damage that I could possibly unleash and to inflict upon the North Korean and Chinese enemy. I felt that I could finally get into some real combat action to slaughter as many of those animalistic bastards that I could get my sights on. The *Stars and Stripes* newspaper had documented stories and pictures to match of the North Korean Army having captured our soldiers, forcing them on their knees, tying their hands behind their backs with barbed wire, and were shooting them in the back of the head, execution style. Things like that and worse being reported caused me to have a purple passion hatred for all North Koreans. And the South Koreans didn't seem much better at that time. I have a different view point about them now.

I felt good. Like Sargent York of WWI going off to fight the Germans, I had visions of sugarplums in my naïve mind, watching them drop in front of a machine gun that I hoped I would be able to be assigned to. Then we were loaded up in to trucks to transport us to the railhead that would take us north. They mustered the remaining longshoremen that were staying behind in a company formation, lowered the flag at half-mast, and played a stirring, inspirational bugle piece with the troops saluting and standing at attention. As the several trucks loaded with soldiers drove slowly out of the area to the train station, I felt proud to be an American. That would be the last good or patriotic feeling I would have for a long, long time.

THE GOON SQUAD OR GESTAPO ENTER THE PICTURE

When we arrived at the railhead, there was no such a thing as a Mr. Nice Guy greeting us with open arms and a decent attitude. The way we were being treated now, by those in authority, lacked anything approaching a decent treatment of soldiers, that were about to be shoved into combat against the overwhelming onslaught of the Chinese army meat grinder to face such enemy wave attacks where the sound of bugles and burp guns filled the air, and your blood ran cold just thinking about it and knowing what was coming.

Suddenly, I no longer felt like a soldier; instead, I felt as though I had been turned over to a hostile government that was now herding us like mindless convicts to extermination. Thoughts of Nazi Germany and Hitler's gas ovens crossed my mind. Thinking back, it reminds me today of the Omaha stockyards in Nebraska. A squad, or maybe even more of military police, were herding us around like cattle, most of them armed with automatic .45 caliber Army grease guns. Why didn't someone tell them we were all American soldiers? It was a heavy dose of reality that was being dumped upon us, and it didn't feel good at all.

NO FRIENDLY FACES IN THIS CROWD

The MPs were standing at a ready to fire if anyone wasn't doing exactly as they were being ordered to do. Funneling us into a line, they loaded us into old dilapidated civilian-type rail passenger cars. The only thing missing to make us feel more like animals were electric cattle prodders, with the windows all boarded up and nailed down tight shut. I was beginning to feel more like how a boxcar full of Jews felt in Nazi Germany as they were being transported to the gas chambers. The patriotism I was feeling a few hours earlier began to fade away into the reality of what was to come. Where had all of those friendly people that had loaded us onto the trucks gone to? Our fifteen minutes of fame had, by now, all been used up.

ONE-WAY TRIP INTO HELL

It didn't take long for things to get even worse, as the old dilapidated steam engines pulling us along began to cough, snort, belch, and nearly stop every time we came to an upgrade or in going through a tunnel. Being a dockworker at Pusan, I was familiar with these old steam engines as they shuttled railcars back and forth for us as we moved needed supplies to the front. Some soldiers had scribbled names on their sides. One I remember was "Old Wheezy" and the other one was "Old Farts." These pulling us now were in even worse shape than the shuttle engines back in Pusan. On steeper grades, they sounded as though they were about to give out and quit. Then another snort or two and we would be moving again.

It was only by the grace of God that we were able to stand the ride into hell on earth; it's a wonder that we had not all been overcome and passed out in unconsciousness from those smoke and fumes in those sealed-up railcars or had died of carbon monoxide poisoning before we ever got the opportunity to fire one shot at the enemy. I felt really fortunate to have my good buddy Ernie Lee along on the trip into hell on earth; it helped in dulling the senses to have company you knew and liked to communicate with. Ernie and I had been together in the same outfit for a long time, and we had enjoyed a lot of fun and interesting times interacting with each other.

YOUR SOUL MAY BELONG TO GOD, BUT YOUR HIND END BELONGS TO UNCLE SAM

Going through the tunnels and having all the windows boarded up and nailed tight shut, we wondered if we would ever make it to the front. Anytime we would stop for piss call or anything else, the MPs would jump out ahead of us and surround the cars we were in, with drawn grease guns at a ready. Still today, a menacing, ugly, and unpleasant sight in my mind's eye as they would pick the high ground to keep their sights on us. Giving us time to relieve ourselves and herded right back on board the old passenger cars. I never was able to understand where we were supposed to run off to if they didn't keep an eye on us. It wasn't like we could catch the next bus home; we were in the midst of the a—hole Orient.

Reality was now setting in big time; we had all signed our names over on the dotted line and given ourselves to the United State of America government. They were now letting us know that we could give our soul to God, but our hind ends belonged to them. Reminding me of a cherished gift I had received of a carved eagle head cane given to me by the Michigan Wood Carvers Association, for my service in the military. The below caption has been etched into the staff:

Richard Lamphier and The Michigan Wood Carvers Association *thanks you.*

A veteran—whether active duty, retired, national guard or reserve, man or woman—is someone who, at one point in life, wrote a check made payable to the "United States of America," for an amount "up to and including my life."

AT LEAST NOW, I HAVE BEEN GIVEN A WEAPON

They took us as far as the train could go then unloaded us into a holding pen that felt as though we had become slaves and were waiting on the auctioneer to begin the bidding. In essence and in fact, we really had all become slaves without any rights whatsoever. That is just the way it has to be in the military; otherwise, we would never know who our authorized leaders would or should be. Herding us again, now into trucks for the final leg of our journey up to the frontlines. Taking us as close as they could and dropping us off in the edge of a cornfield, still no cold-weather clothing had been issued to most of us. I know I didn't have any.

By this time, however, they had issued our weapons to us. I had been issued an automatic .30-caliber carbine, along with ammunition. I had already modified it somewhat as I noticed others doing. I had two curved banana clips that each held thirty rounds of ammunition. I had taped them upside down from each other. When one clip emptied, I would pull it out and insert the other end in the rifle for another thirty live rounds to fire. It worked good doing it that way to eliminate running empty in the middle of a firefight and having to take the time to reload, which would give the enemy an edge on you that he could take advantage of.

MISERY 101 BEGINS TO SET IN

I noticed that those in authority had waited until the military police had left before issuing us any weapons. One thing you learn really quick in a war zone, attitudes change in a heartbeat when you also have a deadly weapon in your hands. This moment is where the real pain, misery, and extreme cold all became a factor to deal with. A bunch of us were dropped off in a cornfield without anyone in authority, no officers or even a squad leader—only a bunch of people you didn't know, everyone appearing to be just as mixed up and confused as the next guy. There wasn't any use to ask any questions about anything. Everyone that knew anything had already left, giving us orders to stay right there until someone came to pick us up.

With no protection from the brutal cold and wind, they left us there in a hurry, in the middle of the night. It was a good sign that we were pretty close to the front lines. About the time I thought it couldn't get any worse, it did. My best buddy Ernie Lee, that had gone with us, and myself, tore a corn shack apart, and we tried to cover up and protect ourselves from the brutal below-zero weather and get out of the cold and snow. It didn't work, however; we just got all the colder and more miserable. It was getting pretty close to what seemed to me to be impossible conditions for one to continue to exist in for very long and still live. I did, however, later on during the next couple months on the front line, find out through experience that you are able to stand way more than you sometimes think you can.

LET THE CHIPS FALL

I HAD NOTICED OUT FROM THE CORNER OF the cornfield where they had dropped us off, a rural Korean home about a quarter a mile away, or so, as a little swirl of smoke was coming out of the chimney. It was a crisp, clear moonlit night, and had it not been for the existing circumstances of half-freezing to death, I could have enjoyed it because it kind of reminded me of the northern Michigan winters and the surrounding farmlands. I tried to talk Ernie into going over with me and getting inside and warm up a little, but he wouldn't do it and tried to talk me out of it by telling me of how much trouble I would be getting myself in.

The more I goaded him, the more he dug his heels in. I was aware of all the possible disciplinary actions that could be taken against me, and none of them seemed any worse than freezing to death. The army had already drilled the fact into our heads that desertion, especially on the front lines, could very easily earn one the instant death penalty. Never claiming to be the sharpest tool in the shed, I had made my decision. Right, wrong, or indifferent, I would not be freezing to death this night in a Korean cornfield.

ANGELS RUSH IN WHERE FOOLS FEAR TO TREAD

SO, I WENT ON OVER TO THE OCCUPIED Korean home, not sure of what I might be getting into. I didn't even know whether it was behind our front lines or in front of them. I knocked on the door, and an old mamasan came to the door and opened it a little. I could see past her into a dimly lit room full to the corners with young and old people and kids of different sizes all sitting around on their haunches, as the Korean custom is. By the old mamasan's attitude and the guttural noises and sounds from all the way down to her toes and coming out of her mouth, it told me the welcome mat had not been made available to me. I knew I wasn't going to ask anyone if I could come in. I just hunched my shoulders and rubbed my hands together, assuming it was an international sign of being cold, that they would all understand, as I walked past the old woman, looking for a spot where I might fit in.

I spotted a couple eight- or ten-year-old boys sitting with their backs to the wall and reasoned that would be a good place to head for. I went on over and squeezed in between them; every eye in the room was on me, but no one was saying anything. I have often wondered what might have been going through their individual minds. I can imagine the stories being told about it for the past sixty-seven years now. I had been issued my weapon and tried not to act threatening but kept both hands on it for a few minutes. My senses were telling me that all was well; no one was either looking or acting threatening. It was like looking into a lot of empty hole eyes with shocked, confused minds and at a loss to do anything about it. I felt somewhat at peace; the heat felt good, and I had maintained a subtle awareness, hoping it would stay that way for a few more minutes to warm up a little.

CHOCOLATE DIDN'T DO THE JOB

I HAD TWO C RATION CHOCOLATE WAFERS AND gave one to each boy by my side as a peace gesture. They lit right up with a big smile, but the old woman laid down some more serious-sounding guttural commands, and they each handed their wafers back. I had not considered the fact that probably none of them had anything much to eat during that time; food was hard to come by in Korea. I knew then I was most likely unwelcome in their home, but—oh well, tough shit. It was their war that was responsible for me being there in the first place. It was their turn to suck it up and put up with me for a few minutes, if that's what was being required of them.

They are all likely telling others still about their unusual encounter in the middle of the night. By now, since Koreans tend to be little people, they have probably got me eight foot tall and four foot wide at the shoulders. Telling their grandchildren how they had sat their spell bound and, in fear, looking down the barrel of a gun in the hands of some crazy foreign soldier. But all that ends well can become a blessing in disguise. I very much value replaying that unusual encounter with a group of unknown strangers in my memory bank, to which I can look back upon and appreciate as one more experience of life that God not only brought me to but also brought me through. One more encounter with life in an unusual way. In a country I never even heard of and a people I didn't know, somewhere on the other side of the earth where I called my home.

I had no idea whether I was in North or South Korea, but I did know I was close to the front lines and I could be in enemy or friendly territory, but I can still see those people sitting there in a packed room, no expression at all on their faces, with all eyes on me. I said a few words of Korean to keep them wondering how much of their language I knew and understood to possibly prevent them from planning among themselves right in front of me to throw me out or even do something worse. Just thinking about this again as I write here causes me to reflect kindly upon this room full of total strangers who allowed me to warm up a little and share space in an out-of-the-way cornfield home somewhere near the front lines of Korea.

I stayed in there for about twenty minutes or a half hour and had gotten somewhat warmed up, and I had begun to lose my nerve. I also didn't want to miss the truck that would be taking us on up to the front. No one with any military authority had ever said anything to me about it later when I returned to the group. I had gotten up and left the people just as I had found them. I thanked them all before leaving. But again, it all fell on empty eyes and closed mouths. It is one more experience of my life that comes back to mind on a regular basis; unusual things happen to us all at times. I value those memories that could have had devastating and negative effects on my life, but to me, God worked it out to be for my good. It could possibly have been the one thing that helped me to survive the Korean War.

I LEFT WITH A FEELING OF RELIEF

I HAD GONE BACK TO THE STAGING AREA, and within a few minutes, a different set of trucks, picked us up to move us closer to our different destinations to certain individual outfits that we had been earmarked for combat in. But not before I took the opportunity to tell Ernie how toasty warm I had gotten and a few other slight exaggerations, like how cute and friendly these Korean country girls can be. I wouldn't let him forget it either. We had to do everything we could to keep our minds occupied to stand the horrible bone-numbing, unrelenting weather in the coldest Korean winter in a hundred years.

Especially so without any decent cold-weather clothing, thanks to the glory-hound General Douglas MacArthur saying he would have the boys home by Christmas and never ordered any decent cold-weather clothing or footwear. He thankfully was run out of town by my hero, President Truman, who sacked him for insubordination and replaced him with General Matthew B. Ridgway, who led his men from the front, not in some safe zone a thousand miles away from the battle like MacArthur, as he sought out the news organizations to pat himself on the back and make a hero out of himself.

It was probably about two or three o'clock in the morning or even later and the trucks had to go slow and in the pitch-black night, with their lights turned off. There was no such thing as a road; we lumbered slowly along as we just pitched back and forth in the back of the truck, intermittently stopping as they picked their way along as best they could. Within a few minutes, we began hearing our own artillery going over our heads and exploding in front of us. Our artillery had begun the offensive for the day. The very much-appreciated artillery bombardment combined with the Air Force or Marine pilots, with their close air support, was a giant support service for us on the ground that I grew to appreciate, respect, and look forward to at just the right time. It would put the fear of God in Old Joe Chink, and especially so if it was napalm (jelly gas).

WE'RE GETTING CLOSER NOW

We knew we were about to enter a new and different world. A world of reality where your life or death for a large part would depend upon the ability and the skill of the enemy versus yourself and your comrades. Some may be tempted to call it luck, either bad or good luck. I prefer to acknowledge God in the equation. The One in control of all things and all of the time. The first thing that surprised me was the artillery shelling going over our heads didn't sound anything at all like what I had heard in the movies. It sounded like the projectiles were going end over end with a *swish, swish, swish* or a wobbling sound.

Our comrades manning the big guns were sure putting a lot of wobbly death in the air to soften up the enemy for us in the ground pounding infantry. Where we would soon be taking over to keep them off balance with our attack-and-retreat policy that General Ridgeway ordered and had identified it as "Operation Killer." Not to be confused with Operation Rat Killer during the same war. Operation Killer was the start of the second major counteroffensive launched by United Nations forces against the Chinese Communist People's Volunteer Army and the North Korean Army during the Korean War between 20 February and 6 March 1951.

It was light when we found the outfit we were to belong to. I was sent to the Second Infantry Division, Ninth Infantry Regiment Company B. My education in reality was soon to begin. At the end of the battle for Wonju, Korea, we, in the Second Infantry Division, had inflicted eighteen thousand causalities upon the enemy. Then in the spring offensive, after I had been evacuated out of combat with the division, they had inflicted another nineteen thousand more causalities that battle had been identified as "the May Massacre." So, in those two offensives, we, the Second Infantry Division, had inflicted thirty-seven thousand casualties upon them. More than making up for the three thousand casualties they had inflicted upon our division at Kunri.

As soon as we caught up with the squad I was to be a replacement in, as they came trudging down through a wooded hill side, the very first thing I did before they had even got to us was ask to be the machine gunner. A black soldier with a machine gun over his shoulder had asked as he approached if any of us knew how to operate a light .30-caliber air-cooled machine gun. Like a lightning bolt, my hand was in the air. He walked right straight up to me and gladly handed it over, saying, "You are now the machine gunner." I had gotten my own way but was too gung ho, immature, and dumb enough to realize it until I had to carry the forty-seven-pound killing machine, along with the ammunition to make it useful, up and down the Korean mountains in knee-deep snow, in below-zero weather conditions.

Still, it pleased me now to know that I got my way to have a serious weapon that could spew out lead enough to inflict the maximum amount of death and destruction upon "Old Joe Chink," our enemy. I had become too bloodthirsty to consider the weight of the weapon and extra ammunition we had to carry. No one in command bothered to bring me up to speed on instructions of use for the weapon. Manpower was in short supply for any specific teaching for the renewing of the proper procedure. Our infantry training qualified us in its use, but a little updating would have been appreciated. Without one second of reviewing or revealing the expected and acceptable operation of the weapon, I became the squad machine gunner.

Too late I had learned an important and necessary lesson. With the metal carrying canisters or boxes holding 250 rounds per box, that weighed twenty-six pounds per box, our usual supply was at least four canisters and sometimes more, which made its weight 104 pounds. That is along with all the rest of the gear we had to carry also, the machine gun and tripod itself weighed about 47 pounds. I usually carried two fragmentation grenades and another weapon and ammunition for it as well.

We learned really fast how to negotiate and to solve this problem and get things done. As I have already mentioned, the machine gun and tripod alone weighed 47 pounds, now adding another 104 pounds to that and slogging through knee-deep snow up and down mountains, we needed to find us a pack mule to carry the ammunition. Having worked on the docks in both Pusan and Inchon, Korea, I had seen and knew very well how much weight a Korean could carry on his back with what is known as an A-frame. A primitive device, designed to carry really heavy loads on their shoulders, almost every Korean seemed to own one, especially if he was traveling. And as there was usually refugees and misplaced Koreans on the move south to escape the brutal North Koreans, it wasn't hard to find a warm body to help us out.

SECURING AN AMMUNITION BEARER

We would keep our eyes peeled, looking out for a strong looking younger Korean man headed south. We would not at all barter, bicker, or negotiate any kind of deal with them; there was no time for such things as that. We made it very simple and put it into practice immediately. They would suddenly find themselves conscripted into the United States Army, under the threat of immediate death if they tried to run off. We knew they would be strong and durable by the size of the load they would be carrying on their A-frame.

We would strip them of everything personal on their A-frame, beyond anything of necessity for survival in the weather conditions, and set it aside and load it up with machine gun ammunition. Whatever room left for personal effects, we would let them take along with them. The rest of it was just left behind on the ground for others to find and to be to put to use as they may have saw fit. My mind-set was, if we have to be there to defend and fight for their freedom, it is not going to hurt them to share in it also.

We were able to draw extra rations most of the time, or they would end up eating the ugliest C ration (canned food in the pack) that no one liked and that was hard to choke down. The corn beef hash was only a notch above starving to death, during the extreme weather conditions that existed that winter. It would stick to the roof of the mouth and often be frozen in the can and had to be chiseled out with a bayonet. But it would at least feed them until we ran into an intense fire fight with the Chinese and while being occupied in defending ourselves against them. As soon as they got the chance they would be gone and out of sight, doing the well-known "chogie-chogie" bug out as it became known in the Korean War. Then we would have to start all over again in selecting another ammo bearer.

Even though we would, in advance, have our Korean interpreter translate for us in telling them if they ran off, we would not think twice, we would drop them dead in their tracks, it was no different than the military rules and regulations for our own soldiers. It might seem wrong to the mind of someone reading it here, and maybe it is wrong, but it is just another example of the decisions having to be made to fit the present circumstances that any soldier finds himself facing, if he wants to survive and do his job. For wars to be won, as bloody as it always is, there has to be those with the balls to step up and make things work. As well as the officers to be up to the task of giving the orders in extreme life and death situations.

Battlefield conditions and ways of operating are altogether different in normal military procedures then they are at any other time. A leader or any regular soldier has to step up and make hard and instant decisions when the situation calls for it. To hesitate could cost lives of your comrades or a close buddy, and your own as well. Too late we often find out the hard way when we have made a bad decision. My chomping at the bit to be the machine gunner caused me a lot of woe and misery. Now that it is all over with, I am glad I took it on and that God had brought me through it. I learned lessons that I would not have learned in any other way. And as I continue to remind you here, God has used it all for my own benefit and overall well-being.

I GUESS YOU CAN'T FIX DUMB

My going from a rear echelon outfit without any recent combat training at all was the beginning of pure hell on earth. I was soft from being a booze- and beer-drinking PX commando in honky-tonk joints and out of condition from supervising and working Korean dockworkers to do all of the grunt work. It had caused me to be out of physical shape, even though I was only eighteen years old at the time. My stamina had been depleted, and in a short time, just putting one foot in front of the other one became a struggle. Mao Zedong, the Chinese big-gun dictator at that time, had decided to take Wonju, Korea, no matter the cost in lives. Wonju was of the utmost importance, a great strategic railroad and crossroad area that was exceptionally beneficial to those who controlled it.

He gave orders to his generals in charge to eliminate completely the Second Infantry Division, which I had become a replacement in. They, the generals, sent three divisions against our one Indianhead Division, giving orders to annihilate our division at all costs, stating that everything else was to become secondary. As they began to throw everything they had at us. Fortunately, President Truman had sacked the glory-hound General Douglas MacArthur by that time, for which President Truman became my lifetime hero, for so doing. No one can deny the value of MacArthur's great military leadership and the hard decisions he had to make in beating the snot out of Japanese during WWII. But he went one step beyond in exercising his insubordination against President Truman.

MacArthur was always somewhere way back in the rear and out of any danger, looking for a photo opportunity in front of news reporters and cameras to promote himself. He was already thought of as a god by the Japanese, and I think he believed it himself, but I was glad to see him go. The stage had been set and the early spring offensive had already begun. Pure hell on earth was now about ready to begin for me. So many things beyond the imagination of men began happening around us and within our midst, now on a regular basis. Each one seemed to be more mind-boggling, bloody, and shocking than the one before it. The carnal human mind, it seems, will never run out of the diverse and differing ways in which to kill and destroy each other.

GENERAL MATTHEW B. RIDGEWAY TAKES OVER

General Matthew B Ridgeway, who led his men from the front, in my opinion was a much superior general in combat than MacArthur ever was. MacArthur led from the distant rear while looking for a photo opportunity that would allow for him to praise his own abilities and cement his imagined godlike status more securely in his own mind. Soldiers liked General Ridgeway because he could be seen right up front. He gave the order to attack and withdraw, in what he had termed "Operation Killer." Keeping the enemy off balance and able then to inflict the maximum number of casualties upon them while keeping our own casualties at a minimum. Ridgeway was a great general that led from the front; he turned the tide of the Korean War around.

A fact that endeared him more to the troops that had to be there themselves. It was a night-and-day operation in the coldest Korean winter in one hundred years. As a replacement, I never was issued any decent cold-weather clothing, and our weapons didn't work properly. It was a guessing game when you needed them, wondering how they would be working this time. I never spent any time inside a building of any kind for two months, except for about five minutes one afternoon when we had been pulled to the rear for a supposed rest that turned out to be anything but. It was one of the most miserable near-death experiences that myself and my assistant machine gunner had spent pulling guard on a tank in the area after our squad leader had pulled myself and assistant machine gunner out to guard a tank against any night time attack.

MORE ON THE TANK GUARD MISERY

I HAD LOST TRACK OF TIME AS ONE day just melted into the next one, of how long we had been on the front lines in action on a 24/7 basis. We had left the line this one day to get some rest and recuperation, a short distance in the rear. We withdrew a couple hundred yards to the rear and spotted a Korean dwelling. The squad leader approached and knocked on the door to get us all inside and to warm up. The older Korean man, probably in his midforties, fought to stay in his home. The squad leader grabbed him by the front of his clothing and threw him aside like a bag of potatoes into the drifted and arctic gale force blizzard snow that was swirling and drifting around his home. But he got back up and fought to get back into his warm home.

THE CAUSES OF A DAMAGED MIND

THIS TIME THE SQUAD LEADER WAS IN NO mood to play patty-cake. Wanting to get the job at hand done and inside to warm up, he hit him a hard, solid blow to the head with his rifle butt, and he fell bleeding and unconscious there in the snow. It remains a vivid reminder that I think of often in reviewing and seeing it as it periodically impacts my mind from time to time. They no doubt found him in the spring frozen to death a few feet away from his own home. The worst thing about it was, at that time, it didn't bother me one little bit. You either learn really quick to adjust to the atrocities of war or stand a good chance of going home dead, wrapped in a shelter half, just like so many others I had myself personally handled.

However, it has not stopped that painful and tear-jerking image from coming before my eyes hundreds and even thousands of times, down through the pages of time, that old man *(at least to us young kids)* didn't deserve to die in that way. War has always been fought and won both by the survival of the fittest and/or by the philosophy of "the end justifies the means." If we would like to continue to live in peace, safety and plenty, there will have to be those willing to fight and die for it when necessary. But again, remember this well: war will end on the day that Jesus Christ returns to earth to lead the world into righteousness, right here on our good earth. It is the specific reason that

God admonishes us all to pray this prayer. "Our Father who is in heaven, hallowed be thy name, *thy kingdom come*, thy will be done *on earth* as it is in heaven."

We had fought the Chinese enemy all day long until late afternoon, on a hill where they were really dug in well and was putting up a strong defense. We had begun to make some headway after another barrage from our artillery that was shaking them loose off the skyline ridge. We were advancing at a pretty good pace, and I was one of the first to reach the top. By this time, they most all had fled up past the next ridge, but plodding along behind were three Chinese soldiers that had not yet cleared the area. I was carrying an M-1 .30-caliber carbine at the time, like I said earlier. I had taped two banana clips upside down from each other. Each clip holds thirty rounds of ammunition. I was able to fire thirty rounds and instantly pop out the empty and insert the loaded one.

I had fired one whole clip at them, expecting to see them all three drop dead in their tracks. It didn't look to me as if they even bothered to flinch or change their pace in any way. They quickly just ambled along out of sight and disappeared beyond the skyline. I felt like a dog for missing them all; they would still be there tomorrow to try and kill us, myself or one of my comrades. The one thing I was glad of was no one had yet reached the area to witness the spectacle, and I was thankful for that. But it really bothered me because I knew well how to shoot and where my weapon was shooting. Our mother had bought all of us boys .22 rifles when we were about twelve years old. From that time on, we hunted something year-round.

That episode bothered me for a lot of years, every time I would stop and think about it. Then one day I was able to get some mind relief as I was reading an article about the Korean War and the different battles and the effectiveness of the M-1 .30-caliber carbines during the Korean War. Later on, during the war, the powers that be had concluded that it lacked the penetrating power needed to go through the heavily padded Chinese outer coats the Chinese soldier were wearing or their backpacks.

All field commanders were given orders to have their carbine-carrying soldiers to shoot for the head. So, this did give me a measure of relief to know that I probably did hit them, but it didn't help us any. But I had made up my mind at that point, I would be throwing that carbine away as soon as the opportunity presented itself to make the change. The carbine automatic-fire weapon was good in close weapon, but evidently, not all that good at a distance. Then later on in life, I began to look at things a little differently. It, all of a sudden, felt good to imagine that those three Chinese soldiers may have made it back home alive to their mothers and families like I was able to do. I hope they did.

The opportunity to get rid of the carbine came the very next day as we moved again, on an attack, against the Chinese enemy. We were going through a sparsely covered wooded area, with good vision in close, but not so good at a distance. A comrade at my side that I did not know was hit and dropped stone-cold dead in his tracks, a few feet away from me. I had checked to make sure he was dead, as I took his M1 Garand .30 caliber rifle that could easily reach out and kill at five hundred yards and more, and I had done well with it on the rifle range in basic training and knew how to use it.

I left my carbine by his side as I took his bayonet and ammunition-loaded bandoliers. The *M1 Garand* is a .30 caliber semiautomatic rifle that was the standard US service rifle during World War II and the Korean War and also saw limited service during the Vietnam War. Most M1 rifles were issued to US forces, though many hundreds of thousands were also provided as foreign aid to American allies. It was a good weapon that you could always depend upon in doing its job. It was quite a bit heavier than the carbine along with the ammunition required, but way deadlier at a distance. However, I would have been at a disadvantage in close-up hand-to-hand fighting among those enemy soldiers attacking us in overwhelming numbers.

LOVE THOSE MARINE F-4U CORSAIR PILOTS

We had called in for artillery and air support on this one mountainous area of steep, high ridges and wooded hills that we were having a problem of dislodging the enemy troops from. The awesome Marine Corps pilots, in their F-4U Corsairs that were so good at giving us close air support, had come in and dropped their napalm bombs (jelly gas) on the top of this steep mountain, as we called them—while other natives of Korea were calling them hills. They had done a pretty good job of putting the fear of God in the Chinese army that was busy now evacuating the high areas of the ground retaking from them. It is hard to describe the smell emanating down to us where the Marine pilots had dropped their napalm bombs.

The closer we came into the all-charred up, burned-to-a-crisp, and blackened area, where some of the enemy soldiers had been caught and burned to a charred crisp too, the worse the smell became; and the gorier sights of soldiers burned in grotesque shapes stuck in my mind and caused me to be thankful that they, the Chinese enemy, either did not have napalm, or at least they had not yet used it on us. One dead soldier among them in particular could not to be recognized as a human being at all. He stays in my mind's eye night and day whenever I think back about combat in Korea.

He reminded me of a good-sized shish kabob. Everything had been all drawn up in his middle torso, to about the size of a small watermelon, shrunken down and charred beyond any recognition of being a human being. The positive, if there is a positive in war, was twofold. One for us and one for him. We would not be required to fight him tomorrow, or possibly be killed by him. And his death was quick for him, he didn't have to suffer long. The war was over for him, and his spirit had already returned back to God who had given it to him. If we can look at it that way, we are all winners. We need always to remember that God loves us all unconditionally. Mankind has a way that seems right in their own eyes, but notice what God has to say about it below.

"There is a path before each person that seems right, but it ends in death" (Proverbs 14:12).

"There is a way which seems right to a man, but its end is the way of death" (Proverbs 16:25).

Even considering my past practices during my tour of duty in the Korean War, God has now given me a peace of mind and an inner feeling of tranquility that outweighs and surpasses all that I experienced and was guilty of. Some of it was being dumped on me by superiors that I had no control over. Other things, I didn't need anyone to direct me in doing. I elected on my own on doing things contrary to the will and ways of God. The more badly mangled bodies of dead or even live soldiers that couldn't die and escape the pain and suffering of their awful wounds you witnessed, the more bloodthirsty you became to extract some equal pain and revenge on the enemy.

But still, as I was evacuated out of Korea and immediately began my self-medication and anti-God activity at every turn in the road, there finally came a time after many episodes of playing smashmouth in some den of iniquity with one of my bad-boy counterparts. The world seemed to be closing in on me, and I suddenly realized that God had been working with me and possibly wanted to use me for His own purpose and plan for all of mankind. I began a serious study into His Word and began to see it wasn't at all like what I had heard about in the so-called Christian churches. In fact, it was nowhere near what I was learning from the Bible.

After acquainting myself with the Word of God, I felt that I had found good company in reading about the life of Saul of Tarsus, who became the apostle Paul. It was an enlightening moment when I read about his life story. How he had described himself as the worst of the worst sinner ever. The apostle Paul, according to his own testimony, was a murderer, rounding up followers of Christ to be taken to prison or to be killed. I will always be grateful and thankful for Jesus Christ explaining how this has all been set in motion through the purpose and plan of God before the world began. Now I knew if God was going to pardon the apostle Paul and that Christ would remove his sins as far away from him as the east is from the west (*Psalm 103:12*).

Jesus Christ is able and capable to call and bring the worst of the worst to repentance and a change of heart and mind to be used to the degree that God has used the apostle Paul. And He will not stop, slow down, faint, or even consider giving up on us until every last man, woman, and child ever born on this earth has shed their incorruption and put on the righteousness of God. As we can all read about in 1 Corinthians. So also *is* the resurrection of the dead. It is sown in corruption; it is raised in incorruption (*1 Corinthians 14:52*). We die in all that is rotten, vile, destructive, and unrighteousness; we will be raised up in all that is good, pure, righteous, just, and in step with the Word and the ways of God.

To the followers of Jesus Christ that before conversion have lived life on the edge and have violated every law expressed and commanded against by God, to those that are worried and concerned about losing their own salvation, this becomes a message of absolute and certain joy and adulation toward God and His Son Jesus Christ. To realize and to know for certain that the purpose and plan of God has always been the salvation of all of mankind. Since God is not a respecter of persons, it means that all of mankind will be called, all will repent either during their lifetime or after their death and during the second resurrection, also known as the Great White Throne Judgment. And all will be saved and belong to the kingdom of God. We have all been sealed with the promise of the God that cannot lie.

Eternal life for all is a promised gift of God and His gifts are irrevocable. We can accept this truth from the word of God or we can call Him a liar through unbelief.

"For God's gifts and His call are irrevocable" (Romans 11:29).

"And do not grieve the Holy Spirit of God, in whom you were sealed for the day of redemption" (Ephesians 4:30).

BACK TO THE FRONT

A DAY IN FRONTLINE COMBAT WOULD JUST MELT into the next one as your mind is lying in limbo between firefights that, at times, would require talking to myself, pushing, shoving, prodding, and bearing down on myself to get one foot in front of the other in the nonstop day-and-night misery, wondering if it would ever end. The next enemy bullet or mortar round might have my name on it.

Feeling guilty when the comrade next to you dropped dead in his tracks and it gives you reason to rejoice in the fact that the god of war may have taken his allotted number for the day, and you have been left alive to face another day of more of the same come tomorrow. Along with those feelings, I felt jealous of the person whose misery had, in the blink of an eye, been solved and taken care of. I felt as though I had been cheated out of getting the relief he had just received.

Either keeping on walking and moving or shivering to even approach generating a little blood movement to stay alive. Operating on the very edge of exhaustion, sanity, hunger, and weakness, wondering if today would be the day that the enemy would take me out of the game, or will I be able to make it to one more tomorrow. No friends left. Ernie was the last to go; lucky Ernie! No one left to talk to and ask how any of them in the same condition as I were able to endure it all. Gaining territory and then losing it back to the enemy along with the causalities it took to gain it. All that one could hope for is one more day to stay alive, and to eventually be warm and have decent food and clothing. But that at the time seemed out of the question and unreasonable to even bother thinking about. You are not really living anymore, anyway. You have become a mindless robot just putting one foot in front of the other, waiting for what fate has in store for you whether it be an enemy soldier a few feet away that has just pulled the pin on a grenade, and has his eye on you, or an enemy mortar soldier who has just dropped the mortar down the tube that has your name on it. Maybe a sniper is waiting for you to step in that clearing, to get his kill shot. You curse the weather, and wonder when your C-rations will be delivered, because you haven't eaten anything now for a couple days. You hate all of those fat cats sitting a world away from all this misery making wars happen, but never stepping up and fighting in one.

No hope of getting any decent clothing or footwear, you settle for the fact that in all of the reality of knowing yesterday's death count to be a good predictor of what tomorrows will likely bring leaves you with a mind-set that your life will, in time, end right here along with all those comrades who were killed around you. Thoughts of home becomes an unrealistic dream that diverts your attention away from your job as a government hunter seeking and searching after one more enemy to send to the promised land. The key to it all seemed to be to turn your mind completely off and keep putting one foot in front of the other like the robot killer the military had programmed and trained you to be.

It seemed to me to be an operation of futility. Then it gets dark, and we have to quit for a while, dropping down again in exhaustion, finding out we are in the exact same place we started at in the morning. I remember sleeping, or rather having to be in a hole that night with a squad leader that I didn't much like. I had dug it out the night before; he decided he was going to do me a big favor and stayed in my hole because it looked bigger than anyone else's. He had his poncho and used it to cover our heads with. Then he lit up a can of canned heat to warm it up a little while we sat there in misery, staring at each other, without any conversation, while the condensation from his canned heat dripped down the back of my neck and onto us all night long, or as long as it burned.

It had gotten to the point where an engagement with the Chinese enemy was a welcome godsend. The adrenaline would take over and bring life back into your worn-down and depleted body, at least for a little while. Your heart would automatically beat faster, and the effect on the mind is it would sharpen up and allow you to do your job. We had run into some stiff opposition from the Chinese one afternoon, as we were coming into dusk, not too much daylight left. We opened up on them in the direction the attack was coming from with all that we had. Machine gun, BAR Browning automatic rifle, mortar, and small-arms fire.

Filling the space and the air between us and them with a whole lot of hot lead and firepower. A lot of meeting the enemy in combat is quite often that way. You may only get a fleeting glimpse here and there or not be able to see them at all; you open up on the area that they appear to be coming from. Their firing upon us slowed down until there would be an occasional shot or two coming in. We had stood vigil for a decent time before bedding down in our snow-and-ice bed, waiting for a nighttime counterattack, which never came. The Chinese enemy had it every bit as bad as we did—no decent clothing or footwear, they would have burlap wrapped around their feet, some were even barefooted with frozen feet, hands, and body parts.

We were back on their track the next morning, heading into no-man's-land where their attack had come from the night before. Within a couple hundred yards or so, we began to run into dead Chinese soldiers that the enemy had left behind. This one area of wetlands like a marsh or a shallow, swampy area with a foot or two of standing water in it. It had frozen over solid during the night and was filled with a dozen or so dead Chinese soldiers. It was a grotesque sight to behold. Several soldiers with just their backs sticking out above the now-frozen surface. Probably those who had been killed instantly, not having to suffer on.

Many of them had not died instantly; their heads and upper bodies were poking up out of the frozen water, some with their silent eyes glazed over and frozen open, peering off into space—their bloodstained uniforms, bodies, and faces a testimony for us to know that our firing upon them the night before, that many bullets had found their mark. Over the years it has become a visual image that too often will visit my mind's eye and will run non-stop until, something else comes along to knock it out of the way until the next time. It is as if a scab has been peeled off some old wound and it starts to stink, bleed and hurt all over again. You begin to think you've seen it all and can handle anything that comes at you, as I had come to think and to believe that I could do. I had seen, handled and caused a lot of death and dying. To the point that I thought I was immune to it. Then one day a few years later I had held the hand of my closest biological brother Glade, as he choked and gurgled out his last breath of life in the VA hospital in Durham, North Carolina. I had been wrong, the scab had been ripped off, the ugly, the insanity, the pain and the unexpected hit me like a ton of bricks. I begin living it all over again. It was the most traumatic and devastating feeling that I have ever had in my life. But still, considering all of this, I could not cry or show any emotions for more than a year later, when a mutual friend of myself and Glade, more like a brother, came to visit and drink a couple beers, then I broke down and cried uncontrollably for a long time.

This vision stays in my mind and heart today, in remembrance of the bloody outcome that happens when men take up weapons against others no different than themselves—killing, maiming, and destroying those made in the image and likeness of God. Thank God we have a Savior in Jesus Christ that has already pardoned us, and God has forgiven us for all sins committed and for all of time. Our final destiny is to become like God and Jesus Christ.

"JESUS CHRIST CAME TO EARTH TO BE LIKE US, THAT WE ALL WILL BE AS HE IS."

THE RUSSIANS CALL ARTILLERY "THE GOD OF WAR." Because of the devastation it can inflict upon the enemy from rear positions miles away from the front lines. Our Second Division Artillery in Korea was one deadly, accurate, and effective weapon against the swarming Chinese bonsai attacks. The Chinese soldiers would come in the first wave, in overwhelming numbers, with Russian burp guns that fired seven hundred rounds a minute and bring cold chills up your spine just hearing them. The Russian burp gun was responsible for the death and dismemberment of more of our soldiers than any weapon that we had to counter back with.

They put a lot of hot lead in the air ahead of themselves. A recurring sound along with their yelling, screaming, and blowing of their bugles in their bonsai attacks always got our immediate attention; that made our blood run cold. The following waves may or may not have a weapon at all. They would just pick up a weapon from a dead comrade, go forward, and keep up the fire. The artillery would zero in on them by way of spotters that could hopefully direct the artillery rounds to explode in their midst. When they came at us in elbow-to-elbow overwhelming numbers like flies on a dead carcass, the artillery would have a field day. After an all-out artillery battle, the empty shells would be piled up twelve to fifteen feet high.

PILES OF DEAD ENEMY AND EMPTY ARTILLERY SHELLS

THE AFTERMATH OF AN ALL-OUT ARTILLERY BARRAGE WOULD leave the whole area filled with dead Chinese soldiers covering the ground in massive numbers of blown-apart bodies. It was as if they had attempted to run themselves through a sausage grinder, thinking they would come out the other end unscathed. Actually, it was their commanders who gave them orders to do it, like our commanders did to us. It was a gruesome sight to see. A field full of broken, busted, beaten, and mangled human flesh, bone, blood, and fragmented body parts, with the steam still rising in the air from their warm and all-blown-to-hell bodies.

Whenever we would be hunkered down in our holes, waiting for our artillery to soften up the enemy that we were soon to face, it really sounded good to hear the shelling going over our heads. We knew as bad as it would have been without the artillery, it was going to be a lot better now to go on attack. For this and other reasons, there was no doubt whatsoever of who won the Korean War. The combined firepower of our military, Army, Navy, Marine, Seabee, and Coast Guard action, according to western sources estimate Chinese casualties at 400,000 dead and 486,000 wounded. In comparison, the American battle deaths were 33,652, an 11 to 1 deferential.

We were fighting back and forth with the Chinese in the battle to defend Wonju, Korea, from falling into the hands of the Chinese Communist Forces. We would push them back and put a big hurt on them long enough for them to catch their breath and come at us again. A seesaw operation where each time, men were paying the price with their lives. Both our comrades and the enemy soldiers. They had us outnumbered three divisions to one. It had gotten severely cold, and the ground was frozen up as solid as steel. Our entrenching tools couldn't even put a small dent in it. As usual, for the most part, we were on the constant move during daylight hours, either attacking or retreating. Then at night, we just lay down on the ice and snow bed without any blanket or anything else to cover over us and tried to get some sleep that never came.

At one point earlier on in the battle for Wonju, Korea, we had no snow to melt for drinking water; we were required to travel long distances over difficult terrain, running into frequent skirmishes with the enemy with nothing at all to drink. This had gone on for a long time until my tongue and mouth felt like somebody had put a big dry sponge into my mouth that had sucked every bit of moisture out of my system that could be taken, while my tongue felt about three times its size. I remembered our drill instructor in basic training telling us about serving in WWII and at one time giving forty dollars for a canteen of water. I had not believed him; suddenly now, I did. I would have given all that I owned for a good drink of water.

We had come down off the higher ground and was crossing this rice paddy when I had noticed where an ox had crossed through it and had broken through the ice in different places. I got out my canteen cup and knelt beside a hoof track that had sank down into the paddy. It was frozen over slightly, and I could see it had settled down and looked quite clear. I cracked the ice and scooped it out and threw it aside. It had settled down from being stirred up by the ox, and to me, it looked pretty clear. Even though I knew their rice paddies were being fertilized with gook poop, *human excrement*, I dipped me out several good long swigs of water. The best I have ever tasted in my life. I never bothered thinking about how many different parasites, germs, or anything else that might have been in it. When it comes to survival, one has to learn to do whatever it takes to get there.

One day, we found ourselves on top of a mountain. I remember it because it was an unusually sunny, not so brutally cold, bright, and upbeat day. We had ended up there after chasing the Chinese off it. Another unusual aspect of the day and time was one of our own tanks was up there too. We didn't often have the opportunity to be with or interact with the tankers. We were all taking a break, laughing and talking and enjoying the moment. We had a good view of the whole surrounding area; as we looked around, we noticed way off in the distance a couple miles away, a normal everyday Korean home within our sight. Since it was in the direction we were pursuing the Chinese army, it could become a place where they could rest and recuperate in warmth and relative safety.

The tanker in charge spun his .50-caliber machine gun mounted upon the tank around and zeroed it in on the Korean home. With every fifth bullet being a tracer to allow the tanker to know where his fire is going, he opened up on the building that, like most country homes in Korea, have rice straw roofs on them. It, in no time, burst into flames and burned to the ground. There didn't appear to be anyone living in it; we didn't see any motion around the area. We had exercised what the Russian call "scorched Earth" where you burn everything behind you that the enemy does not have the opportunity to use it in any way against you. We instead had burned it in front of our attack, so we wouldn't be able to either if and when we got to it.

THE COWARDS AMONG US

SOMETHING HAPPENED THAT I WAS NOT PREPARED TO experience one day. We were in a bad situation for quite some time; we were pinned down by the Chinese, unable to move as they were throwing mortars and small-arms fire into our area, and we were waiting for our own artillery to respond to the coordinated location from which their fire was coming from. We were dug in well and keeping a low profile in our foxholes when one of our own men begin begging for someone to bring him a drink of water. Still to this day, I do not recall ever seeing him or knowing what he looked like. He just kept his crying for water and help incessantly, getting more loud, whiny, intense, and more aggravating by the minute. He was bringing a moral decline and a "Woe is me" atmosphere that began to hang over the area.

I knew he was a regular in the outfit that had been with the division for some time because a lot of the other guys kept yelling at him to be quiet. First from one direction, someone would yell out, "Shut up Stoner" then from someplace else. I could see where he was dug in, but he was afraid to poke his head out of his hole. It was really affecting the whole squad; how did such a person as this ever get put on the front lines? It had gotten so aggravating that it crossed my mind to lob a grenade in his hole and put him out of his misery. It was at the time by far the worst example of cowardice that I ever had seen or ever hoped to see. I did live long enough, however, that God had softened my heart and had given me an empathy toward him. Also, I had to realize later on what real debilitating fear can have on an individual, so much so that I then looked at him in a different way.

The last I seen of Stoner was seeing his hind end running down through the woods to the rear, as fast as his legs could carry him. Someone had yelled out, "Would anybody like to go to the rear for a shower?" He left there like a rat shot ass. I never seen or heard any more about him. I don't know where he came from, but ten to one if I had to guess about it and he made it home alive. He has probably been telling war stories of his great courage and bravery on the front line in combat in the Korean War to his family, friends, and acquaintances now for the past sixty-seven years. I found out there are a lot more cowards in the military service than I ever could have imagined.

I went to school with two kids from my area in Fife Lake, Michigan. Both of them had been drafted into the service during the Korean War. I knew them both very well; both of them were my neighbors. I had been in the Korean War, had been wounded in action, and had been sent home to spend about a year in Percy Jones Army Hospital in Battle Creek, Michigan, to recuperate from frozen feet and to gain back weight and strength from the effects of the severe, below-zero sustained weather conditions that existed in Korea the first year on the front lines. There came a day as I was going to the chow hall to eat when I saw one of these guys sitting and talking with another patient. He had his arm in a sling and was bandaged up. I assumed he had been wounded in Korea as well and asked him about it.

He wasn't ashamed or shy about it at all; he just started spilling his guts. He told me that he had been drafted and had gone home on a delay in route from basic training on his way to Korea. That he had talked to one of his brothers and came up with a plan to keep him out of the war. His oldest brother, Elmer, had suggested that Earl put his hand on a block of wood and he chopped off some fingers. Earl wanted to make sure it would definitely keep him from having to go to Korea and instructed Elmer to make sure he got his trigger finger. So, with the plan in motion, Earl put his hand on the block of wood, and Elmer chopped down on it hard and took his trigger finger off on his right hand, along with two other fingers, leaving him with only his thumb and pinky finger on his right hand.

That, however, is not the end of the story. A few years passed, and Earl and his whole family moved out of our area. One day a couple decades or so later, Earl pulled into our driveway; he came to the house and knocked on my door. We had a good conversation reminiscing about the fun times of growing up together and a few good belly laughs about the dumb things we had done. I was glad to see him, and by now, he had a very nice wife with him, along with a son. He asked if he could hunt on our land and acquaint his son to the enjoyment and fun of deer hunting. I told him to go right ahead; it was all right with me. A couple days later, he came back over and told me how his son had been able to shoot a deer on the property we had let them hunt on.

It didn't stop there. We got to visiting again, and during our conversation, he revealed how he had been getting a VA pension for some time now to compensate for the lost fingers during the Korean War. The other acquaintance named Robert, that I had also known all of my life, didn't fare quite so well. He had been sent to Alaska and was also home on a delay en route before being shipped to Korea. He took his father's 30-30 deer hunting Winchester and shot himself in the foot, but instead of becoming a Korean War veteran receiving a VA compensation check every month, they gave him a dishonorable discharge. He went on drinking and fighting in every bar in the area until he was barred from them all. He died in his forties or fifties, with a worn-out body that had been busted up too many times because of his drunken and fighting lifestyle.

I have one more case of blatant cowardice of a soldier during the Korean War. As we were all being assembled at Wonju, Korea, to be dispersed out into combat companies that had lost many men and needed replacements fast, to bring them back up to fighting strength, there was no one who appeared to be in charge as we all milled around, looking to get out of the weather. The part of Wonju we were in was pretty well bombed out and deserted. Several of us had found a deserted home to get in out of the weather. We were tearing things apart in and around the house to build a fire to warm up the house.

Two of our soldiers there were in a conversation together that I wasn't listening to and didn't care about. It became evident that they were hatching a plan of some sort, I just happened to be in their proximity and saw it happen with my own eyes. One had put his flattened-out hand upon a solid windowsill, and the other one hit it as hard as he possibly could with an entrenching tool, a *steel shovel*. I don't know what happened to this guy, but I would be willing to bet that he too most probably ended up with an honorable medical discharge. And all his life, like Earl and Stoner, he has probably been telling war stories about himself as a brave and courageous frontline combat veteran and has drawn a good pension of VA compensation to prove it.

There are many things that go on behind the scenes that we are never aware of; since this is true, I thought you needed to hear about it. Cowards exist in the military, if I can expose this many by myself, imagine how many others there must be throughout the different military outfits. I have never heard other combat veterans talk about such things. It is hard for me to understand how it is possible within a group of the many comrades you have known and served with for some time and then allow yourself to be exposed as such a spineless and cowardly person that they have living among them. Shame and disgrace on such cowardly actions would drive most men to crawl into a hole and pull it in on top of themselves.

PROGRAMMED WITH A KILLER INSTINCT

THERE IS A PRICE THAT HAS TO BE paid in the mind and heart of those that witness, experience and become a part of all of the brutal atrocities of war. It can for the moment be blocked out and dealt with during the time that it happens, but later on as you unknowingly or unwittingly let that stuff back into you head, it can and often, will start all over again. The kid next to you that has been mangled and dismembered and will never make it home. Your close buddy bleeding to death in front of your eyes that you cannot help.

The job of or the sight of dragging frozen, stiff bodies off a hill can cause the mental breakdown of a brother who can no longer control his crying because his mind has reached its capacity to absorb one bit more of it and not any more remain sane. Many combat veterans come home appearing alright, just fine and dandy on the outside but a mixed-up boiling pot of frustrations, nerves, guilt complexes, and suicidal tendencies on the inside where no one can see them. They left home and family because they were asked to go and serve their country. None of them being aware that they would never be totally normal again. They left home with high hopes and dreams of success, adventure, and personal achievement. They came back a different person with a troubled mind and many with a broken spirit. I put all of my army gear in my duffel bag and put it in the chicken coop of Nancy's folks. Where over the years it all disintegrated and ended up in smelling like chicken shit, until all that was left was the duffel bag. When you would slip up and say anything about your time in the service, it became fashionable for some to ridicule and make fun of anything you had to say, and I wasn't alone. The Korean War veterans were treated bad enough but the Vietnam veterans were being treated even worse than us. Neither was popular and the Korean War identified as a police action by President Truman, caused it soon to be known as, "The Forgotten War". The military were not necessarily looking for the sharpest tool in the shed to join the services, and we may have been a little naïve, gullible and easily taken in by different service recruiters, but for the most part we had stepped up and put our individual lives on the line for our nation. Basically, good kids in a uniform that are programmed and trained to go forward at any cost, to be turned into wild, untrained animals with the killer instinct. Your military leaders making certain that you develop a deep-down red-hot hatred for those that they will be sending you against, that the spirit of revenge automatically takes over to see that the job you have been given be taken care of properly.

Then when you do finally come home alive after surviving it all, and you hide your uniform and all other paraphernalia that would identify you as a soldier, you put the memory and experience of it in a spot way, way back into the corners of your mind. You keep your mouth shut tight because you have already learned that to mention anything about it in a group setting will cause folks to get anxious and fidgety, looking at you sideways as they get up and leave the area for one of two reasons. What you have to say is unbelievable to them, or they are about the same age as yourself and they have to start finding excuses why they never served in the military themselves.

I have great respect for all who have served in the military during peace or war. They were there when needed and asked to, and ready to serve in any capacity. Anyone willing to step up and shed their own blood on the battlefield for others to be able to live in peace, I gladly and willingly call my brother or sister, and the real heroes are those who give their last breath of life that others may live in freedom.

Which has been etched into the Korean War Memorial Inscription stating, *"Freedom is not free."* As long as man is the authority that runs and governs the world on which we live, there are bound to be wars of expansion. Mankind is always ready to step on the rights of those they feel they can conquer, overcome, and expand their own borders by taking what belongs to someone else. At the same time trying to make the conquered believe it is all for their own best interests.

Many veterans that I have talked with acknowledge that later on in life, many of the encounters on the battlefield with the enemy that is hell-bent on taking your life, while you hope to kill him first, comes roaring back into their mind with a vengeance that is hard to dismiss or quit thinking about. The value of having learned how important it is to get that nasty-to-the-core junk of being in a war zone or in frontline action. Out in the open and symbolically exposed to the bright sunlight of the healing power of understanding, to know all that we can about it, to be able to live with it. The Veterans Administration is helping more veterans in this area now, with programs aimed specifically to address and deal with post traumatic stress disorder (PTSD) caused by what is being required of military personnel whose job it is to do the dirty work of killing others made in the image and likeness of God, as same as ourselves. In other words, we are actually killing, maiming and destroying our own brothers and sisters. Leaving others in authority to try a determine what untold damage this is doing in the mind, body and soul of the combatant involved. *Some find help, and many have no idea of where to go looking for it.*

In my case, after trying to gut it out alone for over a half century, I found a group of combat veterans' meeting with a posttraumatic stress disorder group in the Traverse City, Michigan, VA, where everyone in the group has been there and done that. A place where you finally feel at home with others of like mind and experiences, to interact with and to reveal things you have never revealed to another living human being. For the most part, they simply do not want to hear it. Finally, you know you have found others that know exactly what you went through, and now are going through because of it. It somehow is a healing process to both to hear what others have gone through and to let others know what you have experienced as well.

CHISELED IN STONE MILITARY RULES AND REGULATIONS

My good, longtime buddy Ernie Lee, a little Frenchman from Louisiana, that had transferred with me into combat, was in the same squad I was in, and we would walk along and be reminiscing about the good times back in Pusan or Inchon before we had been transferred into combat. Our company officer kept chewing us out for not keeping the proper distance apart from each other, that one artillery round, a grenade or automatic rifle fire had a good chance to kill several men that were bunched up. We had come from a military outfit where they more or less gave us the run of things to make our own decisions. We had developed an independence away from military rules, regulations. and procedures that didn't sit well with a second lieutenant.

We had lost our master slave perceived connection between officers and enlisted men that was being taught from day one in our training, and now adding to that, we were in a 24/7 combat situation where we were being shot at from all sides, at a moment's notice. No assurance of our next breath or heartbeat. It was something that didn't seem to us to be of such of an earthshaking importance to be quivering at an officer's command. So, we didn't pay very much attention to his attempt at keeping us from having some little bit of pleasure within a world of killing and grunge. We more or less kept on visiting as we walked along as we tried to keep our eyes on where he was at.

Going up this hill one day, Ernie and myself were slogging along and not being too concerned about anything. We had not been in contact with the enemy in a while, and it was a reasonably pleasant day for a change; and as usual, we had closed up space between us and were walking along together. We were in the process of passing this pretty good-sized bush when the officer I mentioned stepped out from behind the bush with his .45 automatic pistol in his hand, and for effect, he racked a live round into the chamber, with these words to match, "If I ever catch either one of you two sons a bitches grouped together again, I'll shoot you myself." We sort of put on a scared act and hit him with a couple weak-kneed, "Yes, sirs," as we moved on.

THIS OFFICER HAD EVENTUALLY SAVED MY LIFE

We might possibly have believed him if it had happened in a Pusan alley, where no one ever had to account for anything, but I do not ever remember a green-around-the gills second *lieutenant* trained as a gentleman involved in killing his own men. Even though I knew it had happened during combat. We had more things to be worried and concerned about, sense at any moment now—our next step might be on a land mine, or in the crosshairs of some Chinese sniper, or some other enemy Oriental gook might have us in the sights of his machine gun right now or a mortar in the hills aimed directly at us at this moment too.

Maybe just beyond our sight, an enemy had already pulled the pin and was getting ready to throw his hand grenade among us as we stood there, or then again, I might turn around and stumble over my own feet and break my neck. I was not planning on becoming a career soldier. I would do my duty to the best of my ability, but at the same time, I am all done turning my mind over to anyone other than God to lead me into righteousness, on His terms only. We both knew the officer was right and that we were wrong but had become accustomed to regulating our own way of doing things of this nature.

This officer evidently knew he was spitting against the wind in his attempt at scaring us into submission, and in time, I have learned to really appreciate his military, spit and polish position of subjecting one's self to authority. As a matter of fact, that officer was probably responsible for saving my life later on as we were in the process of taking another hill under heavy burp gun and small-arms fire. I had crested this hill immediately after hearing all hell broke loose when those ahead of us came under heavy and sustained burp gun fire. I could hear the bullets as they rattled on down through the woods, hitting trees as we moved forward.

The officer had separated Ernie and myself and put Ernie in a different squad. I came up over the crest of the hill, and looking over to my left about sixty or seventy feet or so away, a medic had Ernie propped up against a pine tree, ripping his upper-body clothing off and administering first aid. Ernie was the last friend and good buddy that I had known for a long time that was still in our outfit. Everybody else around me were replacements, like I had been.

I didn't know or even care to become acquainted with any of them; then I had to witness their death or dismemberment just as I had seen other replacement men alive in one moment and be stone-cold dead in the next instant or some of the original group that had come from back home. It was a sad moment that I didn't dare to dwell upon. I knew not to get into a lingering mind-set of grieving the loss of a good buddy that could take my concentration off the business at hand, but I instantly knew that life from here on out, in such miserable conditions and without a meaningful friend to talk to, is going to get harder and more difficult, starting right now.

The blood splatter covering the snow surrounding Ernie had reminded me of my father killing and dressing out a pig during the wintertime months back home in Michigan. Being on an assault, I wasn't able to stop or do anything for Ernie. I was expected and needed more up front somewhere. I don't know whether Ernie lived or died, but in the passing of time, it finally occurred to me that the second lieutenant that I had had the problem with, no doubt, with normal military procedure, *had saved my life.*

A Russian burp gun that got Ernie fires so fast at seven hundred rounds a minute, that if we had been together, I would have almost certainly been hit myself too. The Russian burp gun fires at a rate so fast it sounds much like a magnified sound heard when ripping up blue jean material, with a distinct sound that made shivering chills go up your backbone. We would instantly know that we were in for a bonsai attack from the Communist Chinese Forces. *(CCF)* The automatic rate of fire that the Russian Burp Guns that were carried by the Chinese soldiers could and would belch and spit death into the air and space around us, and often into us in their pathway, at an unbelievable number of rounds per second. That would get our immediate attention and we knew we were in for bullet bath coming from their bugle blowing and frenzied bonsai attack.

-All thanks go to God, for bringing me home alive-

I remain today in grateful thanksgiving for the officer that may not have made it home himself, but most assuredly did probably save my life. However, in the bottom line of all that is I personally give all of escaping death in Korea or otherwise to God alone. He is the One that knows beyond any shadow of doubt exactly how many years, months, weeks, and days we are all going to live, and we will not surpass that God-preordained plan. God, it seems, must have had plans for me beyond Korea.

Job 14:5 You have decided the length of our lives. You know how many months we will live, and we are not given a minute longer.

Psalm 139:16 Your eyes have seen my unformed substance; *From before our birth* And in Your book were all written the days that were ordained for me, when as yet there was not one of them.

AN EFFECTIVE KILLING MACHINE

When in the hands of a Chinese soldier, though relatively inaccurate, the Chinese PPSH (burp gun) has a high rate of fire and was well suited to the close-range firefights that typically occurred in the Korean War conflict, especially at night. United Nations forces, in defensive outposts or on patrol, often had trouble returning a sufficient volume of fire when attacked by companies of infantry armed with the PPSH. Some U.S. infantry officers ranked the PPSH as the best combat weapon of the war: while lacking the accuracy of the U.S. M1 Garand and M1 carbine, it provided more firepower at short distances.

As infantry Captain (later General) Hal Moore, stated, "On full automatic it sprayed a lot of bullets and most of the killing in Korea was done at very close ranges and it was done quickly a matter of who responded faster. In situations like that it outclassed and outgunned what we had. A close-in patrol fight was over very quickly and usually we lost because of it."

Our own tommy gun, a Thompson submachine gun, could come close to matching the fire power of the Russian burp gun, but we were not being issued many of them, and they could not match the durability of the Russian burp gun and the misuse by the soldiers that used it. It (the burp gun) was virtually free from the normal defects of other weapons. It was being mass-produced in large numbers at a much less cost and worked well every time it was needed to do so. Even the sound of an approaching burp gun attack struck fear in your mind, caused your heart to beat faster, and anxiety spiked in anticipation of what was about to be right on your doorstep because of the amount of lead that was going to be filling the air.

Once we heard that sound—*Burp! Burp!*—it was a frightening sound. Gerry Farmer, a British veteran of the Royal Fusiliers who served in Korean War from 1950 to 1953, said in video for the UK's National Army Museum, "It meant the Chinese were there. I think the sound of the burp gun and what it represented was more frightening then the rounds that came out of the weapon."

Somewhere along in mid to late February 1951, we were fighting to keep control of Wonju, Korea. I was being worn down to a frazzle myself and the rest of the guys were too. Never had anything warm to eat; rations were not catching up with us. When they did, they were often frozen and had to be dug out with a bayonet; never were we issued the proper cold-weather clothing. The military command had taken all mountain sleeping bags away from the troops after the Chinese had overrun and laid waste another outfit caught in their sleeping bags. Having been too comfortable and probably in a sound sleep after a day of seeking and destroying the enemy, the Chinese CCF had decimated the outfit in a sneak bayonet and bonsai attack.

THE DAZZLING BRILLIANCE OF THE MILITARY LEADERS

The military answer was to keep us half-starved and awake by letting us freeze to death, which some had done. I didn't even have an army horse blanket to cover over me, I had nothing apart from what I had walked and sweated in all day long. Our rations were failing to catch up with us. Inside, I cursed those who had put us in this situation under these conditions. Folks back home would have been arrested and locked away in prison for putting their animals in such brutal conditions as these, in the first winter in Korea. The fighting against overwhelming odds was the easy part; it was the extreme weather conditions that was inflicting greater damage upon us than the enemy ever could.

Back home in Percy Jones Army Hospital in Battle Creek, Michigan, where I and a large portion of the Korean War frostbite victims ended up in, it was fairly common to have frozen body parts of a soldier dry up, turn black, and just fall off after a month or so of letting the doctors and nurses document what all was happening inside the person. I had several operations on my insides where they clamped off the nerves that went to my feet, to allow for me to serve in cold weather, but it didn't work and has caused me a lot of grief in life. And eventually, they sent me back to duty to finish my enlistment in a warm climate at Camp Rucker, Alabama.

HERE, TRY THESE ON FOR SIZE

THE MILITARY ANSWER TO PREVENT FROSTBITTEN FEET IN Korea was what they called shoepacks. Boots with a rubber bottom and leather tops—that only made things worse. Your socks would freeze to the bottom of the boots, and we were being pushed too long and hard to take any kind of care for them or in drying them out by putting them under our arms. We would have frozen to death even trying that. We were, for the most part, being required to survive without any decent clothing or food to produce energy enough to live on. Yet we had to engage the enemy on a daily basis that sapped us of what little we might have left.

Including those worth less-than-nothing shoepacks that replaced the combat boots. As soon as you would start walking in them, your feet begin to sweat, then when you stood still for any length of time, your socks began to freeze on your feet. While they were intended to be the answer for keeping our feet from being frostbitten, they instead, in my opinion, were the primary cause for 5,300 frostbite cases of combat soldiers during the first year of the Korean War. Just one more blunder of General Douglas MacArthur in not believing or accepting the facts of his own intelligent sources telling him about the CCF Chinese troops massing at the Yalu River, preparing for their surprise attack against our fighting troops on the ground.

OPENING UP PANDORA'S BOX

While I am trying to tell others here some of the sights, sounds, and mind-boggling atrocities that happen on a regular 24/7 time frame during frontline battle conditions, still, I am holding back a lot that are either too painful, to graphic, or I am just too ashamed of things that I had allowed myself to take part in, to reveal it to anyone. I believe other combat veterans I have talked to feel the same way also. A portion of it only God and myself know about. By my own choice, I will keep it to myself, and God tells us that He will remove our sins away from us as far as the east is from the west. Getting things off our chests is therapeutic when we meet together as a group in our PTSD meetings in the Traverse City, Michigan, VA facility.

Among others that have been there and done that, but even here, there are some that cannot bring themselves to open up their own Pandora's box to anyone. Sometimes after years of attendance, a comrade will feel comfortable enough among the group to finally, out of the blue, reveal a closely guarded traumatic event he has been holding inside of himself since his mind-boggling war experiences. Those times in the group are much appreciated and quite often will allow another comrade to reveal and get their own rot-gut memories and experiences out of their mind and on the table to be dealt with too. In this way, we are able help one another.

Over a half century now of putting all of the mind-boggling and bloody images of men killing men in every way we have learned to do it, out of memory as much as is possible, then after a few attempts at talking about it with friends, relatives, or acquaintances, only to find out they just do not give a damn about hearing your sob stories, nor do they believe you. You just close off your emotions and put them away, back into the deepest recesses of your memory and mind. You go on with life and try to keep it from coming back into your mind. But we human beings are not made that way and have no control over it. A certain sight, smell, sound, or a similar experience will suddenly snap you back into the past.

Where in my case those memories and experiences remained for over fifty years, before I came into contact with a program the VA had implemented and put into effect, they were forming groups of combat veterans to meet with other combat veterans to interact with and to be able to reveal things to each other that we found had been impossible to do with anyone else on earth, including noncombat veterans. We finally found a place where we could go and listen to the combat experiences of others while also learning to get that built-up horse manure and bullshit of killing, maiming, and destroying that no one else cared about listening to off our chest. This is helping us to get over and to get through some very bad things.

To heal old festering wounds of the mind and heart, it is good to get these things off your chest. We don't need to feel like a weakling or a failure to do so; it sometimes takes a man to admit he has limits. One thing along these lines that has helped me along for quite a few ears, is a telecast one time of Oliver North and General Norman Schwarzkopf Jr. Both combat veterans having been in command and spending a lot of time at the front.

They were having a conversation about being in combat action. General Schwarzkopf was telling about being in such fear of putting one shaky foot in front of the other and having to, actually, physically lift a foot up with his hands and then sitting it back down as carefully as possible, going through a mine field, being in such great fear of the next step that would quite possibly be blowing himself into a million pieces. Just the recall had brought tears to his eyes. But I remembered about how just hearing him talk about it helped me at the time too. So then, the VA programs, they have put in place to help us cope with these things on a regular, daily basis.

Then if we magnify this as something that happens day after day, night after night as we see our comrades who haven't been as fortunate as ourselves, and we have had a hand in carrying them off the battlefield, it begins to slowly weigh us down and cause us to wonder when our number is coming up. I have to admit here that I didn't have as much fear as I probably should have had. That is why the military likes to have a bunch of kids to take into battle. They usually don't question things; they came right from home and are used to being under discipline and don't have sense enough to be afraid. They have not reached maturity, feel invincible and are in possession of "the devil may care" attitude.

"Old men make war; young men fight and die in it."

And so go the normal acts of desperation and the desire to survive during all wars that we fight against others who are made in the image and likeness of God, just as we ourselves are. We were fighting either night or day in the Korean War, which did generate a little heat in our body as long as we were moving; but as soon as we quit walking or being in enemy contact, my teeth would be chattering from shivering. This, I had learned later on, turned out to be very important in staying alive. I don't know how much heat shivering generates, but it isn't insignificant, it is life-saving. The heat generated isn't there to heat all of your body, but enough to keep the blood flowing, which is important to keep your extremities, like your hands and feet getting some blood that they otherwise would not be getting.

A LITTLE RESEARCH REVEALS SOMETHING IMPORTANT

If your body comes into a very cold environment, the blood vessels near the skin contract, in an effort to preserve energy. Now as the cold goes more than skin deep, more vessels contract. That leads to an oxygen shortage in hands and feet. To prevent them from dying, they need oxygen. Shivering produces just enough heat to widen the blood vessels enough to keep the hands and feet supplied with just enough oxygen. Unless you don't care about your hands and feet, calling it insignificant is far beside the point. I was most fortunate, it seems, in discovering that my feet were being deprived of oxygen long enough to have begun the process of frostbite. Thanks be to my assistant machine gunner who had seen frostbite on the front line in WWII. He knew what it was and encouraged me to have it attended to.

I had hobbled down to the company commander's control tent area to see about having my feet looked at. He just looked at me in disgust and, shaking his head began, to rattle on. Finally, he said, "Okay, you go on and get them looked at, then you get your f—n ass right back up here." I knew that we were always short on manpower to bring our company up to strength, but since it would be my last contact with them, it would have been nice to hear some sort of an acknowledgment of appreciation or at least a "Thank you for serving under my command." Officers are trained to be no-nonsense tough and in command of the situation. Any empathy, sympathy, or compassion is definitely not a part of their character. But there wasn't any such foolishness such as that coming from him to have any part of it that day. Looking back, I wish him well and hope the ungrateful a—hole made it safely home himself.

I had learned too during this time that fifteen minutes of shivering eats up as much fat, as one hour of exercise. This answers a question I have had in my mind for many years. How was it even possible for me to lose as much weight as I did in the time frame during my battlefield experience of 24/7 activity, without any decent sleep at all, no decent cold-weather clothing, and the lack of warm food at all? I now have that answer: we were either on the move, which was losing fat from exercise; or we were lying down in our ice and snow bed, shivering so loud and steady as to worry about giving our location away to any enemy that might be in proximity enough to surprise attack or throw a grenade on you.

This set of circumstances that I was required to serve my country in both exercising and shivering uncontrollably, had been responsible for my rapid loss of weight. I weighed barely over one hundred pounds when I arrived in the Army Hospital in Osaka, Japan. Today, I weigh in at 240 pounds, I am overweight now and I am happy with it. I do not miss any meals, and I eat until my forty-two-inch belly feels full and comfortable. And I don't feel a bit guilty and am not ashamed of it or I don't try and hide in the basement to keep others from looking at a reasonably overweight, fat guy. I have earned it, I have it coming, and that's the way it is here in Fife Lake, Michigan. Good night, Chet!

Sleep was just a word in the dictionary; we never got any real sleep. Lacking food and having everything that kept one alive sucked out of us was taking its toll on my body. I was skin stretched over a rack of bones. Then on March 7, 1951, I couldn't stand up on my feet in the morning; they had been frozen during the night, and the toenails were sliding back and forth on top of my toes. I thought that things couldn't get any worse, but thanks be to God, it all worked for my own good. Two days later, I was being loaded on a C-47 plane, on my way to an army hospital in Osaka, Japan. A few weeks after that, I was flown back to the good old USA. My own tour in hell had ended.

AT THE DAYS END

My assistant machine gunner at the time was a black man whose name I cannot remember; we didn't dare to get to close to anyone or each other because they usually didn't last very long. The soldier you see and have helping you at your right hand in the morning, there might very well be somebody else taking his place in the evening, after the former assistant has been either killed or wounded and evacuated to the rear, before you fall dead dog tired and exhausted in your ice and snow bed, after a day of kill or be killed. I will never forget my black assistant machine gunner friend and comrade. He had saved my life, and I had saved his.

Without being able to hug my black comrade, my assistant machine gunner, during that one night in those blizzard conditions, without one speck of protection against it, then to suck in a little bit of heat from his 98.6 temperature body, as we did from each other during the nights to survive. Wherever my black friend is today, if he made it home alive, I thank God that you were there in that god forsaken country in that time frame, that helped me to survive, to go home, to have a wife and family, and to live out a normal God-fearing life. I hope that you made it home as well. I hope you also lived long enough to see how it felt when segregation was outlawed and integration came into vogue.

THANKING GOD FOR SIMPLE THINGS

I am convinced that neither one of us would have made it. I am still amazed that the human body is able to stand such trauma and abuse as it does and still remain alive. This time frame was about ten years before integration of blacks and whites in the United States. The Korean War is where they first put blacks and whites together in the military service. I came home and about a year later, after recuperating in Percy Jones Army hospital, I went back to duty at Camp Rucker, Alabama, a state that still practiced segregation and being hell-bent on keeping black folks under their subjection, bowing and scraping to white folks as their masters of superior intellect and stature. The black people were good enough to fight and die for their ex-Southern slave owners, but drinking a cup of coffee with them—now, that is something else, altogether different.

WHILE WE FIGHT FOR THE RIGHTS OF OTHERS

Had I have come into contact with my black assistant machine gunner friend and comrade at arms in Alabama, it was still against the law in these United States of America for blacks and whites to intermingle in public places. Hugging him in the open public as an equal and thanking him again for being there when needed most likely would have caused us both to be arrested on the spot, maybe even tried and sent to jail. We would not have been allowed to drink from the same water fountain, use the same bathroom, ride on the same bus, or have a cup of coffee together in the same restaurant. While we were fighting a war for others and their causes, we needed some work done in our own country.

JIM CROW, ALIVE AND WELL IN ALABAMA

Going back again now into battlefield mode, before I was evacuated, it still grieves my mind, body, and soul whenever something reminds me of those conditions and feelings that we had to endure at the death or dismemberment of a familiar face, that suddenly is no longer with us, either dead or having been wounded and sent to the rear and being replaced by someone you had to learn to know all over again to trust that they would not turn and run while under attack. I had learned well how to value and respect courage, strength, and bravery while under attack by the enemy. Just as I also had learned to hate, despise, and to be in proximity with weak-kneed, spineless cowards.

I had outlived several assistant machine gunners, and as it turned out, every last one of them could be counted upon to be there every time they were needed. Certain sights, sounds, smells, or similar backgrounds or like conditions that existed during a traumatic event in battle will, at times, cause one to experience a fleeting breakdown in emotions. I am always glad when I am alone when a moment like that comes into my mind that causes me to quiet down, tear up a little, and allows me to just keep it all to myself. You hope it is not evident to others as you try and hide it. You shake it off and move on because you think there is nothing at all honorable that you can do otherwise.

THE CARE AND CONCERN BY THE JAPANESE

During my short stay in Osaka, Japan, in the US Army Military Hospital, being stabilized to be sent back home, I very much did appreciate the care that was given us there by the good and extremely welcome abundance of good foodstuffs, and they also brought in young and pretty Japanese girls to sing and to entertain us, keeping our minds off what each of us may have been suffering at the moment. It was exactly what we needed to get the ungodly smell, sight, sound, atrocities, and memory of the Korean battlefield out of our minds to help us to heal. This was only a few years after we had fought the Japanese in World War II, an Oriental race of people that know very well how to inflict pain and misery on their adversaries.

Our military leaders, in conjunction with the Japanese social services, did the best they knew to do in providing a diversion away from the reality and brutal acts of war. I still very much appreciate and give thanks to all those serving Japanese people and our own social activities personnel. The Japanese had all suffered untold pain, misery, death, and destruction from our military during WWII, brought on by their attack on Pearl Harbor. Yet they now became our cohorts in the war against Communist aggression. I became acquainted with several Japanese people in Korea and had preferred them over Koreans. But seeing now how the Korean people didn't squander the freedom that our military fought and died for, I have a whole different attitude toward them.

I remember what tasted better than anything else to me that we had not been given in Korea. It was milk and ice cream, and we could get it any time we wanted to and have as much as we wanted. I have many fond memories of my time spent in recuperating within that pleasant atmosphere of care and concern. By that time, I had forgotten how much I had hated the Japanese for their surprise attack on Pearl Harbor and the death and destruction they had caused there or remembering a couple close buddies that were a little older than I was that fought and died at their brutal hands. We are all the handiwork of God. Your Father is my Father, and my Father is your Father; we are all brothers and sisters of our brother Jesus Christ.

BLACK FEET AND LEGS

THOSE MEN AND BOYS THAT CAME HOME FROM Korea as frostbite victims, some as young as fourteen years old with severe frostbitten extremities that came first into the Osaka hospital, would not have limbs or body parts surgically removed until it became evident how far the frostbite had grown on a limb for example, and then were determined where to amputate. Consequently, at Percy Jones Army Hospital in Battle Creek, where many of them had ended up, including myself, there would be frostbite cases several weeks or even months later where the feet, ankles, and legs up past the knees would be all dried up and black. They would still be hooked to their body, but seemingly, without any life or feeling in them at all.

Since I had spent several months among them in Percy Jones and had watched them progress to this point, it still shocked me one day when I watched this guy come humming along down the hallway in his wheelchair. Moving along at a really brisk pace and suddenly, he had decided to turn into the doorway I was standing by. His foot had hit the door casing a pretty good solid whack, and half his foot, about up to the ankle just fell off and rattled across the floor. He just laughed about it; being black dead flesh and bone, it evidently had not hurt him at all.

DOING MY OWN SHARE

AFTER BEING RELIEVED OF FRONTLINE COMBAT DUTY ON March 7, 1951, for frostbite of my feet and extremities, on March 9, 1951, I was carried onto a C-47 plane at Wonju, Korea, and flown to a hospital in Osaka, Japan, in a hospital filled to overflowing with the worst frostbite cases possible. Men lying on their backs, suffering and crying out in pain, as they would try and relieve the excruciating pain from their blackened-to-their-knees legs by curling their arms around under their legs then holding them up and off from the bedding. Still within all of the pain and suffering that these guys were having to endure, they all remained in a positive attitude because they all knew that their war was over, and they were all going home. But being happy about it and knowing it didn't do anything to ease the pain they were all experiencing.

I AM GLAD I DO NOT HAVE TO HANG MY HEAD, I SERVED

I SPENT MOST OF A YEAR RECOVERING AND regaining my weight and strength back, later at Percy Jones Army Hospital in Battle Creek, Michigan. An army hospital that treated us all like war heroes. Their kitchen and dining room area was to be envied by the best restaurants in the world. Steak and lobster was a common item on the menu. When I was evacuated out of Korea, I weighed barely over one hundred pounds, and still today have to deal with other serious side effects caused by the extreme weather conditions and the emaciated condition of lacking enough food to sustain a person. With all this being said, though, I do feel I did my own share. I am sorry that for myself to live, others had to die; my military job required having to do things to other human beings made in the image and likeness of God. Much of it replay again and again in my mind and heart at night mostly.

I felt at the time that I passed the test. I didn't faint, run away, or quit in the face of adversity, as I had witnessed a few others doing. One was a good guy that I liked; he had been transferred into battle with me, and I had known him a long time and, up to that point, had trusted him to be steadfast. I had not expected him to turn and run, but he did. As soon as the Chinese began to swarm upon us, he dropped his rifle and ran like hell. I never saw him again; one of our own men or an officer may have shot him. One of the worst things an officer in charge can let happen is to lose control of a situation like this. If it is not addressed immediately, others might be tempted to follow.

For the most part, I was able to control my fear and function as I was required to do. I met the enemy without any shame to myself at that time. I did, though, value my German blood flowing through my veins from both sides of my family; it has always given me the character trait of cold German logic when needed. I can always stay steady and calm in the moment. I can take the unforeseen tragedy of bad accidents, blood, and gore in stride for the most part and deal with it in a calm way. If I come apart at all, it is always after the fact, after all the dust has settled and my mind and thoughts play overtime. Looking back even years later may haunt me at times. However, in battle, I prevailed and did my duty as long as I was physically able to do so.

I found out then to my own satisfaction that I had proven to myself to have had the courage and bravery to stand and fight and keep my own mental and emotional self under control. In my emaciated and worn-down-to-a-thread physical condition, I wasn't able to do much about, moving one foot ahead of the other as it became a 24/7 day-and-night struggle, where we could stand still and fight, either attacking or being attacked, was a welcome engagement with the enemy. The adrenaline would take hold for the moment, allowing one the benefit of being able to calm down a bit while forgetting about the never-ending misery you were in, right there in the middle of a heated battle.

The wood on my M-1 Garand rifle would actually get hot enough to smoke during those sustained firefights and would produce some little temporary heat to be grateful and thankful for. I read about another Korean War veteran not prone to exaggeration telling of his M-1 Garand catching on fire twice during sustained and rapid fire. It was a trustworthy weapon that did what it was designed to do. The light .30 caliber air-cooled machine gun barrel that I had carried had turned red hot too many times from the sustained use also, and it became warped and useless. But still. we couldn't leave it for the enemy to fix up and use against us, so we still had to carry it.

I had grown to hate that machine gun that I had most desired to use on our enemies and having to carry the heavy and useless thing in knee-deep snow up and down those rugged mountains and steep hills. My feet would slip out from under me, I would drop the machine gun and my heavy piss-pot helmet would fall down off my head and sap the little energy I had left in my body to get squared away and pick it back up to put back on. It became a thorn in my side and was pissing me off to the max. I wondered how I might be able to get rid of the thing.

Going up this steep grade one day, after slipping and having my helmet and machine gun drop in the snow and my helmet fall off my head several times, I slipped again; and it was really steep, so I just nonchalantly gave the machine gun an extra little nudge and watched as it slid a long way down the slope. I had put my helmet back on and was in the process of moving on and keeping up with the squad. An officer or a squad leader had seen the whole thing and made me go after it. It took me forever it seemed to retrieve it and catch up with the squad.

What I once had wished and hoped for in becoming a machine gunner, I began to realize I should instead have had my head examined. What had weighed about forty-five pounds with the tripod now began to feel like it weighed over a hundred pounds. It finally had been taken back to the rear for upgrade and repair. Things immediately became much easier without having to deal with a useless piece of equipment that only sapped what little strength you had left inside to do your job with. It had been like feeding a dead horse.

I did what I was asked to do, under the most severe, unrelenting below-zero blizzard conditions and circumstances possible. Never being inside or having anything warm to eat, and adding to that, never being issued any decent cold weather clothing or footwear. Every ounce of strength being sucked out of us, without being replaced. But still, when the smoke and dust settled at the battle of Wonju, we had decisively won the battle, we had maintained control over Wonju and had inflicted eighteen thousand casualties upon the Chinese enemy at the battle to secure Wonju. For which our outfit received a presidential unit citation, which reads as follows:

> The 2nd *Indianhead Division was awarded the presidential unit citation for its action in Korea. The unit must display such gallantry, determination, and Esprit De Corps in accomplishing its mission under extremely difficult and hazardous conditions so as to set apart from and above other units participating in the same campaign.*

The Second Indianhead Division lost more men in Korean the war than any other military division, either Army or Marine. In fact, now after the signing of the Korean War Armistice sixty-five years ago today, as I write these words on July 27, 2018, the Second Division remains still, in Korea today, to be the first to meet any initial surprise attack by their North Korean neighbors as they did on June 25 of 1950. We pushed them back where they belonged and where they remain today. With their heads handing and their communist tails between their legs. My comrades didn't have to die in vain or die for a tie. *We won that war*, there is no other way for a sane person to understand it.

> The 2nd *(Indianhead)* Infantry Division is a formation of the United States Army. Its current primary mission is the defense of South Korea in the initial stages of an invasion from North Korea until other American units can arrive. There are approximately 17,000 soldiers in the 2nd Infantry Division, with 10,000 of them stationed in South Korea, accounting for about 35% of the United States Forces Korea personnel.

Our combat troops fighting in the Korean War during 1950–51, of which I was one. Within the severe below-zero weather conditions that existed during that time frame, 5,300 fighting men on frontline duty experienced frostbite of extremities, to a lesser or greater degree, that were visible on the outside, while overtime it has become obvious many other serious afflictions have grown and developed within that are invisible and beyond the eyes of untrained doctors, who do not know or understand what symptoms or telltale signs to look for. This still today is the cause that prevents many deserving veterans of Korea in being able to apply for and receive compensation for ailments caused by the extreme weather conditions and lack of proper food and clothing during that first winter in Korea.

Beyond that, it could be the VA's solution to keep from paying out claims to needy and qualified veterans who have earned it and have it coming to them, but the VA may purposefully shies away from hiring doctors qualified to deal with the aftereffects of frostbite on the extremities and the inside organs and their inability to act in accordance with their created ability because of the damage of the extreme below-zero weather conditions, lack of food, and decent cold-weather clothing to protect the body against exposure to abnormal stress and damage that has caused many to suffer. Many soldiers are waiting for filed VA claims, asking to be compensated—in vain. Until the meat-wagon pulls into the driveway to remove one more stabbed-in-the-back veteran by a VA that has long ago forgotten the promise of our country to take care of a military person that served when our country needed them but turned their collective backs upon them when the veterans needed something in return.

Declining in old age now, the Korean War veterans are suffering still because of this. Tired of filing for any compensation papers from the VA. They have heard it all now, as their papers come back rubber-stamped one more time with *"Your claim has been denied."* They are becoming a dwindling number of deserving old people now, with nothing left to do but to wait for that long black car that will transport them one last time to their final destiny. While the VA beats their chest and tells us what a great and wonderful service they are doing for our veterans. Somehow, there seems—in my mind at least—that something is wrong with this picture. However, I must say now after many years of trying to get someone in the VA to listen and act, I now am being taken care of in great fashion. A little late, but better late than never.

This is the outfit below that I later became a replacement in during January of 1951. It tells of their being caught in a Chinese trap at a six-mile pass, south of Kunri, Korea.

On November 28–29, 1950, at Kunri, North Korea, the Second Infantry Division fought a rear guard of the retreating Eighth Army and were ambushed by thousands of Chinese and overrun. American losses totaled five thousand killed, wounded, and captured. It was a devastating defeat. Not having time for replacements to arrive from back home in the United States, the powers to be elected to do the only thing that seemed to be a viable solution. They scraped up everyone they could get from those serving in rear echelon duty, of which I was one of them. One day I was a fat cat living a lifestyle of relative ease, supervising and working stevedore crews of Korean dockworkers at the Pusan waterfront in Korea or serving as a security guard on the water front of Inchon, Korea.

Abracadabra! In a blink of an eye, the next day, I was serving as a frontline machine gunner with the Second Indianhead Infantry Division against three divisions of Communist Chinese Forces that had been given the order from the Chinese Dictator Mao Tse-tung to completely annihilate our division, that everything else was to become secondary. But it didn't quite work out that way for old Joe chink. When the smoke and dust settled at Wonju, we maintained control and had inflected eighteen thousand causalities upon the Chinese Communist Forces. They had come against us with the overwhelming force of three divisions to our one. "It is not the size of the dog in the fight, it's the size of the fight in the dog" (*General Eisenhower*).

A LITTLE MORE HERE

To recap a little here, my name is Leith Lyman Cunningham, I am a husband a father, a grandfather and a great-grandfather. I am also an eighty-six-year-old combat veteran of the Korean War. I love my family; I love my precious little innocent grandchildren as well as other little children that I may or may not ever know. I believe we owe those we have brought into this world some insight into what to expect as their own lives unfold before them. What life is really all about behind the scenes that most have never experienced. I hope for the purpose of this letter, if you are a young person, that you will just try and think of me as your own grandfather. A lot of young people in my area are used to calling me Grandpa.

I am no different than any other person; after all, I was once a kid myself as I anxiously awaited my chance to experience life away from the northern Michigan farm on which I was born and raised up in. At age sixteen, I begged my mother to falsify my age so I would be able to join the US Army. She did what I had asked her to do, and I was on my way to fame and fortune—at least in my mind. However, the deception was discovered, and I was released from service. I would be required to wait a little longer for my anxiously awaited destiny to begin. I whiled away my time waiting for my seventeenth birthday, peering into the future exciting life's journey that I would soon be on.

As soon as I turned seventeen, my mother signed the papers again that legally allowed me to enlist in the US Army. Billy Magee, a friend of mine from home, joined along with me; his serial number was one digit before mine. We shipped out immediately to the Tenth Mountain Infantry Division in Fort Riley, Kansas. We began our fourteen-week basic training there in June of 1949. Reality set in immediately as we learned from our drill instructor that we no longer had any personal identification other than our serial number. Being reduced to a number seems to me to be something a rancher might do to identify his cows. But now, I had become #16297131 Billy was #16297130.

No rights at all unless they gave them to us. We belonged to the United States government; we became known as a GI, "*government issue.*" Our drill instructor told me, "*You can give your soul to God, but your hind end belongs to me.*" Then the indoctrination from civilian life to the government killer that we were to become began in earnest. Teaching us all the latest military techniques in how to go about defending our nation and our country against all possible enemies. Looking back at it, it seems the first qualification was to learn and apply every vulgar vocabulary of cursing and throwing the F-bomb around that you could think of, and to take up smoking, drinking, and raising hell till the cows came home.

How to most effectively kill, maim, and destroy the enemy with the arsenal of weapons they would keep loaded and in our hands, to complete our assignments. Weapons of destruction that I had never even heard of or seen before. Mortars, machine guns, Browning automatic rifles, hand grenades, bayonets, tommy guns, rifle grenades, .45 caliber handguns, automatic .45 caliber Greece guns, landmines, shoulder-fired .57 recoilless rifles, Jeep-mounted .97 recoilless artilleries, and others I didn't even know about. We were being highly trained USA government hunters. All we needed now was for a war to break out to give us the chance to apply what we were being programmed and trained for. North Korea stepped up at just the right time for us to apply all that our Uncle Sam had taught us.

Topped off then by being trained with the know-how and ability when necessary to be able to do the job required in hand-to-hand combat. All part of the insanity of war where mankind, from the beginning of time, have found reasons to kill and destroy another one made in the image and likeness of God. I am sorry to have to tell you that this is all real; it is what happens in all wars. It is not the way that it should be, but it is the way that it is. If you have any plans at all about staying alive, a person must immediately adjust to being a part of every atrocity known to mankind, the squeamish, delicate, soft-natured and the conscientious objector that do not and cannot adjust to the blood and gore often can be the first to fall.

A year later after finishing basic infantry training at Fort Riley, Kansas, and during the summer and autumn of 1950, I was in Pusan, Korea, as a longshoreman with the US Army 153rd Transportation Port Company. The brutal, battle-hardened North Korean Army, with their superior numbers and equipment, had us at their mercy with our backs to the Sea of Japan. We were in grave danger of being forcefully shoved out of

Korea altogether. Our military officials in fear that if that happened, we would never be able to get our already dead comrades out of Korea. So, a program began immediately; as our soldiers were being killed daily, they began digging up the burial ground used as a temporary cemetery and hastily began sending the decomposing and mangled bodies into Pusan in boxcars.

A GRUESOME BUT NECESSARY DETAIL

WITH THE WEIGHT OF BODIES STACKED ON TOP of other bodies, these railcars came rumbling through the hot autumn sun with blood and body fluids oozing out along the tracks. The most unimaginable and lingering sight and smell that can enter and stick with the human mind and psyche. Since they wouldn't allow the Korean dockworkers to handle the bodies of our dead comrades, it became our duty to transfer them onto pallets and load them onto ships back to Japan. To be processed and sent back home. We worked two twelve-hour shifts around the clock to get this done. This was an extremely tough assignment to be involved in, but one I valued greatly. It would be the very last thing that I could do for my comrades.

NOT FOR THE SQUEAMISH OR FAINT OF HEART

THE UNEXPLAINABLE, UNIMAGINABLE AND GHASTLY, HORRIFIC SMELL EMANATING from all these dead, rotting, mangled, and decomposing bodies permeated the entire dock area, including the ships that were tied up and docked there in the process of unloading their cargo. We would load their dead bodies in tiers of four on a pallet in one direction, then four in a tier in the other direction to a layer of four tiers per pallet. One man would take a hold of the feet while the other guy would take a hold of the head as we layered them on the pallet. Many of them were so mangled that we could feel the grating of their broken bones scraping together as we piled them up on the pallets. I started looking at their dog tags to see if I knew any of them, but there were to many that made it an operation of futility to continue, and we were being pressured to get the job done.

Some bodies had been so mangled and blown up to a point that only a handful of flesh and bone could be located, in which case, they would wrap the scraps of bone and flesh up with the grave cross to indicate there was part of a body within. There was no place to go to escape the ever-lingering smell. Even our lodging in an old Japanese barracks on the waterfront that housed our three different companies of about seven hundred total enlisted men couldn't escape the awful and constant smell as the bodies were being loaded onto smaller Japanese ships, to be taken to Japan to be processed, to then be taken back to the United States.

The smell couldn't be washed out of boots and other clothing. When the detail was finished, we had to throw them away and get a new issue. Actually, I stole a pair of British hobnailed military boots off British supplies we were handling from off their ships. Something that had nearly done me in later as a ship was coming in to dock and unload its supplies. Those on board the ship had thrown in a small line with a lead-filled center on the end and the other end attached to the much larger mooring rope that ties it off on the dock area.

The lead-filled center about the size of a baseball had been thrown in quite short and was quickly sliding back out across the dock and into the water. I ran as fast as I could to grab it before that happened, to prevent the sailors on board the ship from having to bring it all back in to do all over again. I was able to grab the ball with the rope attached to it and tried to stop, but with those hobnail boots on against the smooth concrete, I just kept on sliding and was barely able to stop before going right off the dock and into the dirty, nasty gook-poop-covered water below.

So, I gave my hobnail boots away and stole me another kind of some sort. This might seem like an awful way to operate, but it is quite often something that happens in a military company that men are passing through in transferring to different outfits. You notice a shirt or another item of clothing of yours is missing, you automatically know that someone your size has stolen it and is probably on his way out of town. No problem; you just scope out someone else your size, and voila!

The process has been repeated. It is not right, but it is the way that it is. I got a promotion to corporal one time for doing it back in the States after the war. Someone had stolen a shirt from me, and I needed to get mine like he got his. The only guy in the outfit that already had owed me money on a car radio was a corporal and also my size. Since I was a private, I had instantly promoted myself to a corporal. But I had to tear the corporal chevrons off to keep from getting myself into big trouble. However, I still come out the loser because he owed me a lot more for the radio than the shirt was worth, and since I was transferring out of the outfit, I knew I would never get it or see him again. In hindsight, I should have taken a nice dress uniform I had seen him wearing at times.

HIGH-LEVEL EXCITEMENT AT PUSAN, KOREA

Before I move on from life in and around Pusan, Korea, I would like to tell you of another event that happened during that time frame. There was chaos and turmoil erupting in Pusan one day, around the dock area where we worked unloading war supplies and goods. Evidently, a spark from one of their old steam engines or a North Korean saboteur had slipped in unnoticed and set the POL dump on fire. Where we kept all of our fuel, gas, oil, and such. It was rapidly getting out of control with the entire dock area in danger of going up in flames.

Fifty-five-gallon drums were exploding and being blown so high in the sky that they looked about the size of little tin vegetable cans in the air. It was an awesome sight to behold as the area was filled with onlookers that couldn't get enough of it as military personnel along with the local authorities were running to and fro, trying to figure out what to do next to get things back under control. Firefighting ships were being brought in from the sea to do their share in containing the now-blazing inferno. There didn't seem to be anything I could do, so I just stood and gawked around like many others were doing.

DURING WAR, WE LEARN TO EXPECT THE UNEXPECTED

The Korean carpenters had made toilet trenches about thirty feet long and three or four feet deep. To be used by the Korean dockworkers. They had built regular wooden-framed structures to enclose them for privacy purposes. Fearing the fire was getting too close to this one outside toilet structure, a crew of Korean dockworkers just physically picked it up and moved it off and away from the hole to keep it from catching fire. The only officer I ever saw all the while I was in Korea in their OD dress uniform, dressed to the max with gloves and a swagger stick in hand, came along about then, looking like a million dollars and gawking off skyward and taking in all of the sights, sounds, and excitement going on around him and in the sky above; and he walked smack-dab into the end of the uncovered ditch full of dockworker poop.

AN OFFICER HAS BEEN HUMBLED

The very first thing he did to keep from falling headfirst into the mess was to put his pretty squared-away gloved hands out in front of him to prevent that from happening. Then he immediately looked quickly around himself to see what exactly had happened and if anybody else had noticed it or seen it happen too. I'm glad he didn't see me looking at him. By that time, I was laughing so hard I could hardly stand up. Fate could not have found a better candidate to administer a little humility too. I can still see the bewildered look on his face as he began to wade through up past-his-knees Korean poop, with his poop-dripping gloved hands held high in the air. I would have given anything to have had my camera with me at the time.

AN OFFICER, A HIGHLIGHT OF MY DAY

FIRE-FIGHTING SHIPS HAD BEEN MANEUVERED IN CLOSE TO the harbor dock area as they sprayed water on buildings and other things to keep them from catching on fire also. Pandemonium and chaos broke out as folks were scrambling here and there and all over the place; nobody seemed to know what to do. A lack of anyone in authority to be able to quell or diminish the problem added to the problem. But as mankind always finds a way to get things done, in time, it was all put down, and Pusan returned to its normal day-to-day activity. The excitement for the day was over, and I returned to work with a unique memory in my mind that still puts a smile on my face every time I visualize again the officer that had gone wading in a river of nasty.

THE ROUTINE RESUMES

THE STREETS OF PUSAN, KOREA, AND THE WHOLE area was being flooded by the poor and destitute homeless refugees being driven ahead of the brutal North Korean Army—those looking only to spend another day alive on planet earth. The North Korean Army—for psychological effect I imagine—were exercising animalistic and sadistic brutality beyond human reasoning as they swarmed through towns and villages, leaving on the streets and gutters in their wake bodies of men, women, children, and even babies. Causing many of us to adopt a mind-set of reasoning that told us, "The only good Korean, is a dead one." Since we couldn't tell by their looks which was which, we didn't dare to trust any of them.

Something I want to reveal here to you causes me to be so ashamed of myself now and others who took part in it. I hate to even think about it, and yet it is something that did happen as we created our own private entertainment in Pusan. Right outside the big old Japanese barracks that our three transportation port companies were being housed in, not more than twenty feet away, was the waterfront and where we kept our garbage cans to throw any leftovers that we didn't eat, and where the little Korean kids hung around to go through it for something to eat. Along the edge of this waterfront, within the same proximity, the Korean carpenters had built outside toilets for the dockworkers to use. Where the poop just fell into the water and floated all around on top of the water.

Those little kids were strong, tough as nails, had no fear of anything, and were really competitive with one another; they were becoming survivors in an environment where others were giving up and dying. We would gather around where they would be assembled and throw Korean money into the deep, dirty, slimy, and poop-covered water as they would scramble to be the first one to dive in and retrieve it. Often coming up out of the water with a big pile of shit on their head, still they showed a willingness to work hard for everything they got. They had found a way to blank out the awful nastiness of what they were doing and was able to end up with a little money to help themselves along in the life that had been thrust upon them through no fault of their own.

TO IMMATURE TO BE SERIOUS

WE WOULD LAUGH AND CHEER THEM ON AND make bets on who would get to it first. The kids as well would be laughing and having fun doing it. It is another one of those things that I would like to take back and have a do over, that it be removed from my memory bank. I can be just as sorry and repentant as I can be for my past actions as much as I can possibly be, but it doesn't change anything in the past. But I have lived long enough to realize that our mistakes and sins in this life are being used by God for our own benefit, if we accept, believe, follow and love Him, as seen here in Romans 8:28: *"And we know that all things work together for good to them that love God, to them who are the called according to his purpose."*

God uses our own sins, mistakes, and shortcomings to bring a change into our heart and mind to cause us to be usable for His purpose and plan for all of mankind, for all eternity. We don't recognize it at the time when we are going through our life being pummeled around by the forces of nature that God has placed in our path to knock off some rough edges to cause us to be useful for His service after we have suffered and have prevailed. One by one, He will place us on His potter's wheel and begin the change He desires in each one of us. He has pounded me down again and again, and He isn't through with me yet. Looking back at those little kids in Pusan, I can imagine God was letting me, in life, sink lower and lower in my own dealings with my fellow man.

It is as if He was throwing money into a bottomless cesspool of filth, disease, and slimy water, allowing me to get a dose of my own medicine, to see how it feels to others.

As I have explained in this writing, He is stripping the years of filth off me, a layer at a time, as He renews my body with His Word that will in His time make me acceptable to belong in His kingdom. As God is my strength, my rock, my mentor, my Savior, and my everything, there is not anything He will ever do to me or anyone else that is not ultimately and evidentially for our own good. The Korean War itself, in hindsight, was just another tool being used by God to eventually steer me in the direction He would have me to go.

But within the conditions of war that was going on in Korea and being privy to the knowledge of how the enemy was misusing, abusing, slaughtering, and killing our soldiers and even their own race of people, the teenage mind in me was being prepared, programed, and set in motion to be all cocked and primed to do almost anything that comes into mind to even the score, get even for all that evil carnage being brought against us. In a country we had never even heard of before and a people that we did not know, we were being primed to do all that our military leaders were asking and commanding us to do, and even more.

WE WERE BUSY EXERCISING OUR PHILOSOPHY

ON TOP OF THAT, PICTURES BEING DISPLAYED IN the *Stars and Stripes* newspaper documenting our comrades being captured, forced down on their knees, and having their hands tied behind their backs with barbed wire and executed with a pistol shot to the back of their heads were these lingering vision and image that kept festering and playing on my mind that caused me to eventually volunteer to be a machine gunner against them on the battlefields of Korea. I was as bloodthirsty as anyone could be. I wanted to be a part of the system that made the enemy pay in their own blood the price for their taking of our blood. I would visualize them piling up in front of my machine gun, knowing how they were treating our captured comrades.

I HAD NOT CONSIDERED THEIR FIRING BACK

BEING UNABLE AND UNWILLING TO PURGE THOSE HORRENDOUS atrocities from my mind and heart while remembering the pathetic and pitiful old women, children, and pregnant young women shuffling along in hopelessness and for a spot to rest in and some already with babies wandering the streets and byways of Pusan with that thousand-yard forlorn and pitiful stare, being naked to the waist as their bulging milk-filled breasts hung down on their bellies and oozed out milk trails that left snake tracks down across their baked, crusty, and dirty skin. Too used up, physically spent, and exhausted to even brush away the flies that competed for her milk—I had the desire to be on the frontlines to rid the earth of such inhumane cowardly dogs that, in my mind, should be denied the right to live.

GIVE ME A WEAPON AND POINT ME TOWARD THE FRONT

It never even entered my mind that in the attitude that I was adopting against others made in the image and likeness of God, I would become one of them myself. Man's inhumanity to man through the insanity of war, obvious and apparent as far as the eye could see in any direction, my eighteen-year-old mind at the time, too young and immature to grasp the awesome magnitude of what I was in the middle of and was a witness too, and like it or not, was a part of—I hope I can make up for that a little here by at least revealing some of it to you now so that others might become more aware of the cost of peace. Should you, the reader, ever be subjected to such things, you might be more prepared to understand what happens during wartime.

A HAPPY AND ENJOYABLE MOMENT

As good, bad, or indifferent as it most certainly is on a regular, daily basis, and yet, there are periods of relief. Just to show how within the most horrible of times, there can, along with it, be a bright ray of sunlight, a light at the end of the tunnel, a silver lining if you will, to make one want to live another day. During this time frame in Pusan, on a hot and humid summer or autumn day, myself and three or four other fellow soldiers were walking along on a dusty road on the outskirts of Pusan. Other than the reason for us being there—to help free South Korea from the grasp of the North Korean dictator wanting to attack and enslave the South Koreans—it was a nice and sunny day otherwise.

THOUGHTS OF KINDNESS ENTER MY MIND

The area was filled with refugees and displaced persons of every nature, struggling to just survive, milling around in a confused stupor, desperate to find some relief somewhere. In my mind, I can still hear the rattle and clank of tanks, trucks, and equipment pushing toward the front lines only a few miles away. The North Korean Army had us with our backs to the wall. We were about to be thrown out of Korea back out into the Sea of Japan. A group of little girl war orphans caught up with us and were begging us for things, maybe mostly for attention I suppose. The image of those helpless little innocent girls in a struggle together in their effort at attempting to survive grown-up man's atrocities of war have never been to far from my mind. I can plainly and clearly see them all at this moment in time; may God had given them refuge and a safe place to be away from it all back then.

MY FAVORITE MEMORY OF PUSAN KOREA

While we walked along, one smaller little girl was running along, crying and trying to catch up but was falling farther behind. She was dressed in a traditional Korean dress, a cute little girl who became more and more distraught as she tried to keep up. I went back and picked her up and carried her along as I teased and played with her and gave her a stick of gum or something else I had to cheer her up. She cheered right up and was having a good time like the rest of them. Then within a little while, five or ten minutes, one of our company trucks came alongside and stopped to pick us up. I cuddled her up, gave her a little hug as I sat her back down on the roadway. We jumped in the back of the truck as the driver moved on down the road.

MY ADOPTED KOREAN DAUGHTER

I looked back and through the swirling dust at this little girl came running after the truck with tears streaming down her face and her arms outstretched, crying out in her strained and pitiful, tear-jerking, and sad little voice, "Obahgie, Obahgie, Obahgie." As soon as I got back to our unit, I looked up a Korean interpreter and asked him what the word *obahgie* meant. He said it meant *daddy*! Being born and raised up of a cold-blooded German background, not easily subject to emotions of the moment, yet the hearing of "Daddy, Daddy, Daddy" still now—some sixty-six years later, coming back to memory from the distraught little innocent Korean girl—continues to tug at my heartstrings and is one more thing that has helped shaped my character since that time so long ago.

DADDY, DADDY, DADDY

This image has returned to my mind multiple thousands of times. Sixty-six years later now and my eyes cannot stay dry whenever she comes back into my heart and into my mind's eye. She had no other place to look for any care, peace, joy, love, kindness, safety, or comfort; she, within minutes, had adopted me as her father. It tells me too how important it is that we should never hesitate to show our love and concern for others. It is a good time to remember the golden rule: "Do unto others as you would have them do unto you."

In the war-torn city of Pusan, where love seemed to be nonexistent, it had a positive effect on one of God's precious little children. I think of her often. I wonder as well if God might make us known to each other in the hereafter. These thoughts cause me to pray, and I ask God to return His Son Jesus Christ to earth to right the wrongs that mankind has achieved in their own governing of this world and its ways. Where under His (God's) rule and reign, all wars will cease to exist. When the judgment of God is in the earth, the inhabitants shall learn righteousness.

> *"At night my soul longs for You, Indeed, my spirit within me seeks You diligently; For when the earth experiences Your judgments The inhabitants of the world learn righteousness"*
>
> (Isaiah 26:9)

A FRESH CHICKEN DINNER

Pusan, Korea, was a culture shock to all of us young kids back in 1950; it was nothing at all like the pictures we see today. They even changed the name now to Busan. My good buddy Ernie and myself was downtown Pusan this one day, where a restaurant was offering French fries and fresh fried chicken. We went on in and sat down as the waiter came to take our order. We both ordered the fresh chicken dinner; he had gone back then into the kitchen and returned with a live chicken, to supposedly assure us that we were getting a fresh chicken. We had given him the nod as he disappeared to prepare the chicken back somewhere in the kitchen I suppose.

TRUST BEGINS TO RUN RAZOR-BLADE THIN

We were licking our chops, anticipating a fresh chicken dinner. It came out looking like a million dollars, all golden brown and looking delicious; but as soon as we took a bite it became obvious it and the French fries had been cooked in fish oil. We had gagged and choked it down the best we could until we began to wonder if we had really got the fresh chicken he had showed us. Or were we being taken advantage of by a Korean bait and switch deal. We got to talking about that and how he probably had a good-looking live chicken for display purposes only; the one we got could very well have been one that had died of old age a month ago. It took the edge off the craving we had for fresh fried Korean chicken.

MOVE TO INCHON KOREA

On September 15, 1950, the Battle of *Inchon* was an amphibious invasion and battle of the Korean War that resulted in a decisive victory and strategic reversal in favor of the United Nations. The operation involved some seventy-five thousand troops and 261 naval vessels and led to the recapture of the South Korean capital of Seoul two weeks later. It became a different war at this time; we had split the enemy and was able to attack them in different directions. Now they had outrun their supply lines, and the war had swung over to our advantage. We immediately moved our longshoreman outfit to Inchon, Korea. To be in proximity to supply the frontline, battlefield action with their much-needed materials to fight a war with.

The Orientals are, for some reason, big on going underground to hide and protect themselves from the invading enemy. The Koreans were no different in Inchon as MacArthur's surprise amphibious landing at their port had taken the North Koreans all by surprise. Where many had gone into their automatic mode of hiding and escaping in their ratholes, where many of their rotting and decaying bodies are still entombed today, the Army and Marines came in with flamethrowers and burned them out, and the engineers came in with bulldozers and buried them alive within the holes and tunnels that they were counting on to save themselves.

APPOINTED A SECURITY GUARD AT INCHON

Arriving at Inchon, our new location for receiving war materials required a different strategy and approach altogether; because of security reasons, Inchon had not been cleared of all enemy operations of subversion to be inflicted upon our military and dock operations now under way. The Koreans, both North and South, were notorious thieves that required keeping a constant eye upon. I imagine they became that way under the selfish and brutal rule of the Japanese for so many years. Japan would confiscate the goods, food, and other things for themselves, leaving very little for the Koreans to thrive and exist on. Therefore they were forced to adapt to a way of life to live in and to raise their families, which stealing seemed to be a part of it.

There was no noticeable difference that anyone could discern between the North Koreans and the South Koreans that let us tell them apart. Consequently, to play it safe, we had to assume that any one or all of them could be North Koreans or North Korean sympathizers. I was one of about twenty soldiers picked to be a security guard. To guard the docks and waterfront against any sabotage, thievery, or suspicious activity that needed to be looked at a little closer or brought into check. It was good duty that allowed for a reasonable amount of time off that we often used hunting out in the Korean countryside or the buying and selling of money, which was all legal and aboveboard.

We used script money to buy things in Korea; greenbacks were not allowed overseas. Script money looked somewhat like Monopoly money; the Koreans didn't have any trust or confidence at all in it but accepted it in order to do any business with our soldiers there. We would accumulate as much Korean money as we could afford to then go into Inchon and negotiate with the Korean merchants to take the script off their hands at a very substantial loss to them, about fifty cents on the dollar if I remember right, but something that they were more than happy to do.

After we had used all of our Korean money in buying back script money, we would flag down one of our trucks carrying supplies to the frontline troops in the north that had to go through Ascom City, Korea, where the post exchange was located to buy Korean money, the desired currency of the Korean merchants. We would then, after changing the script back into Korean money, have doubled our money amount and head back to Inchon to buy more script back for another supply of Korean money in which to buy back more of our script money.

A process that was perfectly legal and aboveboard, and a much-appreciated service to the Korean merchants. We took advantage of our security guard position that allowed for this to take place. I guess you could have called us "entrepreneur," "longshoremen." We were learning how things happen in this world. After a day's work like this, we would end up with a pretty good size pile of brand-new crisp Korean paper money in the back of an army truck we would flag down to take us back to Inchon to our billet area, where we would store it in our footlockers as we waited for our next day off to either go hunting or buy and sell money.

WE WERE AS CLOSE TO BEING OUR OWN BOSS AS WAS MILITARILY POSSIBLE

UNLIKE OUR MILITARY LEADERS AND THOSE IN AUTHORITY now days, we had been given almost absolute and complete authority to maintain the laws that were being established and set down by our military leaders at that time. Military man power was being spread pretty thin, all bases needed to be covered as best as possible. It was strictly a no nonsense, get the job done, shoot to kill when necessary approach, that our commanders would stand behind us on. We were separated from the soldiers that worked crews of Koreans to unload the ships that had tied up at the Inchon docks.

We were being billeted in a separate building, in a different part of the city of Inchon, away from those we had previously served with as stevedores? ourselves. We had been equipped with an arsenal of varied weapons to take care of most anything that would require an intervention of any possible magnitude. We were, however, really short on any training in educating us on how to use some of it; we would just have to punt at times. It was as if they were letting the blind lead the blind by turning over such almost absolute control and authority to a few teenagers. By giving us an armband and a helmet liner that identified us as security guards with an *SG* on it. We now had become law enforcement professionals. We outranked any civilian or military Korean official at our guard post, which was the whole dock area and the edge of Inchon itself.

WE WERE DOING ON THE JOB TRAINING

AS UNUSUAL AND UNORTHODOX AS IT MAY SOUND, any real law in Incheon had been suspended. For the most part, it was also that way in Pusan. The guy with the weapon in his hand was the law. But it was even more so in Inchon, because our Army and Marines along with all military support systems on alert and involved had just assaulted their waterfront, taken over the city, and ran the North Koreans out of town, but still we were not able to detect exactly whom the enemy or North Korean sympathizers were. So, we carried our weapons with us just in case. We—that is, us, security guards—we didn't accept or recognize any Korean police officer, soldier, or any of their military officers or enlisted men or the Korean government, civil or official authority over us. We made the laws and kept order. Our military superiors gave us nearly complete authority in doing so.

DON'T DO WHAT I DO—DO AS I TELL YOU TO DO

Especially so whenever we were in our assigned area to keep things under control and humming along on an even keel. We had absolute control and were in total charge of that area. We were taught that on our own square yards or square feet of real estate under our charge, we outranked even the president of the United States of America.

One night as I manned a gate into the dock area, an officer approached at a brisk pace. When I challenged him with the normal "Halt, who goes there?" he mumbled his name was Colonel So-and-So and kept right on walking. I racked a live round into the chamber of my weapon and repeated in a loud and distinct voice, "Colonel So-and-So, if you don't stop and be recognized immediately, someone is going to have to pick about thirty rounds of carbine ammunition out of your dead ass."

GETTING A SUPERIOR OFFICER'S UNDIVIDED ATTENTION

It is amazing the amount of authority there is in the sound of a bolt slamming shut in the hands of someone you do not have the foggiest notion how stable or unstable they might be or become. I didn't want him to go away with any questions on his mind that he might have wanted to pass on to his superior or those under him. I made him go through the drill of interrogation and the guard laws in existence that I had been trained to understand. I checked his papers, and I don't recall for certain, but I probably asked him questions like, who was pitching for the New York Yankees that year, or who was the most decorated soldier of WWI and WWII? I still wonder how he might have felt inside if he had known the facts, that an eighteen-year-old high school dropout with a ninth-grade education was exercising authority over him, a full-bird colonel of the United States Army, and was putting *his* feet to the fire?

I ENJOYED THIS ENCOUNTER WITH AN OFFICER A LITTLE TOO MUCH

During daylight hours one day, in the same general area talked about above, close to where us security guards were billeted, there was a sudden commotion from outside of our rooming area, mixed with gunfire and yelling coming from outside. I and several guards scrambled outside to see what was happening. The shots had been coming from the dock area, as a Korean dockhand, or at least that is what we assumed that he was, was running in our direction—all humped over, but still running at a pretty good pace.

He ran right up to go around the building we were standing by, and he collapsed and fell on his face, right by my feet. I could tell he had been hit in the lungs because of all of the air-filled blood bubbles coming out from his mouth. He was still alive, but it was obvious he wouldn't be for long. We all just stood there and watched him bleed out and suffocate there in a puddle of his own blood that was coming from his mouth and into the dirt. No one made any attempt at all to roll him out of the puddled blood coming from his mouth. It remains another haunting image that will forever be taking its place among all of the other war memories that have been cemented permanently in my mind, heart, and being.

THE INABILITY TO FORGIVE, EVEN IN YOUR MIND

I HAVE PLAYED THAT SCENARIO THROUGH MY MIND thousands of times down through the years. How is it that a person can become so cold and emotionless and not have the will or character to act in any way to relieve someone that may be going through the last minutes of life on this earth? He was just an expendable Korean, and now in our mind-set, he had become a good one. It has haunted me for sixty-seven years now in the way I felt about other human beings that didn't look or act like us. Fellow inhabitants of the world that God had made so we could learn to live together in love and acceptance. Not someone to look down upon without any empathy, sympathy, or the ability to look kindly upon or have any warm feelings for.

I wish I had had the maturity and presence of mind to have knelt down and placed a hand on his arm or shoulder, and if he had any life left in himself, to let him feel a measure of comfort in his hopeless and ending life? That he might have felt a fleeting moment of perceived kindness from another human being. Whether he was a poor family man that had stolen a can of beans to feed his kids or a North Korean saboteur. We stood there for a little while and then turned and walked back into our billet. We didn't as much as throw a cover of some kind over him. He lay there where he fell until the next day, until someone had removed him. A sad way for any life to end.

A MISSED OPPORTUNITY TO OPENLY SHOW ANY SYMPATHY

THESE THINGS HAPPENED ON A REGULAR BASIS ON the dock area where ships were unloading all kinds of food items and war supplies. One of our duties was to walk a post within the dock area, to prevent the dock workers from stealing things that were being earmarked for our military. The dock area had about an eight-foot-high cyclone fence around the whole perimeter, with wooden pallets stacked up near the top of the fence. Alleyways cut back and forth through and between the stacked pallets, where it made it easier to patrol the area. At night, the Korean dockworkers would steal some sort of goods, hide it on themselves, and then run along the top of the pallets and jump the fence and make a clean getaway.

CAREFUL WHERE YOU ARE STEPPING

One of our guards was a bloodthirsty guy named Cantrell. He would even volunteer to take over other guard shifts in order to actually hunt and kill Koreans. He would file notches on his rifle butt to keep score as he built a bigger, better and more grandiose image of himself in his mind. I didn't care for him at all, but we walked the same beat at different times of the day and night. I had relieved him one night and was walking the familiar pathway around and in between the stacked pallets. We got in the habit of looking up at the skyline at night, making it easy to spot the silhouette of someone against lighter sky background that was attempting to cross on the pallet tops and jump to safety on the other side of the fence.

A GOVERNMENT KILLER THAT ENJOYED HIS JOB TO MUCH

I suddenly tripped over something in the pathway, lost my balance, and fell down. I shined my flashlight on the ground to see what I had stumbled over. Cantrell had shot a Korean dockworker attempting to escape detection. I could tell by the position he was in that Cantrell had shot him in the stomach; he was hunched up on his knees and holding his arms around his belly. He was dead, and rigor mortis had set in, causing him to be rigid. He had to have died in severe, overwhelming pain and anguish. No one had informed me about it, and even though the person brought it upon himself, it has always bothered me that Cantrell seemed to be an individual that just relished seeing his victims suffer unbearable pain when they were dying.

A CRY IN THE NIGHT

My very good friend at the time was a likable young guy about my own age and size by the name of Bronson, and with the same hell-raising attitude as me that tends to get one into trouble, from time to time. We would often walk our beat together for safety purposes and just to have someone to visit with along the way. Our patrol that night included a little edge of the populated section of Inchon. As we walked along, we heard a weird high-pitched sound that made the hair stand up on the back of my neck. We began looking for the source and location of where it was coming from. We zeroed in on a door front belonging to a business on the street. We approached it carefully and found a little Korean boy sitting naked in the doorway, with only an army shirt around him that some soldier had probably given to him.

JUST ANOTHER THROWAWAY KOREAN KID

A HIGH-PITCHED WHINE BORDERING ON CRYING WAS COMING out of him, and he was starting to turn blue and rigid. Things of this nature are not being covered in a war zone by the big brass; we didn't know what to do. Looking around, we noticed a makeshift dwelling a few hundred feet away that had a little light coming out between the cracks. We decided to take the little boy over and get him inside out of the weather to keep him from freezing to death. Inchon had been bombed out recently, and no one had much of anything left to take care of themselves. I knocked on the door, and an old mama-san came to the door; and as soon as she saw the little naked boy, she began loudly protesting, saying, "Domi, domi, domi," with all kinds of negative hand gestures. We knew that it meant "no" in Japanese, because all Koreans spoke Japanese.

DOES THE END REALLY JUSTIFY THE MEANS?

IN SITUATIONS SUCH AS THIS, YOU LEARN TO be decisive, bold, and in charge. To get straight to the point, because there is not any good solution to it here and now. I shoved the little boy into the shelter with old mama-san's mouth running ninety miles an hour, and she shoved him right back out. Again, as with the colonel at our guard post, I racked a live round into the chamber of my carbine rifle, pointed it right straight at her head, and, through sign language that she obviously understood with the motions I was making, told her if we saw that little boy back out on the street again this night, we would be back to shoot her. I had to make up for being an eighteen-year-old kid that wouldn't be taken seriously, by being loud, in charge and demanding, and believable.

These things I write about here are the reason why those of us who have seen combat or know what it is like to live life in a war zone, stay away from discussing such things among others that have not served within areas of total lawlessness such as this. It is not believable to them, and the squeamish cannot bear to hear about it, or to even know that it exists. It changes a person little by little; you become a different person when the population surrounding you seems to be void of decent character traits, and many it is that begin reverting to a basic animal instinct of survival of the fittest. I hope that I am getting the message out of man's inhumanity against his own kind, that others will be able to learn things without having to go through them.

TOO MUCH RESPONSIBILITY FOR AN EIGHTEEN-YEAR-OLD KID

As security guards at the Inchon waterfront and dock area, we were expected, and ordered, to maintain a professional and strict military code of conduct, honor, and dress. We had to be squared away at all times, to back up our position of being in authority. We wore an armband of a black background and white lettering of *SG* (Security Guard) with *OD* colored helmet liner with *SG* on the front in white lettering and two thin white lines that encircled the middle part of the helmet liner. Our fatigues or khaki uniforms, I can't remember which, were being worn with a sharp crease where they belonged on the pants, shirt, or jacket with a web pistol belt lacking any Sam Browne–type leather chest strap, and we bloused our boots in airborne style.

Consequently, our clothing was being sent out to a local laundry or an individual Korean woman that always picked up and delivered our laundry back to us at the guardhouse. I had the opportunity at one time to go to her place of business. The primitive level that she was required to sweat, struggle, and work in surprised me. It was all being done by hand. And she was several months along in a pregnancy that didn't slow her down or hold her back at all. One thing most all Koreans do have to be proud of is their work ethic, and this little lady was no exception. It was fun to watch her work; she made every move count and was super-efficient in her trade without any modern tools to work with.

LOOKING FORWARD TO THE FINAL RIGHTEOUSNESS OF ALL MANKIND

She was a reasonable young lady that obviously had been taught the work ethic well. She had to use as an iron a small cast iron skillet filled with hot coals. I don't know how she was able to manage such a heavy and awkward thing all day long, but the finished product was far and away the best and most professional job from any laundry service I have ever seen, either before or since, and I later on had worked eight years in a laundry myself. There was no comparison whatsoever.

This brings me to a gut-wrenching experience of unimaginable scope or reason. Things like this happen way too often in an area of war, or of the lawlessness within a war zone that often prevails. Where the only law being exercised and being obeyed is coming from the person holding the gun. Whatever it is inside of us that quickly reverts to survival of the fittest for self-preservation during times of stress and disorder. There is a way that seems right to men as we see here in Proverbs 16:25, but notice where it ends. *"There is a path before each person that seems right, but it ends in death"* (NLT) and again here in Proverbs 12:15. *"The way of a fool is right in his own eyes, but a wise man is he who listens to counsel."*

Mankind has been created a carnal creature, with enmity against the will, the way, and the avowed purpose of God. Something that allows our mind and heart to totally turn our backs on decency, integrity, care, and concern for our fellowman or woman, or any common sense whatsoever. It is the exact reason why we need our Savior Jesus Christ to return to earth, to set up the coming Kingdom of God, that we may finally learn the way to righteousness and eternal peace on earth. It will never happen with fallen mankind at the helm of our government, They, or we ourselves, *all of us*, are all too easily corrupted by the pull and sway of the devil and Satan. Take God out of the equation and we would immediately return to dust. Yet! *With God* all things are possible.

The Word of God tells us that it is not in man that walks to direct his own steps. And how true that has shown to be over the past six thousand years of man's attempt at ruling this earth. We have now brought ourselves to the brink of cosmocide *(the total and complete destruction of the earth and everything on it)*, that unless Christ should return to put a stop to it, there should be no flesh saved alive. But Christ will return to stop unrighteous mankind from completely annihilating themselves off the face of this earth through their gross disobedience of the Word and way of God. And to usher in the kingdom of God.

Cosmocide—world leaders and scientists are frankly *frightened* by the prospects of the future. They warn that man now possesses the means of committing *suicide* of the whole human race" and even talk in terms of "overkill." They realize something totally unforeseen must soon occur to *stop* the present trend of world events, or humanity will finally destroy itself!

PAYING A DEBT WITH YOUR LIFE

Too many people lack any empathy at all for their fellow man or woman. This wonderful, dedicated, and hardworking Korean laundry lady that I talked about met with a fate that sixty-seven years later on still brings tears of sorrow and frustration to my eyes whenever I stop for a moment and bring it back into my mind. I am haunted still by the whole scenario that led to her untimely and senseless death by an individual who had allowed his mind to shut down to the point that it determined that he spend the rest of his life locked away in some prison. Caused by a weak moment that had come into his mind that told him it was all right to kill another human being made in the image and likeness of God and His Son Jesus Christ.

IT IS IMPOSSIBLE TO WASH SOME THINGS OUT OF OUR MINDS

This nice, pleasant, and well-mannered little pregnant Korean laundry lady had come into our guardhouse to either pick up or to deliver clean clothes, or both, when a security guard sitting on his bunk and playing around with his .45-caliber handgun suddenly, without any warning or notice, purposefully loaded it up and shot the little laundry woman in the stomach. It killed her and the baby both instantly as the place erupted in all kinds of chaos and traumatic things taking place, as the guard that had done the shooting was overcome, subdued, and taken away. Sometimes the remorse, the magnitude, the mystery of it all, and the attempt to come to some kind of understanding of why such things as this can happen leads me to blame it on Satan, the adversary that God has placed here, for us to learn to resist him so he will flee from us, as His Word tells us in James 4:7.

A PROBLEM IN NOT UNDERSTANDING THEIR CULTURE

It all didn't end there. A few days later, as several of us guards were resting and lounging around the guardhouse where we relaxed and slept, someone had made us aware that there was a commotion going on outside, coming down the street. We got up and went outside to see the unusual spectacle heading our way down the street. It looked like a parade back home where men, women, and kids, and even babies, were in a celebration and having a good time. Thinking he could win the Korean War on his own terms apart from any unwanted input from president Truman. And still being all puffed up with an extra helping of vanity, pride and superiority, after recently winning the war against the Japanese, he elected to go forth with plans of his own that he felt were superior to anyone else's.

They were all walking along singing and chanting and waving sticks with tassels at the tops, and we just felt good about it and decided to join in, probably more like to mock them, I suppose. We had also begun to dance around, sing to our hearts' content, and grab anything in sight to wave around in the air, when suddenly one among us was alert and smart enough to finally figure out it was the laundry woman's funeral possession. To which we say—

YOU CAN'T FIX DUMB

IT STILL HURTS WAY DOWN DEEP TODAY WHENEVER I pause for a moment and think about it. When I first became a security guard at the Inchon waterfront docks, I didn't know exactly how to deal with some things that would come up from time to time. On this one particular day, I caught a dockworker trying to get through with stolen goods. I didn't know that he might also be a North Korean or a North Korean sympathizer. Rather than issuing punishment that we had been authorized to administer, before letting them go on their way, I decided instead to take him to the South Korean police station to get a feel for how they operated and dealt with these kinds of situations.

ONE OF THE BIGGEST MISTAKES OF MY ENTIRE LIFE

THE POLICE WASTED NO TIME IN GETTING RIGHT to the business that all Orientals seem to be very good at. It didn't take me very long to decide I had just made a really big mistake, and it was too late now to undo it. The several police officers in the room descended upon the dockworker like sharks in a feeding frenzy. The Orientals just automatically seem to know every severe torture trick in the book. The truth be told, they probably wrote the book on torture themselves. I recall the horror stories about the Japanese and how they had treated our prisoners of war. No kid gloves being used here as the routine jumped off to a good start. Letting the caught-red-handed thief know without any question that he was in for some of the most severe and very high-level Oriental abuse and torture beyond his imagination.

NO ONE ON EARTH SHOULD EVER BE TREATED THE WAY THIS GUY WAS

THEY TOOK THIS POOR GUY AND RAN HIM through the rack. They made him get down on his knees, more like throwing him on his back, yanking and slapping him around until he was on his knees. Then they put a sledgehammer handle behind his knees and made him squat back on it on the inside crook of his bent legs, as the man in front of him jumped up and down on each end of sledgehammer handle while at the same time he kept hitting him in the face as hard as he could with a hard rubber hose. The Korean policeman doing the over-the-line beating on the victim was running his mouth a hundred miles an hour in a loud, threatening, and demanding-sounding voice. He kept it up nonstop for several long minutes.

The man was bawling and frothing at the mouth as his eyes rolled back in his head; he was making sounds that were more like those of a badly wounded animal than a human being as the snot blew out of his nose and drizzled down his face. It is the worst beating of either man or animal that I have ever personally witnessed. His knee joints at this point had no doubt pulled themselves out of there sockets. Even my cold German blood would not allow me to stay and watch any more of it. The man may have been a North Korean, I don't know. But it appeared to me that they were hell-bent on beating him to death, and I am quite sure that they did.

FORGIVE US, FATHER—WE KNOW NOT WHAT WE DO

SOMETHING THAT I AM PROBABLY MOST ASHAMED OF all, beyond any other thing that I have ever done in my life, happened at the guard post in Inchon, coming off from the dock area where the Korean dockworkers did their twelve-hour shifts before changing shifts and going home while the new shift came on to work. We had swing-open gates of about fifteen or twenty-feet-wide, closed up until the shift changes, as the going home shift lined up at the gate, waiting for its time to be opened. Then we would swing it open wide and let them all go through on their way home. If we suddenly, without notice, stopped them and closed the gate, they instantly knew that we would be frisking them for stolen goods. When we would close the gate in that way, you could hear all sorts of cans and different things rattling, clunking, and hitting the ground, all the way back down the line of workers.

BURY THE PAST, PUSH FORWARD TO ACHIEVE

WE WOULD MAKE THE LINE OF DOCKWORKERS MOVE to one side, which would then expose the whole line of stolen goods. Since this had become a daily routine because we were dealing with family men with wives and kids at home that were most likely starving to death because there simply was not enough food and needed supplies to go around in the city of Inchon at the time. It was an extremely difficult time for the South Korean families in their trying to survive and raise their kids in such an atmosphere of near hopelessness.

For that reason, we did try to cut them a little slack in certain cases, but in other cases we dealt pretty harshly with them, in order to somewhat stem the tide of their blatant thievery. But our punishment, however cruel and out of balance, never even approached the threshold of what they would have received at the hands of their own police force. In fact, we were taking on the character traits of the exceptionally cruel Orientals ourselves. But we justified it because of how they were treating our own captured soldiers. Hate, revenge, get even, do it to them before they have a chance to do it to you—it's a big part of our natural carnal mind and heart. It is a part of what *Satan*, the god of this world, has been feeding his flock identified as "the Babylon of Confusion," also known as Orthodox Christianity.

HORSE-FACE, MY KOREAN SOLDIER FRIEND

OUR MILITARY SUPERIORS IN INCHON, KOREA, IN 1950 had assigned a South Korean soldier to our guard post to learn the specifics we were having to deal with on the waterfront, dock, and warehouse complex on a regular, daily basis. Since I had spent a lot of time with him and had the chance to appreciate his personal character traits and the comical way of doing things I wasn't used to, I began to really enjoy his presence, and we began to have fun teasing each other even though we couldn't understand very much of what the other one was saying. We compensated for it by doing all sorts of hand and facial gestures. I had already learned really quick in dealing with others that cannot understand what we are saying that smiling, laughing, a handshake, and a pat on the shoulder is in itself a well-understood universal language, so we used it a lot.

For whatever reason that I cannot remember today, I started right out calling him "Horse-face." It may have been that he reminded me of one of our big workhorses we used back in Michigan on the farm. It stuck, and I never remember calling him anything else. In a short period of time, I looked at him as a friend that I had a good time with, and I know that he did me as well. I had earlier gotten a hold of some really warm sheepskin aviator pants and had taken them to a tailor and had them made into a sheepskin vest. Horse-face liked them and had tried to talk me out of it to give it to him, but I wouldn't ever do it. One night, Horse-face had gotten hold of some, at probably ten cents a gallon, rank and rotten-tasting Korean whiskey and wanted to share it with me. I somewhat remember having a good time up until I didn't remember anything anymore.

When I did wake up, it was morning, and I was about halfway over a barb-wire fence. All humped over with my head on one side of the fence and my feet on the other side. I didn't feel good enough to die. I had the worst headache I ever remember having. I began shivering and looked around for old Horse-face, but he was nowhere to be seen. About that time, I realized that my vest was missing too. Suddenly a light went off in my head and I now realized why Hoses-face was so liberal in sharing his cheap Korean whiskey. I soon found him back at our guard post with a big smile on his face, with his feet up on a table, all reared back just as proud as could be, wearing my sheepskin vest. We had a few words together before I took him down and took it back off him. We had a good laugh about it, and all's well that ends well.

POWER CORRUPTS; ABSOLUTE POWER CORRUPTS ABSOLUTELY

The proverbial saying "Power corrupts; absolute power corrupts absolutely" conveys the opinion that as a person's power increases, their moral sense diminishes. I have already told about us security guards in Inchon, Korea, having way too much power in any direction we were looking in, that this power was bound to be misused considering the nature of war and never knowing what tomorrow would bring upon us. We security guards in Inchon had been given power beyond what eighteen-year-old kids were able to handle at times. But the powers that be didn't have much choice. Most of us were still kids.

AN EYE FOR AN EYE, A TOOTH FOR A TOOTH

As a security guard in Inchon, Korea, I had decided never to take another human being to the South Korean police station for punishment. I would administer it myself and then turn them loose. On two different occasions, I had gone way overboard on the punishment to fit the offense. It had been swift and brutal beyond common sense. It is something I cannot or will not ever forget or discuss with a living soul, beyond what I am doing here and now.

I am just too ashamed to admit and to accept the fact that I was quickly becoming as brutal and as sinister as my surroundings, and those I was judging and condemning. I went way too far, but at the same time, it was also way short of what their own people were used to dishing out to them. I hurt them bad but didn't cripple or kill them. At least as far as I know, I didn't. I have confessed to God, and He has forgiven me. Jesus Christ died to take away the sins of the whole world, mine included, *My salvation is certain, so is yours.*

JESUS CHRIST IS SPIRIT; WE MUST WORSHIP HIM IN SPIRIT

We had access to all sorts of ammunition at our hands on a 24/7 basis. On our time off, we would often load up with the desired weapon and ammunition of our individual choice and go hunting up in the area of Yong-Dong-Po, out of the Inchon vicinity and up toward Seoul. I have a lot of fond memories of those times, enjoying life with your close buddies and comrades. This part of the Korean experience has always been fun to look back upon to remember the good times we had hunting and playing normal tricks upon one another. To laugh and joke around with friends and putting the war only a few miles away out of sight and out of mind. Never realizing that all too soon I would be a part of the government's dirty job of doing the killing.

A DAY OF SURPRISE LEARNING

On one of our hunting excursions in this general area, near Ascom City, Korea. We came over the ridgeline of what I would call a mountain, but the Koreans called them hills. We looked deep down in the valley or ravine below onto a small village with multiple dwelling places huddled within a compound of sorts. In the distance, the people milling around reminded me of bugs, flitting here and there. The village was on the edge of a substantial rice paddy, where we noticed an occasional person walking out on the built-up ridges that surrounded the rice paddy. We finally figured out they were going to an outside toilet they had built on the ridge. We watched them for a while, until an older Korean man began his own journey going to the pot.

FOOLS RUSH IN WHERE ANGELS FEAR TO TREAD

Finally, we came up with a plan of action. We felt we needed to do a little research; after all, we were all seventeen- or eighteen-year-old kids ourselves and had been given inquiring minds. We mutually agreed to test our theory of how close to the old man's feet would we have to fire before he would get excited and break into a run. We spent several minutes blowing dirt up all around his feet, making it sound as if the war had arrived right here. The old man never even as much as do a slight flinch; he never broke the gait he was walking and never even bothered to look around to see where all the shooting was coming from. This really got our full attention now, and we decided to go on down and check this situation out, to check out these seemingly brain-dead people all out.

DUMB AND DUMBER MOVE ON DOWN THE BIG HILL

There was one long building in the compound that we could see lettering on its top as we sat looking down upon it but couldn't read what it said because age had diminished many of the letters, but it was written in English. In a half hour or so, we had gone on down and were approaching the little village and were really surprised to see the closer we got to them, the more they had all congregated into a pretty good-sized group and were all tickled to death to see us and welcomed us with open arms as they came running out to meet us. Smiling, cheering, and laughing right out loud. We didn't really know what to think; they were happy as could be, but they also were disfigured and physically ugly, with all kinds of scars and missing body parts. We approached them cautiously and carefully, not quite aware of what exactly was going on, but we aimed to find out.

IN FOR SOME SHOCK AND AWE

As we came closer to the crowd that had assembled there, I spotted one middle-aged man standing up and behind the main group. He had a big ear-to-ear grin on his face, but he also had one hand inside his shirt, like the pictures of Napoleon we had seen. I didn't know what he might be hiding. I alerted the other guys, pointed him out and told them to cover me—I was going over to check him out. I just nonchalantly took my time and edged over by him and quickly grabbed his hand and yanked it out from his shirt. Talk about shock and awe. I was thunderstruck and felt like the world's biggest fool. I still had a good grip hold on his wrist area, but most of his hand had been eaten away by something, or at least it was missing. Suddenly, one of the guys, obviously more alert than the rest of us, had finally figured out what the writing on top of the big building was all about. We had stumbled into a *leper colony*.

WE CANNOT DISCUSS REALITY WITHOUT DISCUSSING GOD IN IT

These poor crippled-up and disfigured men, women, and kids, alone and lonely creatures never having any visitors, cut off from the outside world, living for the most part in this out-of-the-way, godforsaken shantytown of misery, within such horrible maggot- and rat-infested conditions as these open-air dump-type enclosures not fit for an animal to live in. It was, and still is, enough to pray to our Almighty God of all heaven and earth to look down from above on such pain, misery, heartache, despair, hurt, and hopelessness that the misguided rule of mankind has brought upon themselves. And for God to hasten the day of the return of Jesus Christ, to right the world of all its evil nature and to hasten the return of the righteous rule that He Himself and the elect of God will be spending time bringing about during His thousand-year reign. Beginning at the first resurrection.

GETTING BACK TO 1951 INCHON, KOREA

Realizing then that we had come into a leper colony being isolated in an out-of-the-way secluded location, where outsiders were forbidden to enter, this pitiful gathering of human beings stuffed off in a corner and out of sight and mind jerked at our heart strings. Our being there, up close and personal, to touch and to be among them must have been a totally unexpected once-in-a-lifetime occasion for them all to experience. Because of how much these friendly, loving, caring people, enjoyed, and appreciated our visit, we determined that any damage to ourselves, if any, had already been done. We just hung around and had some of the best and most memorable time of our lives in Korea. It seemed like the good and proper thing to do.

MORE ON THE LEPER COLONY

One buddy with us had one of the first Polaroid cameras in existence at that time. It took pictures and developed them at the same time. We took a lot of pictures and showed them to the happy group, which left them beside themselves laughing and dancing around, being delighted about the whole thing and beaming all over in excitement and appreciation for having us as their company. I would give a lot to have access to some of those pictures of back then. It really would fulfill the old saying that one picture is worth a thousand words. But they have not all been lost in time; in my mind's eye, I can see many of them yet today. Evidently, they are periodically just waiting for that recall, that future time when God calls all His children home to Himself.

Maybe we were able to be a little strength or a hope to them, if only for a fleeting moment, in our being able to share a spirit of love, fun, and togetherness with those who likely need it most. These people grew their own food—meat and vegetables. We bought a duck from them on our first visit, and on another occasion, we bought a little pig of about twenty pounds. We took it back to our cooks and asked if they would cook it for us. They said they would, so we left it in their hands. We rigged up a little pen to keep it in until Thanksgiving. The cooks agreed to look after it and keep it fed and watered in order that they might share in it at Thanksgiving dinner too. Consequently, we went away with our mouths watering for the taste of fresh pork again.

Looking back now, it reminds me of a Jewish father and his attempt at teaching his only son about trust. One day, when his son was just a small lad of two or three years old, the father had placed him on a high wall; and as he sat there, the father held his arms out and ordered the little toddler to jump into his arms. He said, "Come on, Abby yump, yump. Yump Abby, you father will, catch you, yump, come on Abby yump."

But the little boy was too scared to do so. The father kept on reassuring him that he was right there to catch him. Saying again and again, "Jump, Abby. Yump, your father will catch you."

Finally, the little boy did as his father had coaxed him into doing. He jumped. The father in that instant stepped back, and *splat*, the little boy hit the ground hard and began to cry.

The father picked him up and said, "Abby, you learned a great lesson today—never trust anyone, not even your own papa."

Those brownnosing cooks had jumped the gun while we were busy at our other duties and slaughtered the pig for their personal gain. With visions of sugar plumbs bouncing around in their head, anticipating making brownie points with the company officers, they put their diabolical plan into motion. By stuffing the little piggy and putting him into a roaster, they had made up a nice meal of fresh pork, mashed potatoes and gravy, and all the trimmings to feed the company officers. We never got so much as a smell. So the moral of the story that day was learning the lesson of the old Jewish father. Never trust anyone, not even you own papa. And especially, never again trust our cooks.

We didn't have much time to be mad at and offended by the cooks, though. A few days later, the CCF (Chinese Communists Forces) that had massed at the Manchurian border and the egomaniac General Douglas MacArthur had refused to believe his own intelligence sources telling him that it was exactly what they had been doing for a long time. The CCF began their bloodcurdling, bugle blowing bonsai attacks on our unsuspecting troops in overwhelming full force on every front, and we were soon run out of Inchon and all of North Korea, with our tail between our legs, and our longshoreman outfit had to retreat back to Pusan to reestablish our longshoreman duties there.

GENERAL DOUGLAS MACARTHUR (THE GREAT ONE) BITES THE DUST

THE BIG MACARTHUR BLUNDER COST THE LIVES OF many men. The Second Infantry Division, the division that I would soon be a replacement in, was fighting a rear-guard action at that time to allow the marine and army units to retreat out from the trap that the CCF had caught them in at the Chosin Reservoir. The Second Division suffered altogether over five thousand causalities that day because of a self-centered glory hound looking to cement the image that he had of himself recorded in the annals of war as the great General Douglas MacArthur. Always supposing himself to be of superior intellect and of having the ability of directing a war beyond what anyone else could, including the President of The United States of America, President Harry S. Truman. MacArthur stepped into a big pile of doggy do do, in his lack of respect for the chain of command. In being disobedient to the orders of President Truman. MacArthur wasn't used to taking orders, he was the one who usually gave the orders. It didn't work out to well for him this time.

He received his just reward for insubordination when President Truman fired him for his thinking and acting as if he could override, go past, and make a mockery of the direct orders of the President of the United States of America. It needs to be pointed out here as well, to balance out the real skinny on MacArthur: he really was a great general and war tactician who more than earned the right to be praised for all that he was responsible for during the Second World War against Japan. That can never be taken away from him, and we will all be indebted to him for his long and faithful service to our country and the part he played in defeating the enemies of our country and his awesome move at Inchon, Korea, where he changed the course of the war by breaking the supply lines of the enemy and giving us a giant advantage to move forward with a will to win the Korean War. Do not let anybody ever tell you that we didn't. We put them right back where they came from.

THE WORD OF GOD IS JESUS CHRIST

WE PRAY FOR AND ASK YOU, FATHER GOD, to return your Son Jesus Christ, to put an end to the unrighteous rule of mankind on this earth. That Christ and His special elect people, known as the first fruits, will then rule with Him for the next thousand years, to bring all of mankind into the righteousness of God. Where God then will <u>be all</u> in <u>all</u>. Listen well here, my spiritual brothers, sisters, and friends. *Please* do not let your church or the minister that is masquerading as an angel of light that teaches in your church continue to feed you the ungodly slop of God sending even one of His children to the raging flames of hell, to suffer day and night forever. It is one of the biggest Satan-inspired and Christianity-believed lies ever against the Word and way of God.

WE ACCEPT, BELIEVE, AND FOLLOW EITHER GOD OR SATAN

IT IS A VIRTUAL IMPOSSIBILITY FOR JESUS CHRIST to lose even one person that the Father has given Him, and God has given all things into the hands of His Son Jesus Christ (John 3:34–36). *The one who comes from above is above all; the one who is from the earth belongs to the earth and speaks as one from the earth. The one who comes from heaven is above all. He testifies to what he has seen and heard, but no one accepts his testimony. Whoever has accepted it has certified that God is truthful.* (I have accepted the truth of God) *For the one whom God has sent speaks the words of God, for God[b] gives the Spirit without limit. The Father loves the Son and has placed everything in his hands. Whoever believes in the Son has eternal life, but whoever rejects the Son will not see life, for God's wrath remains on them.*

THE WRATH OF GOD HAS AN ENDING

Ezekiel 16:42

Then my wrath against you will subside and my jealous anger will turn away from you; I will be calm and no longer angry.

Isaiah 54:9

For this is like the days of Noah to Me, When I swore that the waters of Noah Would not flood the earth again; So I have sworn that I will not be angry with you Nor will I rebuke you.

Isaiah 54:10

For the mountains may be removed and the hills may shake, But My lovingkindness will not be removed from you, And My covenant of peace will not be shaken," Says the LORD who has compassion on you.

Ezekiel 5:13

Thus My anger will be spent and I will satisfy My wrath on them, and I will be appeased; then they will know that I, the LORD, have spoken in My zeal when I have spent My wrath upon them.

Ezekiel 21:17

I will also clap My hands together, and I will appease My wrath; I, the LORD, have spoken.

LEAD, FOLLOW, OR GET OUT OF THE WAY

IT NEEDS TO BE POINTED OUT HERE THAT the wrath of God remains upon the person refusing to believe the Word of God, but only so long as they stay in their unbelief mode. At that future point in time when God puts His hand to the plow of redemption, He will call and open the heart and mind of all people to be completely receptive to His truth. So, my friends, be of good cheer. No one ever born upon this earth is ever going to spend even one iota of a nanosecond in the Christian-contrived literal hell that they use as a scare tactic. It is meant to be used for that specific purpose—to keep the dumb sheep in line and keep them scared to death of losing their own salvation, and to keep the tithes and offerings flowing freely and plentifully into the coffers of their particular church. Into the money pot that the one at the top digs into as pleases him.

BELIEVE ONE OR THE OTHER

ONE OF THE FORTY-ONE THOUSAND OTHERS WHO CLAIM to be the true church of God. Hoping they have been successful enough in their deceptive teachings of hogwash and outright lies, that no one will bother to read their own Bible for themselves, that they might discover that the church they attend has taken the place of God in their mind and hearts. That they continue on feeding the goose that has been laying all of those golden eggs for their church. Putting their faith and confidence in the hands of ministers masquerading as apostles of Christ as recorded here in 2 Corinthians 11:13–15. *"For such people are false apostles, deceitful workers, masquerading as apostles of Christ. And no wonder, for Satan himself masquerades as an angel of light. It is not surprising, then, if his servants also masquerade as servants of righteousness. Their end will be what their actions deserve."*

GOD IS THE SAME, YESTERDAY, TODAY, AND FOREVER

THEIR MOTIVATION IN FURTHERING THE SUCCESS OF A false gospel is to control minds and hearts and to bring ever more money into their bulging coffers. We all go through the symbolic fire of God that Hebrews talks about (Hebrews 12:29). *Our God is a consuming fire.* To purge us of all unrighteousness. But much of the Word of God is written in symbolic, figurative speech, parables, and /or metaphoric language. It is not intended to be taken literally. But the plan of God does not change, He is the same yesterday, today, and forever. He changes not. We are all going to belong to the kingdom of God, right here on earth. He is God the Father of all, and we are all His children.

BE CAREFUL WHEN YOU THINK YOU STAND, LEST YOU FALL

WHAT A GIGANTIC AND MONUMENTAL SIN OF CORRUPTION and evil it is for any church claiming to be a Christian organization that believes and teaches others to accept and to believe as the truth of God, that they have been given the truth to pass on to others, to try to convince their converts that God would treat the children that He loves in such an ungodly way that, according to them, is forever. The truth is the exact opposite: God will save all; not even one person will lose their salvation. It is not something that might possibly happen sometime; it is a chiseled-in-granite done deal that Jesus Christ has already accomplished and paid the full price for all sins of all creation, for all time. When He announced, *"It is finished,"* He had completed the assignment that His Father, God, had given Him to do. All of mankind's salvation is an absolute certainty.

Here is another fact to consider while attempting to understand the truth of God in this matter: God has breathed the breath of life (*spirit*) into all of the god-kind at our birth. The spirit came out from God into the god-kind, causing us all to become a living soul. The spirit can be withheld from anyone, but it cannot die. The spirit has always existed and will continue to exist and live on forever since it cannot die. Us physical god-kind beings received the indwelling spirit at our physical birth here upon the earth. *The Word of God tells us what happens with our spirit when we die. Then shall the dust return to the earth as it was: and the spirit shall return unto God who gave it* (Ecclesiastes 12:7). Easy words to understand—that which came out from God will simply revert itself from whence it came and be absorbed back into God. Where it remains until the resurrections.

BEING SENT AS A REPLACEMENT INTO HELL ON EARTH

THE SECOND INFANTRY DIVISION HAD LOST THREE THOUSAND men in one afternoon in a six-mile pass below Kunri, Korea. U.S. Army losses numbered around two thousand killed and one thousand wounded. Precise casualties for the Chinese are not known but are estimated at thirty-five killed. Upon reaching Hungnam, the veterans of Chosin Reservoir were evacuated as part of the large amphibious operation to rescue UN troops from northeastern Korea. It was the longest retreat in U.S. military history. One Marine officer *(possibly the famed marine general Chesty Puller)* has been quoted as saying, "Retreat? Hell, we are just attacking in a different direction." You have to love those marines.

I have to apologize for getting off track as I go along in my writing down things that cross my mind, but if I don't, I will forget them. I still have more to say about life on the waterfront as an army stevedore or longshoreman in Pusan, where we found ourselves again after MacArthur's amphibious landing at Inchon had been a great success. But because his arrogance and sitting himself up as some kind of a god that the Japanese believed him to be, he ignored the intelligence sources that were informing him of the Chinese forces massing at the Yalu and preparing to attack in full force. Because of that giant MacArthur blunder, we were once again receiving war materials and supplies for those on the frontlines, back down south in Pusan, Korea.

We had been run out of Inchon by the Chinese enemy that had now entered the war in overwhelming numbers that had been massing up beyond the Yalu River in Manchuria by the multiple thousands. Things began to paint a bleak picture for our severely outnumbered and battle-weary soldiers and marines that had borne the brunt of the atrocious and brutal battle practices being inflicted upon them by the enemy and by the severe and never-ending weather conditions that existed at the time. Once again, we had found ourselves in an awkward and disadvantaged position against the enemy. Where our entire military had been driven out of North Korea on a headlong rush to escape death or imprisonment, in the longest retreat in American war history.

Our military had to retreat far enough to regroup, lick their wounds, bury the dead, bring in more replacements from back home, and begin to make plans for the spring offensive. Number one on the list for the Second Division that I now belonged to was to hold on to the geographic and strategic city of Wonju, Korea. That is where I found myself as a machine gunner in the Second Indianhead Infantry Division, and by far and away, in the most mind-numbing, body-punishing, brutal below-zero conditions that had hit Korea in over a hundred years; being without decent cold-weather clothing and lacking in ever having a warm meal, never able to catch any decent sleep at all; against three-to-one odds of Chinese soldiers that had been commanded to annihilate us all. But when the battle was over, we had inflicted eighteen thousand causalities upon them and held on to Wonju.

BACK IN INCHON

Before leaving the Inchon area where I was a security guard, we on occasion would go hunting up in the hills and rural countryside places west of Inchon. Several of us guards found it relaxing, fun, and enjoyable to be together out in the rather secluded sections among the common everyday people. We were in the hills looking for any game we could find. We didn't know what kind of animals Korea had or anything about their hunting season; and in truth and in fact, we didn't care. We just wanted some fresh meat. We came over a hilltop ridge that allowed us to see a lot of area. We noticed a compound of several traditional Korean rural homes down in a big valley. There were chickens running loose all around, picking their own living outside of any pens. We decided to go down and see if they would sell us one.

When we got down there, several of the community leaders came out to meet us. They were friendly and appeared curious as to what we wanted. There was this one real nice big red rooster. We went through the motion of moving our hands to our mouth and fake chewing as we pointed at the rooster. It was immediately obvious they didn't want to part with that rooster. Looking back, I realize the rooster was probably a blue ribbon prize–winning special that had sired all the other chickens we saw running around. They all began to chime in with an adamant "Domi, domi." We knew it meant "no" in Japanese and that the Japanese had made them speak the language while Japan occupied and ruled them.

Japanese colonial rule (1910–1945) was a deeply ambivalent experience for Koreans. On the one hand, Japanese colonialism was often quite harsh. For the first ten years, Japan ruled directly through the military, and any Korean dissent was ruthlessly crushed. So the Korean people had been accustomed to being brutally ruled by Japan, and many, if not most, still used the Japanese language. We offered money and tried other ways of negotiations, to no avail. Just more and stronger still as they repeated their final word of "Domi domi." We were also tired of wasting our time and continued to make arrangements to end the stalemate. One of us, I can't remember which, took the red rooster out with our .30-caliber carbine. We picked his carcass up and put the money down where the rooster had dropped. We knew we had worn out our welcome by that time and left the area immediately.

Now we had a nice big red rooster that we were licking our chops for, but no one to cook it for us. We just continued on with our hunting, and after going over a mile or so, we spotted one little Korean home in another valley. We approached the house and found a family of Koreans living there. A father, a mother, and two kids. We attempted to get a little acquainted a little without either one of us understanding the other. I again made motions by pointing to the rooster, then to my stomach, and then toward the mother. They instantly knew what we wanted and gladly and excitedly agreed right away to do it. Now there was a kind of party atmosphere in the air as we laughed and began joking around.

The mother took the big chicken and went to a different location from where we were, to clean and dress it for the meal, and the father by that time had invited us into their home. We were really feeling welcome and at home using the only universal language that we knew: we just smiled and laughed a lot. The father had caught the bug too and joined right in, saying things we couldn't understand; but with hand gestures and facial expressions, he was getting through. We knew we had made the right decision in coming to their home.

The father called in one of his kids, a young boy of about eight or ten years old. He gave the boy some money and some instructions, and the boy ran off with a big smile on his face. We watched as he soon disappeared over the hill and out of sight. We were in the main room with what they called a *kabocha*, a big clay bowl, about eighteen or twenty inches in diameter, that held the coals from after cooking the meal that was done in another room in the entryway of the house. The coals mixed into the ashes already there would keep emanating more heat than one could imagine. We were enjoying our unusual but very pleasant afternoon.

About the time the mother had the dinner ready to serve, the young boy came back in with a canister in his hand. The father handed it to the mother with some instruction we couldn't understand as she smiled and left the room. In a couple minutes, she was back with a teapot with steam coming out of the spout. The father poured us each a little cup of what he called *sake* and handed it to us. It was homemade and white like milk. We had already known about it—it was a rice wine that the Japanese and the Koreans drink with their meals or special occasions. We knew ahead of time about the gross taste of it, but we all agreed to drink it with a straight face, smile big-time, and lick our chops to show our gratitude for the extra mile they had gone for us.

We were all getting warmed up to the special occasion now as the mother began serving the chicken and other vegetables she had prepared along with some little biscuit-type rolls. At first, we had envisioned a fried chicken dinner, and were surprised to see everything in one pot. There weren't any specific pieces we could identify, like drumsticks, wings, or such. She had taken a cleaver to it and chopped it all into pieces. But as soon as we started eating it, we couldn't believe how delicious and tasty it was. The father ate with us, and the mother served him first. The mother and the kids ate after we were all through, with a lot left over for them.

We hung around for a few minutes, thanking them and shaking hands and enjoying everything to the maximum. This outing is a really powerful and pleasing memory in my heart and mind. I'll remember it as long as I live, things turning out this day that had to be pleasing to God and all of us that were involved. We decided together that we had to do something nice for these kind and loving folks. I gave them my field jacket, and each one of the other guys gave them something too. I imagine that the mother and the father are dead by this time, but I am certain that those little kids had plenty to tell their peers back then and remember it well yet today. They probably have told it to their own kids throughout the years that followed. We soon after were run out of Inchon by the overwhelming numbers in the Chinese army, and we had to retreat all the way back to Pusan.

Pusan at that time became a hotbed for every kind of criminal activity known to mankind. We carried our weapons with us when we went into the city, not knowing what kind of deviltry we might expect around the next corner. Black-market cubicles lined the streets and operated openly with immunity or with impunity. We could buy army- or military-issue clothing and food stuff of any description. The operators dyed everything military a navy blue and all-American food stuff beyond what we were familiar with were for sale and available everywhere.

Pimps, sex peddlers, and prostitutes themselves walked the streets advertising their availability for doing a roll in the hay or to fix one up for an authentic oriental Korean horizontal mambo. They even prostituted, at premium prices, their own innocent little schoolgirls, whom they always dressed in snowy white little blouses and navy-blue pleated skirts. If there were any cops in the city, they probably had to run and hide their eyes from it all, or they quickly learned how to benefit from it all themselves. Being downtown Pusan one day, my buddy and I were walking back to our living quarters by the waterfront when a big black soldier we didn't know came along in a jeep and picked us up and gave us a lift.

We were coming out of downtown Pusan and going through an intersection that had a Korean policeman standing on a raised piece of concrete in the center of the intersection directing traffic. The black soldier said, "Watch this" as he drove close by him at about twenty miles an hour, stuck his arm out the side of the Jeep toward the officer, and, with a doubled-up fist, hit him in the head and face so hard that it was a wonder it didn't break his hand or wrist.

I say this because it is something that really happened, and it should tell you how the military serving in Korea felt about the people in general. They were being looked at as non-human beings, less than dogs. The only good Korean was a dead one. There seemed to be an ongoing attempt to create a deep hatred for both South and North Koreans alike because we were there to kill half of them, and we couldn't tell which was which on the streets of Pusan. We all became too soon old and too late smart, and we don't get a do-over, I sometimes wish we could.

No one in authority ever attempted to modify or change how we disliked them or give us any training in how to treat them as we should have been doing all along. It was as if the powers that be wanted us to develop the hatred for the whole Korean race. The culture shock was difficult to deal with in having them *(the Koreans)* constantly and humbly bowing and saying, "I'm solly, Joe" *(they cannot pronounce* "r"*)*. The only thing we got from other soldiers that had served in Korea caused us to think of them as less than human, because they were poor, they stank of garlic and ate fish heads, and they had learned under Japanese occupation how to be humble and bow down low to any authority.

After I had come home one day, I was listening to the radio, and some Korean War veteran was being interviewed; and he talked about some of these things I am writing about to you now. He was right on point in telling it just exactly like it was. They had immediately stopped the interview and kicked him off the show and branded him a communist propagandist, while I knew that everything he was saying was true. The national news back then was not any different than they still are today. It is almost impossible to get real and truthful news from them today as they put their left-wing spin on things to influence minds along the lines that they serve, accept, believe, and think everyone else should too. They believe in the freedom of the press and the freedom to speak freely, except when it goes against what they believe and accept as truth. Then it all becomes a different story.

At one point in time earlier on, a big stink had gripped the Pusan red-light district, which mostly included the whole city. For whatever reason, it had not been revealed at the time why, but we were told by those seemingly in the know of things that a combat marine had come off the frontline and had taken out his government hunter-trained frustrations on a prostitute in a house of ill repute. He reportedly finished the job off by shoving his bayonet up her vagina, or birth canal. It was all causing a giant uproar throughout the city, and it should have. Who can say what it is that causes mankind to do such evil things to one of their own kind?

We do know, however, that all of us carnal human beings have the exact same proclivity inside of us that can come out in a heartbeat and manifest itself in every evil, ungodly sin under the sun. All it takes is for the right set of circumstances to come into our lives, and we can all become a different person than what we appear on the surface. We, all of humanity, have been made after the god-kind, but we are not there yet in our maturity. Some things such as this and a lot worse, I have written and then deleted it, simply because it may be just too much for certain individuals to take in and digest, no matter the truth of it all. We have all fallen short of the word and way that God would have us all to live a sin free life, and to benefit and be blessed for so doing. All sin has a penalty, and all have sinned, so all have a penalty that must be paid. **Romans 6:23** Tells us that the penalty for sin, is death, but the gift of God is eternal life. Both are true, we are all going to die, or either in a twinkling of an eye at the return of Christ as the elect of God, we will be changed into incorruptible, immortal spirit beings and have life as God and Jesus Christ have life. All of the rest of mankind who have ever lived, the great masses of humanity, many who never heard about Christ, along with those that did hear the truth but rejected it and died in unbelief of the sacrifice of our Lord and

Savior Jesus Christ whom accepted on Himself and willingly died in our stead to free us from that death penalty.

All that had not believed that Jesus Christ was whom He claimed to be, The Savior of all of mankind, along with those that never heard about Christ, will be resurrected at The Great White Throne Judgment, to be judged and then be subjected to the symbolic lake of fire to go through a correction and purging process to burn out all unrighteousness, in what ever length of time it takes, dependent upon the willingness or stubbornness of the resurrected individual. But all of mankind will be saved as God did promise before the world began. (Titus 1:2) The bottom line in the purpose and plan of God requires that every person who ever lived, must come to the belief and understanding that the sacrifice of Christ paid the penalty for all sin for all time. None of us had anything at all to do with our own salvation. Without the sacrifice of Christ, we would all end up as dead as a door nail for all eternity.

Some things I write, I feel like I should delete them after I have already written about them. Then going back and rereading about some of this stuff still rips off all the scabs of pain that have been built up through the overload of time that continues to be inflicted upon my mind and lodged into my permanent memory. Knowing it was all being caused by my own carnal nature made it even worse. To relive over and over. I wonder, should I be as open as this, to cause someone else to suffer it in their hearts and minds? While the reader has the option to turn away and quit reading about it, as many have done, my philosophy is that it is far less traumatic and mind-boggling to read about it as opposed to witnessing it firsthand and having to live it.

But if my calling, desire, and purpose is to reveal what war is really like to serve a good purpose in the eyes of God, in calling others into His truth, knowing that the one and only solution in bringing all wars to an end is the eventual return of Christ to return as Lord of Lords and King of Kings to rule and reign here on earth with the elect of God, then if I claim to be a follower of Christ, how can I do anything else? If none of us are to ever learn to hate evil and unrighteousness, how can we ever learn to love and to appreciate what the real and wonderful truth of God is all about? I have noticed that the more that I hate real down deep inside about the satanic influences that cause all of this blatant unrighteousness, the more I also am learning to love and appreciate the wonderful righteousness that God has purposed and planned for every single one of us who have ever lived on this earth.

And if indeed the end justifies the means and God has used it to call us and impact our mind to bring us before Him on our knees, it might be well to remember what my father used to tell me. He would tell me, "Nothing ever happens so bad, but what it could not have been worse." So if war, absolute misery, and the hard knocks of life is what it took for God to bring me or to bring you to Himself, then so be it. The end really did then justify the means that He had used. Thank you, God, for the awesome revelations that you have taught me, and I am glad it wasn't any worse.

If your mind is bothered by reading these things, do not ever try to understand what you are reading in your own bibles. God is keeping His truth from being revealed to most all of mankind. Because the whole Bible is filled to the brim and to overflowing with the evil actions, foul atrocities, and hateful, godless cases of abuses of every nature against mankind and against God Himself. Still, it is up to you yourself that knows what is best for you and what you can handle in your mind and heart and be able to bear. Jesus Christ tells us that He has much more to tell us, but that we cannot bear it all yet. So, my dear brothers and sisters in Christ, do not let me or anyone else manipulate, shame, intimidate, or drag you to where you do not think you should go. It may very well be that Christ is guarding, protecting, and preventing you from understanding too much too soon.

I don't know if things like this should even be repeated because of the shock and awe from just hearing about it, which will never be washed out of a person's mind. Just the many-years-ago memory of these things coming back into my mind brings back an uneasy feeling of the unending scope of the evil, sinister, and ungodly makeup of us carnal human beings. Which you and I and all of humanity, whether we want to believe it or not, have all been born with, into that same carnal condition as well. But war is always hell on earth, and things like this make it be so. We can only hope that in time it will maybe sink into the minds and hearts of those that stick pins in a map to determine where the next war should begin, and that they will stop to think of what they are about to unleash and load up on the backs of all mankind.

"OLD MEN START WARS; YOUNG MEN HAVE TO FIGHT AND DIE IN THEM"

But, my dear brothers and sisters in our Lord and Savior Jesus Christ, none of this should surprise those of us that God has given the ability to understand His Word and His way written down and preserved within the pages of the Bible. After six thousand years of the rule of man on this earth, it has shown the total impossibility of mankind in being able and capable to govern themselves within the righteousness that His Word would have us to accept, believe, and to follow. It doesn't require that you accept and believe this to be true because I tell you, here is the Word of God on it. "O

LORD, I know that the way of man is not in himself: it is not in man that walks to direct his steps" (Jeremiah 10:23).

The answer that mankind needs to understand and come to grips with as being the truth that God explains to us throughout His Word cannot and will not ever be solved by mankind alone, in our present evil, physical, and carnal condition. To end the scourge of wars for all time and forever then, it all boils down to only one possible solution. There is no other. Jesus Christ must put down all unrighteous rule of mankind and destroy it completely. The elect of God chosen out from the many being called will have a part in doing it and will be ruling here on earth with Jesus Christ for a thousand years. *"If we suffer, we shall also reign with him: if we deny him, he also will deny us"* (2 Timothy 2:12).

The last enemy of man and God to be destroyed is death itself. After which Christ then will subject Himself back under the ultimate rule of God that will forever encompass the still expanding universe. And again, here in Luke 22:9, it says, *"And I bestow on you a kingdom, just as My Father has bestowed on Me."* This is not rocket science, my friends, my brothers and sisters in Jesus Christ. Neither does it take an Einstein to understand it: our God-ordained destiny is now and always has been to be an active part of the kingdom of God, to be set up and administered right here on planet earth. That being the exact plan and purpose of God Almighty since before the world came into existence. *"In hope of eternal life, which God, that cannot lie, promised before the world began"* (Titus 1:2).

BACK AGAIN TO 1950 PUSAN, KOREA

Myself and two or three buddies had gone down into the outskirts of Pusan one evening after dark to scope out the area, as curious and nosey young guys are prone to do. We were being really careful and making our way along in quiet mode. Having that feeling inside that the boogey-man might jump out at us at any moment. It was really getting darker by the minute as we came up on a set of steps that angled up and off to our right, with a kind of slight curve in it. About that time, we had begun to wonder whether or not we should go any farther. One of the guys with us was a slightly squirrely kid from the South that would fight at the drop of a hat—a nervous-type person with a hair-trigger personality.

Suddenly, a voice from out of the dark yelled out some strict-sounding lingo that sounded like someone barking an order in a different language. We later on determined it to have been like our own "Halt, who goes there" guard challenge. We must have approached a military contingent or outpost of some sort. Instantly, this kid with us was up front of our group; his instant knee-jerk response was to spray the area ahead of us with his .30-caliber carbine. He emptied his fully automatic fire, fifteen-round clip of ammo in the direction that the voice was coming from. We didn't have to wonder what to do anymore; we were falling over each other getting out of there and making tracks for places unknown, with all kinds of commotion, excitement, and yelling coming from back up the hill. As one might very well expect, we neglected to report any of it to our officers.

The Wild West didn't have anything on Pusan, which became the wild east during that time. Lawlessness abounded in all directions from downtown main street, side streets, back alleys, and everything in between. Every law of common sense and decency had been thrown out the window as wholesale deviltry ruled and took over in the breaking of every natural and sensible way that mankind was supposed to be conducting themselves. The soldiers all carried weapons in the beginning, which didn't work out well at all. The hand writing was on the wall; all it took for chaos to reign, would be when someone heard the first shot being fired. There would always be someone ready, willing, and able to impose their own will on others.

One evening after working our shift unloading the ships, several of us had gone on down to a well-known honky-tonk joint where there was dancing, drinking, and all kinds of activity going on. One of the first things that surprised and shocked me was when I went to the toilet. This joint was more upper crust than other places we had been into. The Korean toilets are just an oblong hole in the floor, about two and a half feet long and eight or ten inches wide. You just squat down and let it go. I was in the middle of doing my business when a young lady came prancing in and sat down to do her business in the next slot on the floor. I tried not to gawk or act surprised, but I did notice she was wearing ugly OD army underwear, which didn't do too much to excite me. It was no big deal to her; the Korean men and women traditionally use the same toilet. At least they did back then.

We were right in the middle of getting sloshed to the gills with beer that had come to Korea from Wisconsin as a gift to service members. On the top of the can was written, "Gift of the Milwaukee Brewing Company—Not to be sold." It was being black-marketed, hijacked immediately after coming off the ships into the anxiously awaiting hands of honky-tonk joints. They would be selling it for a dollar a can. Suddenly we heard shots being fired, as chaos broke out, and everyone began to scatter fast. No one wanted to be involved in that kind of trouble. The word that came down immediately was that a black soldier had shot and killed a CID investigator—one that may have been investigating the rampant black market business that was doing a land office business in Pusan at the time.

I had been with my buddies, but somehow in all of the turmoil and my inebriated stupor that I had brought on myself in overindulging on one-dollar beer, I got turned around, lost track of them, and got out of there as fast as I could stagger along. Suddenly, out of nowhere came two Korean girls who grabbed me by the arms, one on each side, and pulled me inside off the sidewalk. I don't tell this story to very many people—they simply will not believe it. I wouldn't believe it myself if someone had told it to me; it just sounds too farfetched, but it is true, and I am going to add it here, because it really happened. I want the reader to get an actual feel for the Pusan atmosphere and the way of operating during the Korean War in 1950.

When I woke up in the morning, I again had the world's worst drop-dead hangover ever. I didn't feel good enough to die. I had vaguely remembered being pulled in off the street the night before, but that's about all. Now it was morning, and I found myself lying in bed between two really cute and good-looking naked Korean girls. One huddled up as close as she could get on one side, and the other one on the other side did the same. Their gyrating and heavy breathing told me the story. The writing was on the wall, it was obvious what their expectations were as they slithered around under the covers, waiting for me to pay them back for rescuing me off the streets the night before. All I had the energy and desire to do was to get out of there just as fast as I could. I couldn't afford missing morning roll call and being reported AWOL. I thanked them both and hightailed it back in time to report in for reveille.

HOLDING THE LIFE OF ANOTHER IN YOUR HANDS

Getting back now to my battlefield experience, my mind also reflects back often on a vision that never goes away for very long either. It will suddenly reappear with a vengeance, at unexpected times. Taking this well-defended hill by the Chinese enemy one afternoon while under heavy fire, we came up over a knoll or crest of the hill, where off to my right a young Chinese soldier had his hands up and was attempting to surrender. Half in and half out of his foxhole. By that time, we were right at his hole, as my comrade, whom I didn't know, leveled his M1 rifle two or three feet from the boy soldier and emptied a full clip into his twisting, turning, and convulsing body.

A MOTHER WAITING FOR THE SON

The blood and bone, fragments of flesh and brains splattering the side of his foxhole was unusually gory and horrifying to watch, I didn't know what to say or do, I was a new replacement. As shocking as it was to me, I didn't say or do anything; I just in my mind reasoned that this might be why my comrade was still alive himself, and that it was a lesson I needed to learn. These things visit my mind when something may happen to jar those memories loose all over again. A son of some old Chinese mother that will never see him alive again. Going to her own grave, grieving about a life cut short on a bloody battlefield far away. We all should learn to pray for the kingdom of God to be set up and administered here on earth by Jesus Christ, that wars may cease to exist forever after.

DEALING WITH WAR DEMONS

As we go along, I would like to leave you, the reader, with some of the things that have helped me to overcome my *"war demons"* and be able to move on to being a somewhat balanced, productive citizen, operating conscientiously within the spot on this earth where our God has placed me. I hope that others who might also have been there during their own military duty as a government hunter, being required to hunt down and kill others like ourselves, will be helped in some way by reading some of these experiences. I was doing the best that I knew to do within each day as I lived it. I am compelled to list down as the number one most constant positive influence upon my being as time moved on was to be able to see things and to accept things through a different set of eyes and a different heart that God has given me, to feel with and too see with more clearly.

NO ONE TO TRUST

I came home with a mixed-up, boggled mind. I didn't want anyone to violate my personal space. I didn't want to be around anybody, except Nancy, my wife-to-be. When someone appearing to have a bone to pick with me got in my face, I would be all cocked and primed and be looking for the imaginary target I would aim at to drop him in his tracks. I always harbored a feeling of some unsuspecting force behind me or in the shadows. I didn't like who I had become. I didn't much like anybody else either.

I spent a lot of time back then dreaming about how awesome and peaceful it would be to live alone on some deserted island, never having to see another human being. Then to snap back to the reality of getting up and going to work among others you couldn't learn to trust.

LANGLEY, AN ALL-MOUTH REDNECK FROM KENTUCKY

EVEN YOUR GOOD FRIENDS WERE NOT ABOVE BACKSTABBING you. I had gone to a dance with a good service buddy of mine while we were stationed in Aberdeen Maryland, being trained to be artillery repairmen. We had gone out on the town and were having all kinds of fun and good times when I had asked a girl he had also been dancing with for a dance. She accepted and everything went well, and nothing at all was being said by my buddy as we continued to dance and have fun together. I had later on gotten up to go to the bathroom when he said he needed to go too. I walked into the bathroom ahead of him, as he came in behind me.

As soon as he got through the door that opened into the bathroom, he shut the door with a slam and backed up against it so I couldn't get past him to get out. He had a switchblade knife in his hand, which he referred to as his hillbilly boxing glove. He was frothing at the mouth as he announced through clinched teeth, *"No one ever f—s with a Langley."* He had reasoned the girl was his property and thought I was trying to take her away from him. Never mind the fact he had only known her for an hour at the most. This guy was among many others from the South. I liked their smart-mouthed, kickass jargon, and the Southern drawl they all have, but even though I liked them and had fun being around them, they taught me a good lesson: they quite often have a mouth that spits venom, accusations, and challenges in a loud and demanding style; but when the shit does hit the fan, they most often lacked the balls to back their mouth up.

Which brings back to mind an incident that happened when I was stationed at Fort Eustis, Virginia, and taking schooling as a stevedore longshoreman. Several of us had again gone out on the town in Norfolk, Virginia. Not finding any action in Norfolk, we decided to take the ferry over to Portsmouth, Virginia, which was a dry town, where booze wasn't legal, but someone had told us about a "Blind Pig" in the area. A place that violates the law and serves it anyway. There is usually a high level of action going on in these kinds of places, so we thought we would check it out. About four of us headed on over to Portsmouth. We had one smaller but feisty little guy from Missouri named Keeny; he always liked to lead the way and be in charge. He was a talker and the kind of a guy that needed a little getting used to. We had got to the door of the place, and we had to walk down a long hallway, turn a corner, go a few feet, and enter the club through a door there.

As usual, Keeny had gotten there first, had turned the corner, and was out of our sight; but we could hear the conversation he was having with someone at the door that was checking him out, and Keeny was getting pretty loud and obnoxious. The man checking him in had obviously said something Keeny didn't much like, to which he took issue with as we heard him say, "I'm from Missouri, you've got to show me." We heard a couple of clunks and a thump or two, and then what sounded like a body hitting the floor. We walked on around the corner, and there was old Keeny lying stiffer than a board on the floor. We never did let him forget it either, as we rubbed his nose in it anytime after that when he would get a little mouthy. Someone would pipe up and say, "You've got to show me. I'm from Missouri." We made sure our whole outfit knew it too.

There were just too many dark corners within my past experiences of war and operating in a war zone that I couldn't wash it all out of my inner being, no matter the alcohol content. But by the same token, I wasn't ready at the time to bother doing anything about it either. The problem was always the other guy, and him, they, or them, needing to learn how to get along with me. Thankfully, God knows exactly how to deal with His rebellious children. It would take a few more lumps, a few more years, a little more time to get my undivided attention. He did in time, and for that I will be eternally grateful and thankful. No matter where you are now, He will, in His time, get your undivided attention as well. I hope it won't take as long or the number of lumps that it took to get mine. But still, I had many things to learn yet.

I WAS A GLUTTON FOR PUNISHMENT

Hence, I went to work on a program of self-medication, which I was also to learn included self-destruction, for about a ten- or fifteen-year episode of *Hell Raising 101*. Sitting in some bottom-of-the barrel redneck honky-tonk joint, playing smashmouth with a bunch of others just like myself. Taking my share of lumps while at the same time getting in my own licks too. Always looking over my shoulder for repercussions heading my way because of the lifestyle I was living. I took a certain amount of personal pride in knowing and believing I had stepped up when needed and did for the most part what was being expected of me during my tour of duty in the service.

But in the same breath, even though I was working steady and applying myself as best as I could with the load of baggage that I had built up for myself that seemed to stick with me like snot on a doorknob, I had the feeling that I was slowly spiraling out of control as a husband, a person, and a father. I wondered at what point I might reach the bottom and become beyond the point of no return. My mind wouldn't seem to give me any real rest. Looking back now, I believe the missing element in my life without my understanding it at the time was in my hidden desire to learn, believe, and to follow the actual truth of God, beyond the false teachings of the Christian religion. War brings us face-to-face with our Maker.

Still, I continued on back then in my feeble attempt at managing and running my own life and that of my family. I would not allow anyone, not even a friend, to get in my face and downgrade or offend me in any way, to verbally insult or to physically assault me in any way without one of us having to suffer the consequences. Much of it I still feel bad about and have been sorry for. Looking back now, I hang my head in shame and disgrace and wonder how a few good friends were able to put up with me and still be the friends they continued to be. I would often later on feel like some egg-sucking cur dog that should be euthanized and put away to protect others. I felt walked on enough in one lifetime to bother cutting any slack for anyone that felt the need to get in my face.

I was working on a Canadian freight dock down by the Ambassador Bridge in Detroit at one point. Slim was a tall, lanky hillbilly from Kentucky. I liked him a lot; he was a good guy, and we had lots of enjoyable times together, just talking and telling stories about life and the different experiences we had had. One day, in fun, over a comment he had made, I reached over and pulled the bill of his baseball cap down over his eyes, and he immediately flew into a rage and called me a son of a bitch and meaning every word of it. Without even thinking about it, I popped him a good one in the chops, and he hit the deck. He got up with a confused look on his face, and not wanting to go any further with it, and to save face I suppose. He looked me in the eye and told me never to do it again. I still have many fond memories of Slim. I wonder how he made out in life. But no matter how bad you feel about anything, once it has been said or an action has been taken, it's too late; it can't be taken back.

While working at this same freight dock, I had a problem with a foreman that had touched me in a disciplinary way, and I had thrown him away from me in a corner. He had gone in and told the terminal manager about the incident. The terminal manager, a decent guy himself but into himself big-time as a macho-type guy, came out then and was reading the riot act to me while punching me in the chest with his extended fingers.

I punched him in the mouth and knocked him through a widow back into his office, where lady secretaries began to scream bloody murder. When he had gone through the window, he had got cut up quite bad and had gone to the authorities to have me arrested, and later on had sued me for five thousand dollars. He was unsuccessful in doing so, but I lost my job; and because of it, we lost everything we owned and had worked hard for.

A longtime neighbor kid that I had gone to grade school with—a kid the same age as myself, he and his siblings interacted with me, my siblings and our families neighbored and got along well through the years, and we always enjoyed each other's company. I liked him, and he was a type of person that would do anything for you and share all that he had with others. Being home one day after my Korean War service, I had gone over and picked him up from his place to go have a beer with me. We had gone to the Cat's Paw Tavern on 131 down by Manton, Michigan. He had, had a couple of beers and began telling me and others war stories that he was supposedly involved in. I immediately took him to task on it because I knew he had somehow avoided the military service altogether, and I wasn't in any mood to let him get away with it. I half dragged his wimpy ass out of the bar.

I told him to get into the car, and I would be taking him home. Inside, my guts were on fire, and I was having a problem in keeping things together. I had seen too many mangled and tortured bloody deaths from real combat comrades, and now just the sight of him and his running his lying mouth was causing me to reach my limits. We had gotten to his home, and he was getting out of my car and reached back in the back seat to take a six-pack of beer given to me by the father of my best friend, who was also a Korean War survivor who had stepped on a land mine on Easter Sunday 1951, causing a rock to be blown through himself, and remained in critical condition. He had been evacuated home but was in pretty bad shape. They had operated on him and closed the incision up before letting him leave and go home.

On his way up home to visit his folks, the incision opened up again. He stopped and had it taken care of in some doctor's office. He had an operation to deal with it and then close it up again. But as they traveled along on their way, it had broken open again on the car trip home along with his wife and one little girl at the time. They all had to try to hold his insides in long enough to get him to an emergency hospital to take care of the near-death situation he found himself in. He was as close as any of my blood brothers to me, and I knew well all that he had gone through during and after the Korean War. He had been a paratrooper during the war and had seen heavy and sustained combat. It was another thing that bonded us together. His father had given me the six-pack in the tavern, for my service in the Korean War. It became the straw that broke the camel's back.

I reached over and grabbed my lying friend by the shirt collar and hauled him back into the car, right up close and in my face, looking him straight in the eyes about six inches away. I had jerked him around and slapped him up pretty good as I told him in plain and easy-to-understand language that I never wanted to see him or have anything at all to do with him forever. I went on and told him I didn't even want him to be walking on the same part of the earth that I was on. I advised him to keep his eyes open, and if he ever did see me walking anywhere, to immediately cross over and get on the other side of the street, or I would beat his ass if he failed to do so. Several times I had seen him in Cadillac, Michigan, coming down the street on my side, and he would immediately cross over to the other side. He must have left the area because I had not seen him for about fifteen or twenty years.

One day, I was at my folks' home visiting them, and in walked this guy that had come to visit my folks too. He glanced over and saw me, and it looked as though all the blood had suddenly drained out of his body. He caught his breath and came straight across the room with an outstretched hand to shake my hand and give me a cheerful greeting. I did not want to cause a scene in my folks' home, and I was also thinking it might be time to bury the hatchet and let old wounds heal. So we all had a reasonably decent conversation and talked about old times and other things than that which had happened down in Manton. I have added this personal account to follow through with what can happen to a mind subjected to the atrocities of war that we can see on the caption on the cover of this book cover I am in the process of having published. I will show those of you that read it on our website a copy here below for you to see.

I didn't recognize it at the time as I was being put through wringer of God in His attempt to get my attention, but as the years passed by and finally I had experienced a spiritual awakening, it became clear to me that God was using it all to my own advantage. That is, if we believe the Word of God on it. Since I had now accepted God and had grown to love Him and His Son Jesus Christ, who claims to be the Savior of all mankind, and not wanting to call God a liar, I wholeheartedly believe what He has left recorded in the book of Romans. *"And we know that all things work together for good to them that love God, to them who are the called according to his purpose"* (Romans 8:28). I also accepted and believed the scripture that was telling me this in Romans. *"And these whom He predestined, He also called; and these whom He called, He also justified; and these whom He justified, He also glorified. What then shall we say to these things? If God is for us, who is against us?"* (Romans 8:30–31). The answer, of course, is *no one!*

A HEART OF STONE

I came back from Korea with a mind-set and a heart that had been seared over like a steak on a smoking hot grill or on a cast iron frying pan. A part of me almost seemed to have died; the empathy, sympathy, compassion, and the ability to feel emotions had left me, if I ever had any of them at all in the first place. In a way it served me well at that time in dealing with life. I was glad of the cold, logical German blood I had running through my veins that I had inherited from my mother and my father. I had seen my share of what life and death was all about; being in a nation during wartime, I had been able to endure it all, and like Timex, I had *"taken a licken and kept on ticken."* Close to death at all times, but close only counts in horseshoes.

Seeing way too many dead and dying human beings made in the image and likeness of God, stacking their broken and mangled bodies on top of each other and feeling the grating of crushed and broken bones as we piled them up to be sent home to their families. Or, later on, having to drag their frozen, stiff dead bodies off a hill where they had given up their last breath of life so that others could go on living in freedom and plenty. I felt that it was a good thing now that it had happened and was over with. It will allow me to deal with others that I will have to be around the rest of my life as family and friends die. I felt I was immune now to death and dying. But do you know what? It doesn't work that way at all. Just about time you think you've got it all figured out, reality sets in.

MY EARLY YEARS

My oldest brother, Glade, was a year and eight months older than me. We were always really close; being the oldest, he always looked after me while we were growing up. We didn't have any secrets from each other; we could communicate our closest and most important secrets to one another without fear of being stabbed in the back. He made life on the farm enjoyable in being able to play and work together. Our father was a good man but a taskmaster; we spent a lot of our time planning how to avoid all his strict rules and regulations. That all abruptly stopped when he *(my brother Glade)* turned sixteen years old and left home. Then as soon as he turned seventeen, he joined what was then the Army Air Corps. Being home then with my younger brother, who had always been my father's favorite, became a thorn on my side. He couldn't do anything wrong, and I couldn't do anything right. I wanted out and away from there.

SEEKING A PASS TO GO HOME

I didn't see much of my older brother Glade after that because I had joined the Army as soon as I could too. When I came back from Korea and was sent to Percy Jones Army Hospital in Battle Creek, Michigan, he had gotten in touch with me and told me he was coming home on furlough from Davis-Monthan Air Force Base in Arizona, where he was serving as an air force MP. He was to come through Battle Creek on his way up home to see if I could get a pass to go home too. I was really looking forward to seeing him again for the first time in several years. We had talked about some of the fun things we were going to do, like looking up longtime good friends and to reminisce about the enjoyable times of years now gone by. In due course, he had showed up at Percy Jones hospital as expected, and he went with me to see the commanding officer about getting a pass to go home with him.

WHAT RULES?

Major Traxler, a commander in the Percy Jones Army Hospital at Battle Creek, had denied my request for a leave; and since it had been a couple years since Glade and I had seen each other, I told him not to worry, I would go with him anyway. I desperately wanted and needed to spend some time together—to reminisce, to find out how his life had been going. Just to catch up on each other's life experiences serving in the military. I began to develop a plan of how to go about jumping ship and going home.

I took my brother Glade out to walk around on the hospital grounds and scope out the lay of the land to determine where I would be meeting him after it had gotten dark. I showed him a good spot where I would go over the fence to go with him. I knew most of the MPs because I had been in their lock-up in the hospital basement a couple times for misdemeanors of some sort, usually probably just getting away with anything that happened to cross my mind. I felt as though after surviving Korea, there was nothing at all they could do to me that could even come close to comparing to that frozen Korean hell on planet Earth. I was aware also that they were cutting us wounded men off the battlefield a lot of slack. So the plan was made, and all we needed was for it to get dark.

As we were crossing the grounds where I told him I would go over the fence, we met a couple of MPs whom I knew patrolling the area, and one asked me the question, *"When are you coming down and visiting us again Cunningham?"* Their meaning being to visit their detention center in the basement, to be locked up again. I told them it probably wouldn't be too long, that I would be down and see them as soon as they could catch me, that I would be jumping the fence as soon as it got dark.

They just laughed and moved on. Then as planned, I did jump the fence and go home that night with my brother which I have never regretted for even a moment. I stayed home even after my brother had to go back to duty in Arizona. The military authorities sent my mother a letter encouraging her to see that I got back before it was desertion. I intercepted the letter and showed it to her twenty years later. She got a kick out of it, and called me a couple of choice names in jest.

FOND MEMORIES OF YESTERYEAR

I HAD BOUGHT A TOP-OF-THE-LINE 1946 FORD CONVERTIBLE with all of the bells, chrome, and whistles that could fit on it and was having too much fun to go back right away. I had to carry a big stick to keep the girls out of it. But it all came to an end when another soldier home from Germany had also gotten a new Studebaker convertible, and we were leaving too many black patches around town. The local cop that we both knew finally picked both of us up and took us to the Traverse City jail. But he felt so guilty about it that he would bring his daughter Rachel over to visit me almost every day, to go to a ball game or just to hang out. The sheriff at that time was a WWII vet who had served in the same outfit as me in Korea. He had a soft spot in his heart for me and more or less gave me the run of the jail.

I BECAME A HAPPY CAMPER

SINCE I DIDN'T HAVE A DRIVER'S LICENSE, HE gave me one and paid for it himself. But he had notified the military, and they had sent two MPs up from Percy Jones to pick me up and take me back. It was the same two MPs that I had met on the hospital grounds before I left. We all actually had a good laugh about it, and it was a very enjoyable ride back to Battle Creek.

Like I said, a lot of slack was being extended to returning combat personnel at that time, and I for one took full advantage of it at every opportunity. Just this moment, the name of one of those MPs came back to mind—he was Corporal Dupray. On our trip back to the hospital grounds, I reminded him of the fact that I had told them I was going to jump the fence as soon as it got dark, and I had done just like I told them I would do. They were somewhat to blame themselves for my leaving, because they had not believed me and could have stopped me. But in hindsight, after these sixty-five years later, *"a good time was had by all."* But then life moves on and hands us different things to be occupied with as we are raising our families. We need to learn to count it all as a blessing from God—good, bad, or indifferent—because it is all intended for our own good and the eventual good of all mankind.

GOD PUTS MY FEET TO THE FIRE

Then about eight or ten years go by, and everyone is busy going to work, making a living, raising their kids along with all the struggles of life; and one afternoon I got a phone call from my brother Glade living in Atlanta, Georgia. He was now in the veterans hospital in Durham, North Carolina. They had diagnosed him with a brain tumor and were preparing to operate on him. I asked them to wait and give me a chance to be there, which they did do. I flew out there, and we got to visit and reminisce about the fun old times together for a couple days before they operated on his tumor. It was a few days before Christmas of 1960. There was a party atmosphere in the air as early celebrations were already getting started. It didn't sit well with me because of what was about to take place. My closest brother's life would hang in the balance.

They finished the operation and had transfused him with 32 units of blood before finally throwing in the towel and letting him bleed to death. They told me that I could go in to see him in intensive care, which I did do. They also told me that the only part of his brain that was working was the part that causes one to breathe. I stood by his bed and held his hand and talked to him. I knew they either had lied to me or didn't know the truth of the matter themselves. It was their feeble effort at attempting to comfort me in some way, I suppose. I have wondered thousands of times since that day, what if anything, did the pagan Christmas lie preached by Christianity have to do with my brother's death? Had the hand that guided the scalpel had one too many shots of liquid Christmas cheer?

The tears began to well up in his eyes and run down his face as he gurgled and choked out his last breaths of life but was unable to move at all or to say anything. It was an extremely difficult time for me. I didn't realize it at the time, but later on, as time went by, I felt as though God had begun to work with my hard heart and stubborn mind. I was being put on His potter's wheel to knock off a few rough edges—something that happens to all of God's children that He loves. Here below is what He has to say about that in Hebrews 12:6–11 (NKJV):

For whom the Lord loves He chastens and scourges every son whom He receives.? If you endure chastening, God deals with you as with sons; for what son is there whom a father does not chasten? But if you are without chastening, of which all have become partakers, then you are illegitimate and not sons. Furthermore, we have had human fathers who corrected *us,* and we paid *them* respect. Shall we not much more readily be in subjection to the Father of spirits and live? For they indeed for a few days chastened *us* as seemed *best* to them, but He for *our* profit, that *we* may be partakers of His holiness. Now no chastening seems to be joyful for the present, but painful; nevertheless, afterward it yields the peaceable fruit of righteousness to those who have been trained by it.

I AM NO DIFFERENT THAN ANYONE ELSE

I learned that I was in no way immune to death as I thought I was, especially so when it is your closest blood brother. Then having to go back to his home in Atlanta, Georgia, along with his now-grieving widow and tell his three little kids that daddy wouldn't be coming home anymore; and being in that mix of emotions of hurt, sorrow, and ongoing suffering was heart-wrenching, to say the least. While on the one hand it is tearing the guts right out of you, you still have to step up and try to be the comforter. Put on a happy face when it is the last thing on earth you feel like doing. *One* thing that was exceptionally difficult for me, and still so many years later, was such a mental and emotional shock that sticks with me yet.

After seeing him alive and being able to have fun one day, having good conversation of days and times gone by, and then the next day being instructed to go pick up his belongings he had come in with. The sight and the feelings remain firm and clear in my mind, of having someone reach into a pigeonhole and bring up a cardboard box full of his clothing and personal things, and then having to sign for them. Yesterday he was a living, breathing flesh-and-blood human being, my brother. Today they slide what is left of him across the top of the counter in a cardboard box. This was the initial step on the part of God, I believe, to start my spiritual awakening.

In an odd sort of way, my closest brother had a part in my accepting and believing the Word and the way of God. I believe Jesus Christ is who He claims to be: *the Savior of all mankind.* All of mankind without even one exception. Still it took a couple more years before I could even cry one tear over his death. My mind and my heart had become so programmed and sealed up too tight to show any open grief or emotions at that time. A mutual friend, a combat infantryman, Dale Westcott, in the Eighty-Second Airborne in Korea, serving in the Korean War the same time frame as myself, had come over to our place for a visit one day; he had been more like a brother to both Glade and myself.

We went out and got a snootful and got to reminiscing about all the good times and the playing tricks on one another that we had enjoyed together growing up, and I couldn't quit crying. I thought it would never stop. I embarrassed myself more than ever before. I eventually pulled myself together and got my emotions in check and moved on with life. Then it all went back inside, and I elected to deal with it alone and by myself. The coming to terms with the death of my brother Glade was by all means one of the hardest, most difficult, mind-numbing as well as mental, emotional, and spiritual suffering that I have had to go through so far in life. I got back in the bottle of self-medication and hell-raising. Everything I tried to use to numb the pain only seemed to make things worse. What kind of life was this that I was trying to live and be happy in?

THEN GOD STEPS IN BIG TIME

I BEGAN TO FEEL LIKE A GREAT, BIG slimy rat that had become a bottom feeder in this society that for the most part continues thumbing its nose at the way and will of God and the premises that our nation had been built upon, myself included. A system and mind-set built upon get, take, grab, and receive as opposed to one of give, build integrity, care about, and help your fellowman. There I was, feeding and being in lockstep with others of the same kind, crawling around in the muck and mire of our society, which, in my opinion, included this world of so-called Christian religious persuasions of following after custom, ritual, and traditions as opposed to the Word and way of God.

I anxiously awaited on each day to finish my work and head for the nearest honky-tonk joint to get medicated out of my head and out of own skin into oblivion. Hoping someone would rub me the wrong way and give me the excuse to play a little smashmouth in an attempt to feel a little better about myself. The reality of life and old memories were becoming my constant companions. Then some things began to change—in a word, a change of mind and heart began to *come over me*. It was as if God had decided to give me a hand up and out of these worldly perversions. He symbolically, as I imagine it, rolled up His sleeves and reached all the way down through the filth, slop, and corruption of years of accumulation of this world's Babylonian system of thinking and administering the misguided rule and way of carnal mankind, as opposed to the will and way of our God.

I BEGAN TO FEEL HIS PRESENCE IN MY LIFE

I imagined that I could feel His hand as it rested on my back as I tried to wiggle, squirm, and slither away from any kind of a connection between myself and my Maker. I definitely did not want anyone else telling me what I needed to do and what I needed to quit doing. Having been owned by the United States of America military had not given me much chance to think and operate on my own. I was making a lot of mistakes. None of them could be hidden from God; He must have thought it was a good time to meet me on my own road to Damascus, like He did the apostle Paul. I do appreciate the fact that He didn't strike me physically blind like He did Paul, but in reality, I had in fact and in truth been born and raised spiritually blind. God was beginning to remove the spiritual scales from my eyes; I was blind but now I was beginning to see.

THE AMAZING GRACE OF GOD

Instead of striking me physically blind, though, He then, it seems, grasped me around the nape of my neck and slowly and methodically at first began bringing me up and out of the gutter of this world to strip away the layers of the built-up filth of following the pathway of least resistance but fitting in very well with the direction that our perverse society and our nation were all heading lockstep into as well. God has had to knock a lot of rough edges off me through the years, and there will be more to come. While it is anything but fun while we are going through our trials and traumas that we bring upon ourselves, we should learn to appreciate the changes for the good that we can see taking place within ourselves. For God will always discipline those whom He loves.

> *"For the Lord disciplines the one He loves, and He chastises everyone He receives as a son"*
>
> *(Hebrews 12:6)*

> *"Those I love, I rebuke and discipline. Therefore, be earnest and repent"*
>
> *(Revelation 3:19)*

Going through the fire of God that he tells us he is in: *"Our God is a consuming fire:* (Hebrews 12:29). The never-ending pain and suffering of war and all that went with it in Korea is but one of them. God is the potter, and we are the clay. He is up to the job.

He has the ability, the knowledge, and everything else it will take to put us individually onto His potter's wheel, to mold and shape us into the exact image that suits His own purpose and plan since before the world began. Here is how it is explained in Jeremiah:

> *"Arise and go down to the potter's house, and there I will announce My words to you.' Then I went down to the potter's house, and there he was, making something on the wheel. But the vessel that he was making of clay was spoiled in the hand of the potter; so he remade it into another vessel, as it pleased the potter to make"*
>
> (Jeremiah 18:2–4)

At times it may require that He smash and pound us down and start all over again in working vigorously with this stubborn and difficult lump of clay that we all can be. To achieve His avowed and promised purpose. To make us all in His likeness and in His image (Genesis 1:26). The chastisement of God, knowing it is for our own benefit and eternal well-being, is well worth accepting as needed correction from a loving Father. Our Father God will not do one single thing against a son or daughter that is not for our own good. We have His word on that, and God cannot lie.

> *"And we know that all things work together for good to them that love God, to them who are the called according to his purpose"*
>
> (Romans 8:28)

As I believe the Word of God to be true, let us look at another gift that He has given me that has been of the greatest value in my growth in being a thankful and grateful husband to my wife. It can be found in Ecclesiastes 9:9. *"Live happily with the woman you love through all the meaning-less days of life that God has given you in this world. The wife God gives you is your reward for all your earthly toil."*

Nancy has always been instrumental in giving me the right help at the right time. Having patience, love, affection, and caring about helping me with the problems life had laid upon myself and her as well, as she and I have suffered the aftereffects that we are discussing here. God could not have given me a better wife to love, cherish, and to be there in the thick and thin of life. To have our children and experience what it is to be a family. The peaks and valleys of life have been constant companions with us, as we shared together in them as a family. I have learned a good lesson along the way. There have been more blessings in the peaks of obedience while we have suffered the valley curses of disobedience as well.

Leith Lyman Cunningham

A REWARD FOR OUR EARTHLY TOIL

I remember well the nights that Nancy would have to hold my head in her lap, caressing me and taking the time and effort to love, support, care for, and give me some relief by talking softly and in a pleasant manner. Attempting to comfort me from the long-lasting mental and emotional pain that would suddenly creep up on me without notice. She was instrumental in helping to keep me from losing my mind. And she would continue on as long as it would take for me to get enough relief to finally be able to get some worried and broken sleep, before having to go to work in the morning. She didn't know at the time what the problems I was experiencing were all about—she just stepped up and did her part and more in helping me to deal with them.

I would often have to listen to soft music all night long to be able to get any relief. I wanted to jump right out of my own skin. I tried to get help from a local doctor to prescribe something for relief. He gave me the best advice any doctor has ever given me. Even back then they had all sorts of uppers and downers that would mask over the real problem, and he said he could give me a script for some. Then he told me the best advice he could give me was to learn to deal with it in almost any other way. Telling me things have a way of coming back even worse in most or many cases when one becomes dependent on drugs.

I followed his advice, and it soon led me into a spiritual awakening. I felt that God was beginning to show me a way of escape. I had to feel the security of being able to protect my family and kept a loaded 12-gauge shotgun under our bed at all times. We finally had to quit sleeping together. I would have nightmares, grab Nancy by the legs, and attempt to drag her out of danger. Neither one of us was getting any sleep. Nancy has had to bite the bullet more than once in having to put up with whatever came into my head next. Still we have stood the test of time and ended up here in our old age, being able now to relax and enjoy to the full all that God has given us. We are both happy together and keep on looking after each other.

I do dearly love and appreciate Nancy, the wife of my youth, we having been joined together as one on November 10, 1951. On November 10, 2018, our marriage and becoming one will have stood the test of time for sixty-seven years. Since all good gifts come from God, my wife, along with our God, is and always has been my motivation to rise above the carnal nature that has been created and placed inside every single one of us human beings. Many interpreters have offered suggestions about the symbolism implied in woman coming from the rib of Adam. For example, Matthew Henry wrote, *"Woman is not made of a man's head to climb over him, she is not made of his feet to be trampled on, but from his rib to be by his side as an equal, under his arm to be protected and close to his heart to be loved."* No matter how appealing this symbolism is, it cannot be proven that this was the original intent. Having said that, however, this quite accurately describes how I feel about my wife, Nancy.

THANK GOD FOR HIS FORGIVENESS

IT IS A NATURE WITHIN THAT WE ALL have to war against and bring into subjection to the will and the way of God. Since Nancy is the greatest gift as a wife that God will be giving me for all my earthly toil, I need to appreciate, be thankful for and do the best job that I can to honor, respect, and take good care of that relationship. I accept and recognize her as such and may God continue to bless our marriage and relationship during the sunset of our years together here on planet Earth. We are both getting older now, when everything we do is getting more difficult and riskier in how we go about doing it. We know if we fall down and hurt ourselves bad because of the natural instability of our age, there is a better-than-even chance that from that point on, someone else will likely have to be making our decisions for us. That's just the way it is! It is the best reason that I know of why it is so important that we put all our trust and confidence in God and not upon mankind.

Since I believe it is God who is in control of all things and all the time, I give Him alone all the credit for not only bringing myself and Nancy to that which has happened and shaped our character during our lifetime, but He is the One that has brought us (and will you too) through all the trials, traumas, and hardships as well. God will use and call upon many diverse sources to achieve His purpose for all of mankind. The wife of my youth that He has given me I count as one of the greatest. Jesus Christ tells us that He tells us the truth, but we will not believe Him. He tells us too that the sin of mankind is the sin of unbelief. Our wives then are a reward for all of our earthly toil. That, my friends, is the truth straight from the word of God.

MY OWN FUTURE FORETOLD

ABOUT SEVENTY YEARS AGO, MY CLOSEST BROTHER GLADE and I were downtown in Fife Lake, Michigan. As we walked along, having fun like any young boys might, I noticed a girl jumping rope with other girls. Even though I was only thirteen or fourteen years old, I had, had my eyes on her for a while now. She was probably about eleven or twelve at the time. I pointed her out to my brother and told him, *"That is the girl I am going to marry someday."* I had noticed and liked everything about her; I felt that she would be the exact person I would need to build a life with. One fly in the ointment was that she didn't like me at all. I looked upon that as a small and minor bump in the road to our future of being together as husband and wife till death do us part.

I would need to begin right away to make it become a reality. Looking back now all these years later, I have come to believe that it was all of God. I firmly believe that God had singled her out to be my wife, knowing she was the type of mate that I would need to always be there to help me as I in turn helped her along with our combined trials and traumas of life. To stick it out when things get rough and demanding. I believe God was giving us to each other, just some minor details had to be worked out. God is working in the lives of all His children whether we believe it or not. He knew us before we were ever born, He knew us all in our mother's womb, He knows exactly how many days we are going to live, and we'll not live one instant beyond it. He knows the exact day we'll die and we'll not live one instant longer. Now back to being age fourteen and making plans for life together with the one that I am going to marry.

PLAN A IS PUT INTO EFFECT

First requirement by necessity is that she first would have to like me somewhat. Not a problem! That was the easy part as I put plan A into effect immediately. I knew even back then that absence makes the heart grow fonder. I knew as well that all girls at that time were goo-goo eyed over anybody in a uniform and the mystique of actually knowing and communicating with one such person would be a big feather in Nancy's hat. I talked my mother into signing the papers allowing me to join the Army as soon as I turned seventeen years old. Now that plan A had been put into motion, I immediately embarked upon plan B as soon as I reached my first duty station at Fort Riley, Kansas.

I wrote Nancy a letter and told her what was going on in my life, that I had joined the military service and had become a soldier in the United States Army. I let her know that I had always had good feelings about her and suggested we communicate with each other by mail. We did that, and it quickly developed into a superfun and enjoyable time within our early moments and times of sharing and building a relationship together. I remember how enjoyable, how great and awesome it was to look forward to getting a letter from her and hearing my name being called at mail call, or to see her on those occasions when I would be able to get a furlough to come home for a visit. Along with an occasional phone call to get our individual batteries recharged and to stay in contact. She was always my focus, and we spent most all of our time together on those occasions. Another giant plus factor turned out to be Nancy's dear mother: she liked me right from the beginning, and laughed her heart out hearing my steady supply of jokes and funny stories, until the tears would be running right down her cheeks.

A WILL AND A REASON TO PREVAIL

IT HELPED ME A LOT OVERSEAS IN KOREA during times of struggle and strife. I had something to look forward to back home. The relationship that began back there in the summer of 1949 has of date stood the test of time. Don't let me fool you into believing that it has all been peaches and cream; it has been filled with peaks and valleys. It has not ever been easy. It is not even supposed to be, it is solving family problems, it is dealing with all of life's issues, it is the hardships, the trials, and traumas of raising a family and keeping things afloat that builds strong and lasting character, the dealing with and meshing two minds and two hearts into one. It is never going to be easy, but it is worthwhile and the way that God intended it to be. Therefore, I accept Nancy as my gift from God, as my greatest reward for all of my earthly toil. Unbeknownst to Nancy, her goose had already been cooked way back there in the summer of 1949 and before.

Over time, I begin to see how God was beginning to bless us even when others were doing things to cheat me, to hurt me, tear me down, and cause grief. God was turning it around to be for my own good. I was being sued for five thousand dollars by an irate boss for defending myself as he was punching me in the chest with his fingers, and I knocked him back through a window into his office. It had been the cause of my eventual declaring bankruptcy and losing everything we owned, but in the long run God used it as a way for us to climb out of debt, reminding myself of what Joseph had said to his brothers in Geneses. *"You intended to harm me, but God intended it for good to accomplish what is now being done, the saving of many lives"* (Genesis 50:20).

MY SPIRITUAL AWAKENING

MY SPIRITUAL AWAKENING BEGAN AT ABOUT AGE THIRTY-TWO, when I had read a magazine article on Christian living that encouraged folks to dig themselves out of debt. It made good sense, and I put it into practice right away. I also attempted to get my life and lifestyle in order. Even though I had caused our family to lose everything we owned three different times at this point. It took us eight years of diligent, sustained effort to come out of the hole I had dug for myself and my family. At forty years old, I became absolutely and totally free from any debt to anyone. Our home was paid for, we had acquired another property, we had a brand-new car, and we were now saving money. However, I do give the credit to my God and Savior Jesus Christ for calling me and causing me to be receptive to His truth.

FAST FORWARD

Here it is now, over sixty-seven years later after coming back home from Korea, as I sit in our comfortable home in Fife Lake, Michigan, with the love of my life, the woman that I married, love, and appreciate. God has blessed us greatly over the years in leading us to prepare financially for our old age, to be able to enjoy it apart from debt worries. Our child-rearing days are over for the most part as quietness permeates our surroundings. How sweet it is! Quite often, you will be able to find me lying back in my La-Z-Boy chair, relaxing with my hands behind my head like a lazy farmer, surfing the channels for a good cowboy movie, and reflecting upon how good life with peace and plenty can really be. God has been good to us. He has blessed us beyond any measure or level of success we could have ever expected to achieve on our own, for which we'll be forever thankful and grateful.

Success for us has never been measured in any amount of money a person can lay up for themselves—it is much more than that. To be financially stable is a wonderful blessing not to be diminished in any way. God is blessing us in a manner that allows us to do things we were not ever able to do before. It gives a person the ability, wherewithal, and the reason to do some of the things they've always wanted to do but couldn't. You can reach past the margarine on the grocery shelves that's only one molecule away from being plastic to pick out real butter. Now I reach past the ground beef and select a New York strip steak and if on a whim a bottle of champagne sounds good for that day, I get it. The blessings of God have allowed us to be more independent in our life's decisions, for which we are grateful. But make no mistake about it—we still know how to economize, and it is actually hard to break the habit. My hands still want to reach for the bargain.

A good portion of my energy and effort is being spent on a regular daily basis googling up spiritual websites, reading the scriptures, or something of interest on the Internet or picking a tune on my guitar and attempting to sing some old country tunes or other favorite beer-drinking song of days gone by. Maybe playing euchre with our family members as we sip our favorite champagne and see who can tell the biggest tallest tale to get our card playing opponents off guard, as we enjoy the company of each other, having good, clean fun and enjoying life together, as it was meant to be. I still remember the 24/7 miserable day and night, never-ending kill-or-be killed frontline combat in Korea that my Uncle Sam was paying me eleven cents an hour for, so we have paid our dues and have arrived at a place where we can give a helping hand to our family and others.

REWARDS AT THE END OF THE TUNNEL

Our attached garage made over into a family room now, is my domain, everything in it or on the walls represent things I like and enjoy seeing and being surrounded by. American flags scattered here and there throughout. I love our country and the American flag that represents it, our home is lit up flying flags on white flagpoles. The awesome sight and the feeling one gets watching at night with American flags whipping and snapping in the wind, brings goose bumps up my spine. The walls in our family room were covered with pictures of great meaning and importance to me, pictures of myself and three other brothers for example, in our uniforms, only my younger brother still living. It is for others to enjoy too if they so choose. Sometimes I don't have to bother to even think about anything as I lay back and let the pleasant, warm and cozy atmosphere of this comfortable room, permeate my body, heart, soul and mind. God is great; things are good!

Our home has become a memorial that I have put together in grateful appreciation and thanksgiving for all veterans, and especially so for all of those many that gave up all of their tomorrows so that we can remain free to enjoy all of our todays. I am an American patriot that takes great pains to show my friends, my neighbors, and all passersby that I love and appreciate this still wonderful country that our God has placed us in. Yes, we may have our national and international problems to deal with, our morality is heading right down the toilet full-throttle, and God may have to intervened to keep us from annihilating ourselves from off the face of this earth.

Yes, I can see a light at the end of the tunnel. When mankind gets done destroying this planet Earth, the home that God has given to us. Then Jesus Christ will return to usher in the wonderful world tomorrow, under his rule and reign. Mankind will never again be at each other's throats to destroy, maim, and kill others made in the image and likeness of God. We ourselves will be as God and Christ now are. Peace will reign on earth and throughout the universe for all future time. We will all be as God and Jesus Christ are. Jesus Christ came to earth to be *as we are*, that we might all become *as He is*. My time as a physical person on this earth is winding down, before too awful long God will be calling me home to whatever He has in store for me, just as He will you too. I will hear one of two things, either "Well done, my good and faithful servant," or "Depart from me, I know you not."

With all of this in place, I am a happy man. Looking back at what God has so lavishly given and bestowed upon us through His guidance and direction. The things that are causing our lives together to be fulfilling and peaceful, that Nancy, myself, and our family have diligently worked for and created for ourselves, with the guidance always being supplied to us by our God and Savior Jesus Christ. It gives me a feeling of personal worth, gratefulness, thankfulness, of what our own God-given tenacity, diligence, and accomplishment has given to us. People often tell us how lucky we are, but I have noticed that the harder we work, it seems, the luckier we become. What more on this earth could one ever ask for? Our work ethic and struggles in life to arrive here today as it is, and are paying great dividends. Our goal has never been to be rich with the dollars of this world's wealth, Yet God has blessed us beyond measure in comfort, peace of mind, and a glad heart. We are, indeed, rich and live in peace and safety.

We have been given everything we need to enjoy our declining years. It has all been a wonderful gift from God. All the blood and gore and misery of war in Korea is a thing of the past. Well! Not quite, but it is dimming down somewhat, sort of like looking back at an accident in the rear-view mirror. It allows us now to look forward to the kingdom of God, which He will bring upon this world, in His Own time. Where all of mankind who now live, have ever lived, or will ever live will eventually be resurrected as immortal spirit beings without even one exception, and we all will spend eternity having life as God the Father and His Son Jesus Christ have life. None of us will be going to heaven, as counterfeit Christianity believes and teaches others to accept as the truth of God. God and His Kingdom are coming here to earth to administer His government here among His people. We are admonished to pray thusly in Matthew 6:10. "May your Kingdom come soon? May *your will* be done *on earth* as it is in heaven. *Notice as* it is in heaven, *not actually* in *heaven*."

WAR: And The After Effects On Those Doing The Dirty Work Of Killing

TO ALL VETERANS OF THE FORGOTTEN KOREAN WAR

BUT NOT BY ME! AND I KNOW YOU HAVEN'T forgotten it either. I remember it like it was yesterday. I arrived on Korean soil soon after the war had begun in June of 1950. I was in a United States Army longshoreman outfit; I was an army stevedore in the 153 Port Transportation Company. We received and unloaded ships in Pusan, Korea. As they brought in war materials, weapons, tanks, trucks, and supplies of every nature to fight the brutal, invading North Korean enemy. We worked crews of South Korean dockworkers that worked for fifty cents for a twelve-hour shift. All of them ragged, dirty, and with a smell that would gag a maggot off a gut wagon. A complete culture shock to the mind of the eighteen-year-old farm boy that I was at the time. It was a Korea totally unlike the Korea that we see today.

They were a backward, humble, and subdued people, after being under Japanese domination, intimidation, manipulation, and harsh rule for over thirty-five years and then being set free after WWII. All I had ever seen the dockworkers eat was fish heads and rice, which they carried to work in little tin containers. It always made me wonder where the rest of the fish had gone. I had never seen a dog or cat all the while I was in Korea; it was part of their food source—they ate them to stay alive. I believe it is part of their culture heritage as well.

The area was filled to overflowing with displaced people driven ahead of the well-trained, well-equipped invaders, to escape a certain death at the hands of the North Korean enemy. This was where they left men, women, children, and little babies lying dead and mangled in ditches along the way as they came. War orphans in Pusan begging on the streets and fighting each other for scraps of food we had scraped off from our mess kits into garbage cans. I will never forget the little three- or four-year-old girl that I picked up and held her close with a little hug and showed her a few minutes of kindness before I put her down and had to leave, and how she ran after me with outstretched arms, crying out, "Daddy, Daddy, Daddy," with tears of remorse she was feeling at the time.

Mothers with little babies strapped to their backs, naked from the waist up, with milk oozing out from their bulging breasts, making trails down across their individual dirty and crusty bellies. Too used up and spent with hopelessness and exhaustion to even brush away the flies. Wandering aimlessly about with the familiar thousand-yard stare in their eyes, looking for but finding no relief in any direction. What has bothered me most down through the years is at the time, I had little or no empathy or sympathy for them. However, back deep in the recesses of my heart and mind, there must have been a soft place somewhere that God had created within me; it continues to come back, again and again, in vivid detail, as if it was happening today.

These lower-than-dirt, poor and misused, and forgotten-about pregnant mothers and others with babies were at the mercy of everyone around them. All that many of them had was a thrown-away three-pound coffee can, having been thrown away by our military. They would put a makeshift bail on it for easier handling. They carried it with them as they went, looking for the tiniest bit of scrap that could be burned in them to produce a little warmth for them at night, to heat a little food or while sleeping on the streets or alongside anything they could find as a wind break. They all had to wonder if there would be a tomorrow or be any better than today was. They were being treated as some throwaway human beings, much like our homeless on the streets and back alleys here in our present-day society.

A big part of the problem taking control of my mind and attitude toward the Korean people began before we ever got off the troopship that had brought us to their nation. As the gangway was being put into place to exit off the ship, a large noncommissioned officer wanting to show off his great wisdom and expertise in how to handle the beaten-down Korean population that had just recently been freed from the harsh, cruel, and brutal oppression of the ruling Japanese that had occupied them for over thirty-five years, it had taught the Korean people to bow down low in subjection to the laws of those who ruled them. It is still a pitiful and agonizing picture in my mind as I write about it here.

THIS IS THE WAY TO TREAT THE DOCKWORKERS

This big noncom (noncommissioned officer), a sergeant it seems, took full advantage of knowing this piece of information. He used it to show a whole shipload of newly arrived military personnel looking on from above, still on the ship, the ones that would be working these Korean dockworkers. He was the first one down and off the gangway. There was a huge warehouse on the dock where some thirty or forty Korean dockworkers were taking a break, squatting on their haunches as it was their custom to do. This giant of a man (noncom), in comparison to the smaller Koreans, began going down the line, cursing and swearing sprinkled heavily with the F-bomb, kicking and beating everyone in line that couldn't escape his wrath. It was intended to show us that would be working them how to get work out of these less-than-human animal-like people.

WAR: And The After Effects On Those Doing The Dirty Work Of Killing

My carnal mind and heart had mostly been seared over and shut tight from overload or from any kind feelings for them, another consequence of war, it seems. Open-air markets on the streets without refrigeration, raw fish, and different meats rotting in the hot sun. With flies so thick you would have to keep your mouth closed in fear of inhaling them, before they laid their eggs on the meat and became maggots. It was almost as if I had died and gone straight to hell. It stank so bad; there were parts of Pusan you had to hold your breath and move quickly through to keep from puking. This just skims the surface in describing a part of Pusan, Korea, during the summer, autumn, and fall of 1950. It was on the streets of Pusan, Korea, where I witnessed my very first South Korean drafting process for bringing young men into military service.

My buddy and myself had occasion to be in downtown Pusan one day. The city boomed and bustled elbow to elbow with the refugees and displaced population that was being pushed ahead of the assaulting North Korean Army that lay outside the Pusan perimeter only a few miles away from entering Pusan. There was barely enough room to maneuver around without bumping into someone. All of a sudden, a tumultuous commotion broke out as if the world was about to end. There were young men running full speed in every direction one could imagine. I was thunderstruck at the time, wondering what in the world was going on, what was it that they were all running from?

At first, I felt as though the North Korean Army must have broken through our lines and were mounting a major offensive against Pusan. Within minutes, it became obvious what it was that was causing the chaos and hysteria. The South Korean soldiers—known as Republic of Korea, or ROK, soldiers—were conducting a South Korean–style draft of young people into the army. They would form a big circle in the middle of the city that would take in several blocks of the busiest and most populated part of the city. There were maybe a hundred men making up the circle as they began to close it up and making it smaller and smaller. As they came near to the center, they would close up any escape route.

As they got closer to the center, the young men became aware of what was happening and began to run wild in any direction they thought they could escape in; they didn't want to end up as cannon fodder against their North Korean enemies. But the ROK soldiers would tackle them to the ground, shackle them up, and move them to another area, to be trained for frontline combat to meet the North Korean meat grinder. A day or so later, as we were in town again, we would witness the ROK Army training them how to march and carry a weapon. They would not however let them have a weapon at this point, they trained them with shovel handles, hoes, broomsticks and anything else they could dig up that represented a weapon, and made them look somewhat like a soldier.

IT SOON BECAME WORSE!

Everything about the enemy at the time was superior to our forces there. The battle-hardened troops greatly outnumbered us; they were well trained and with better Russian tanks, planes, and other weapons to use against us. Our first troops to face them were no match at all. Soft U.S. Army troops that had been pulling occupation duty in Japan were quickly sent to slow their advance to keep from having ourselves forced out of Korea altogether. The slaughter of these soft, undertrained, unprepared troops facing a superior-numbered fighting force began immediately.

It appeared as though we might be pushed out of Korea at the time. Fearing if that happened, we might never be able to get our dead comrades out of Korea later on, they, the military, began digging up the battlefield cemeteries, wrapping the bodies in a poncho or shelter halves, with a wire around the ankles, one around the waist, and, if there was enough left of the person, a wire around the neck with their dog tags attached to it. They came rolling into Pusan loaded into boxcars stacked with dead bodies like cordwood. The weight of the bodies stacked on top of each other caused the blood and body fluids to ooze out along the tracks in the hot autumn sun. Something that has been branded like a hot iron into my whole being.

We handled multiple hundreds, and even thousands, of these dead and mangled bodies of young men and boys still in their teens, not yet able to vote or to have a legal drink of alcohol. The stench and smell of rotting flesh and death never left our nostrils. The Korean War Memorial in Washington DC has the inscription, "FREEDOM IS NOT FREE" on it. How well I know firsthand that to be true. We live free in our country because many others have paid the ultimate price to make that a reality. We all would do well to remember and not to ever forget the cost paid for freedom.

The Communist Chinese Army entered the war in overwhelming force and numbers during November of 1950. Our military took soldiers already in Korea to try to stem the tide and beat them back. I was among that number heading into the battle on all fronts that raged on. Again, soft and without any recent training for going into combat. Yet I relished the fact that I was one among many others chosen to go into a combat infantry outfit. I had developed a purple-passion hatred for the enemy, especially so for the North Koreans. Reports came in by way of *the Stars and Stripes* newspaper that for effect they had killed some of our soldiers execution-style, tying their hands behind their backs with barbed wire and shooting them in the back of the head execution. Making certain the grotesque images would reach out and be available for all to see, and to strike fear in the hearts of the timid.

My mind-set at the time was that the only good Korean was a dead one. The more we kill today, the less we'll have to kill tomorrow. A testimony to the ignorance and gullibility of an eighteen-year-old mind that can be programmed and trained to accept the insanity of war, to kill and destroy others made in the image and likeness of God. For the first time in my army life, I volunteered for something I had been advised not to do. All my past military friends and family members, those of World War I and World War II, my uncles, cousins, and friends had advised against volunteering for anything. Yet I could taste blood every time I would see or hear about the atrocities the enemy were afflicting on our troops. I volunteered as a machine gunner with the Second Indianhead Infantry Division. I wanted to shed a lot of North Korean and Chinese blood, which I eventually became able and available to take part in.

I remembered, too late after volunteering as a machine gunner, our basic training drill instructor telling us that the average life of a machine gunner under attack is about three minutes. Because the machine gun can do so much damage in such a short length of time, the enemy will quickly zero in on its location and position, in order to silence it, and then allow for their advance against you. Along with that, I had not planned on having to carry the thing through knee-deep snow-covered mountains and rice paddies at thirty, forty, and fifty below-zero blizzard weather conditions, without proper cold-weather clothing or decent food to generate the energy to do so. The kill-or-be-killed insanity of war ended for me when I was evacuated off the frontlines on March 7, 1951. My feet had been frozen, and the war was over for me.

I weighed barely over one hundred pounds, skin stretched over bone from the extremely cold below-zero weather without proper cold-weather clothing and never getting enough to eat, never getting inside a building of any kind. Forget about ever taking a bath or any way to clean ourselves up. Our sweat-soaked clothing had to be lived in day and night. Some never made it till morning. Almost everything that could be taken out of a person and still remain alive had been sucked out of me on the battlefields of Korea. I spent most all of the next year recovering in the Percy Jones Army Hospital in Battle Creek, Michigan. I come now to a point I would like to make. After losing hometown friends in the Korean War and others I became acquainted with in the service, seeing some of them shot stone cold dead by my side or others having to suffer on in pain and agony.

Our troops, the First Marine Division and the Seventh Army Division caught off guard in North Korea at the Chosin Reservoir, had to suffer greatly in the below-zero weather conditions where the Chinese Communist Forces were waiting to trap and annihilate them all. We see a following piece written by *Time* staff writer Paul Richter:

50 YEARS LATER, THE BATTLE OF CHOSEN ENDS

Korean War: Once-maligned Army troops honored for their actions in brutal attack.

WASHINGTON. In the bitter cold of December 1950, a convoy of 3,200 U.S. Army troops came under withering fire from tens of thousands of Chinese infantrymen massed in the hills east of Chosin Reservoir in North Korea.

Twelve hours later, about 1,500 Americans from the 7th Infantry Division were dead, more than 1,000 were wounded and most of the convoy's 40 vehicles were charred hulks or in flames. The attack was the brutal conclusion of four days of assaults by the Chinese, and when it was over, only soldiers strong enough to stagger six miles to a U.S. Marine encampment escaped capture.

For years, the units involved have been accused of incompetence, malingering, even cowardice. But now, at the 50th anniversary of the outbreak of the Korean War, the military has taken a new look at the battle and officially affirmed the contribution of what came to be called Task Force Faith.

In a ceremony this month, survivors were decorated with a Presidential Unit Citation acknowledging that, even though the Army units were ill-prepared and poorly trained, without their resistance the Chinese likely would have swept south and achieved their larger goal of destroying a Marine force of 17,000.

It makes me feel good when someone comes along and sets the record straight, and it should you too. It wasn't just the Marine Corps alone that had to suffer and die in that campaign. That was just one isolated area of Korea where no one has ever doubted how bad it was and give everyone the credit due them. But some lesser-known but just-as-severe conditions existed all around that area during that time frame. For example, because of the surprise enemy attack upon the Marine Corps and the Seventh Infantry Division. The Second Infantry Division was ordered into fighting a rear guard at Kunri, Korea, to allow other army and marine units to withdraw to the rear and escape their being surrounded. The CCF caught the Second Division in a pass south of Kunri and in one afternoon had inflicted over three thousand causalities on the division.

WAR: And The After Effects On Those Doing The Dirty Work Of Killing

I lost a hometown friend who served in that Chosin Reservoir campaign in North Korea and is still missing in action; his body was never recovered. Now, after sixty-five years of waiting for so-called brilliant, smart, and intelligent presidents that rule and govern our nation to bring our dead soldiers back home to be recognized as giving their lives for the freedom we all enjoy and to be buried with dignity and honor, where President Obama and those before him weren't smart enough, gifted in tough negotiations, beyond talking about it. Now along comes an idiot crossed with being a moron who knows nothing at all about politics or anything else, named Donald J. Trump, who according to the left-wing Democrats and their fake news counterparts is an ignoramus that is guilty of treason and should be impeached. I have a logical question I would like to ask: what exactly does that have to say about those that didn't even come close to measuring up to President Trump's ability to achieve things that none of them could? They need to hang their obstructionist heads down low between their legs in shame and disgrace.

THE WAR DIDN'T STOP AT THE CHOSIN RESERVOIR

Soldiers, sailors, marines, and men and boys of every description stuck with it and continued on fighting and dying for the cause of freedom. Losing arms, legs, eyes, jawbones, ears, fingers, toes, hands, and feet, and all sorts of other body parts and boggled minds. It caused me grief, pain, and sorrow to hear it being reported that we never won the war. But is that really true? Let's take a look at the evidence. The North Korean and the Chinese war machine with all their superior Russian weapons and overwhelming numbers were pushed back to the basic place of their initial invasion, where they still remain today. The North Koreans continues to be an oppressive military regime that rules through fear, intimidation, and manipulation. But again! The proof is in the pudding. We won that war, and the South Koreans did not squander their freedom. The progress and achievements they have taken on and succeeded in is proof positive that our military did not have to die in vain or for a tie. We put them back where they belonged.

The North Korean people still live in abject poverty throughout the country. Under the despotic rule of one, not all that much different than Hitler of WWII. Still hell-bent upon invading South Korea and bringing them into the northern fold in his quest to conquer and gain land mass, power, and control over the minds and hearts of all of Korea. But there is one little problem—the DMZ. The demilitarized zone, where our military stands guard to make sure it never happens. It may be true that the war has never officially ended, but it should not take a mental wizard to figure out and come to a logical conclusion as to who has really won the war. There should never be a question about that at all, and our history books need to acknowledge it. So as not to be politically incorrect, they just don't say much of anything about the Korean War, causing it to be branded as "the Forgotten War."

A night satellite photograph of North and South Korea, for example, reveals a telltale message to the world. The whole of South Korea is being illuminated with the lights of industry, commerce, and progress, by a nation that is producing and exporting world-class products of every nature. While the north remains dark and void of the things that democracy has brought to the south. South Korea has become one of our greatest trading partners. They are a nation and a people to be admired and looked up to for their perseverance, determination, stick-to-itiveness and dogged work ethic.

Their athletes bring a measure of excellence to the Olympics at competition time. They did not squander the lives of my military comrades and friends who fought and died to free them from being dominated and controlled by North Korea. They didn't have to die for a tie, we won that war hands down, we run their raggedy communist asses out of South Korea and have kept them there now for sixty-plus years. How can anybody supposedly known as an educated person continue on claiming the war was never won by anybody? One person evidently started the rumor and made that claim in saying it those sixtysome years ago, and now all of the naïve and simple-minded commentators in lockstep with one another continue to parrot it. Please get it right, dummies: *"We won the Korean War."*

I was in Seoul, Korea, during the 1950s and could see nothing but huge piles of rubble and devastation. A grasshopper would have had to pack his lunch to go through the area. Unfit for habitation, the people had all been driven out in front of the invading armies. Seoul changed hands four times during the war. As far as the eye could see, the city had pretty much been leveled. I don't remember seeing anything higher than a three-story building. I was amazed in 1988, as the Olympics were being held there and we were all able to see maybe the most modern city in the world that had risen from the ashes of destruction and devastation. And it hasn't stopped there; they continue to go forward building some of the most awesome, eye-popping structures on the face of this earth

The skyline is now covered with skyscrapers, superhighways, bridges, and commerce. A bustling city on the move upward and onward. Another testament to a people given a free mind in which to achieve, build, and go forward with. South Korea today is a nation with a population of 50 million people. A full 20 percent of the population live in the city of Seoul. A city with a population of roughly 10 million people—that, my friends, is a couple million more than the people who live in our own New York, City. Interestingly, Seoul's population density is almost twice that of New York City, and eight times higher than the density of Rome.

I was in other Korean cities such as Pusan, Inchon, Wonju, and others, where the same progress has since grown and now thrives as well. The spread of Communism around the world was stopped dead in its tracks in Korea. You can decide for yourself who won the war, but for me, the question has been settled. It gives me comfort and an inner peace on this Veterans Day to know in the deepest recesses of my mind and heart that my friends and comrades did not die in vain, or *"die for a tie"* in Korea. Time has shown that we decisively did win the war. The proof is there for all who have eyes to see with. The South Korean people have made it so; they did not squander their freedom, bought and paid for by the blood of my military comrades, buddies, and friends.

In the 1994 version of its annual publication, *Service and Casualties in Major Wars and Conflicts*, the Pentagon put Korean War battle deaths at 33,652 and "other deaths"—meaning deaths in the war zone from illness, accidents, and other non-battle causes—at 3,262. That yields a total of 36,914. Around 8,000 men were never recovered, whose bodies remain in Korean soil. One such young man was Sergeant David Feriend of Fife Lake, Michigan. He lost his life at the Chosin Reservoir battle, against the overwhelming brutal onslaught from the Communist Chinese forces against an American military force caught unaware because MacArthur had refused to believe his own intelligence people advising him of their massing at the Yalu River. I had gone to school with David Feriend, his two sisters, and a brother. As we remember our friends and neighbors of yesterday who gave up all their own tomorrows that we all might live in freedom today, it behooves us all to do so with a grateful, thankful, and appreciative heart.

These brave and courageous young men and women went and served in a country they had never heard of before, fighting and dying for a people they did not know. To keep a nation free and prevent them from falling into the grasp of oppressive communism. The grateful, thankful nation of South Korea has rapidly, through the pages of time, risen from the ashes of destruction to that of unparalleled growth and development, as a testimony and a memorial to those lost lives. It does my heart good to know that my comrades in the bloody, frozen combat hell of Korea did not die for a tie or in some stinking rice paddy fertilized with human excrement for no purpose to be achieved. We gave South Korea their freedom back, and they have honored our sacrifice by not squandering it.

Thus, gaining the attention of the whole world as a people and a nation to be reckoned with, South Korea has shown itself to be ever grateful and thankful for American service men and women who have served their nation. They put out free publications to veterans to prove where their heart is in this. Among other things as I understand it at this point in time, they will bring any veteran of the Korean War that would like to return for a visit to Korea by paying for all food and lodging and half of the plane fare or travel expense. To show us how much they did then and still do appreciate and are thankful for our sacrifice to their nation.

On this Veterans Day of remembrance, let us acknowledge and pay tribute to *"the many who gave some, and the some that gave all."* Remembering as we do that it is our Almighty God who is in control of all things, and all the time.

Korean War losses

South Korea
217,000 (military)   1,000,000 (civilian)

North Korea
406,000 (military)   600,000 (civilian)

China
600,000 (military)

Source: *Encyclopedia Britannica*

Doing the math here will help a reasonable mind to be able to determine who won the war and the reason why the enemy had been driven to the peace table.

This first is a tribute and remembrance of my two best US Army buddies—Billy Magee and Ernie Lee. They both fought with me in the Korean War. Beyond that, it is a memorial to all who have given their last breath of life, that we might live on in freedom and peace. I have installed a permanent marker on our garage with the dual inscriptions of each Billy and Ernie to cause me to always remember and not to take for granted that all lost, wounded, crippled for all the rest of their lives, and those who have given everything to secure our peace and safety deserve to be remembered and honored for their selfless service to our country and to each one of us individually.

BILLY MAGEE was from Fife Lake, Michigan. He and I joined the U.S. Army together in May of 1949. His serial number was one number before mine. We had gone through basic training together at Fort Riley, Kansas. His bunk was next to mine all through basic training. We had many good times together. Billy was killed in action by the brutal and animalistic North Korean Army in September of 1950. Before he was old enough to vote, have a legal beer, get married, or raise a family. I visit his gravesite up east at Garfield cemetery often; and hardly a day goes by that I fail to remember him. We all need to remember and guard against forgetting that *"freedom is not free."* It always has required, does now, and will continue to demand the blood of many to step up and pay for the never-ending and staggering cost in blood, for others to be able to live in peace, safety, and plenty.

ERNIE LEE was my closest army buddy in the 153 Transportation Port Company in Pusan, Korea. When the overwhelming numbers of the Chinese Army overran all of our military on the frontlines and slaughtered many of them, Ernie and I were immediately shipped up to the frontlines with many others to bring the army divisions up to strength. The last time I saw Ernie, a medic giving aid to him had him propped up against a tree and was ripping his upper body clothing off.

NO GREATER LOVE THAN THIS

He had been hit with a burst from a Russian Burp Gun in the hands of a Chinese soldier. The blood-splattered snow made me think of my father slaughtering a pig during the wintertime back home. In the middle of an assault I wasn't able to stop or help, because I was needed more up front somewhere. The last bloody image of Ernie sticks in my mind; I don't know if he lived or died. But I do know that he was willing, as all the rest of us were, to lay down his life for his friends, comrades, buddies, and nation when the time came. To which Jesus Christ tells us in *John* 13:15, *"Greater love hath no man than this, that a man lay down his life for his friends."*

Another one of my very good friends—a brave and courageous warrior of the Korean War and one to be honored and remembered—the late Robert Hall of Kalkaska, Michigan, and I had many things in common. Although we met each other later on in our lives, we both had quit school and joined the U.S. Army in 1949. We both had gone through our basic training at Fort Riley, Kansas, at the same time, he a month or so later than myself. Our lives paralleled in civilian life too; we were both long-haul truckers. Mostly, I suppose in my case anyway, and in his too, I believe, we didn't do well with having others barking orders at us. After surviving what Korea had to offer, we became quite independent.

THE MACARTHUR BLUNDER THAT CAUSED MANY LOST LIVES

Bob had gone overseas to Osaka, Japan, to take his training to become a combat medic as well as a combat infantryman. We both had been trained for combat infantry at Fort Riley, Kansas. We both ended up in Korea during the beginning of the war. We had both gone through the early days of the war in different outfits without proper cold-weather clothing or decent footwear because of General Douglas MacArthur's huge blunder of bragging he would have the boys home by Christmas, and consequently never ordering any cold-weather clothing, causing us to have to fight against overwhelming, well-prepared, well-trained, and the brutal, no-nonsense combat-ready North Korean and Communist Chinese armies in the most inhumane and mind-numbing cold and blizzard conditions in over a hundred years.

THANK GOD FOR WHISTLING DEATH

We were being ripped to shreds and pushed back on every front. On one of the initial attacks against the Communist Chinese Forces, Bob Hall's unit of seven infantrymen were in the process of seeking and searching out the Chinese enemy when the enemy found them. His unit of seven men on the ground had been attacked by a Russian T-34 tank with its artillery piece. Four of the seven were killed outright; Bob and the rest had been wounded as the tank closed in to finish them off.

Then out of the sky came a Marine Corsair fighter plane at just the right, exact time. The Japanese army had called them whistling death because of the sound the air passing over the gull wings made on the aircraft. The pilot had taken the tank out in a great ball of fire, by either napalm or rocket fire. We learned to love those marine pilots and the close air support they were able to give us.

WE ALL LEARNED THE NEW MEANING OF THE WORD *COLD*

Bob spent a few weeks in recovery in a hospital in Japan and then returned to his duties on the frontlines in the Korean War. I know exactly what Bob had to go through that first winter in Korea, because while I was with a different outfit, I also had to endure the same never-ending misery of blood and gore that was being required by all who had to go through it on the ground. And during that first winter, it was without any proper cold-weather clothing or footwear. As the weather was the worst in over a hundred years, we had to fight and die in thirty and forty below-zero weather where our weapons would freeze up and be useless against the enemy. You could spit and see it turn to ice a few inches in front of your eyes.

THE COMBAT MEDIC WHO SAW TOO MUCH

BOB WENT THROUGH FIVE MONTHS OF THIS HELL and didn't get any decent cold-weather clothing or footwear until the end of March 1951. He suffered greatly through the winter months in leather combat boots, before getting shoe-packs that weren't much better. I and the others thought they were even worse. Bob never opened up to his wife and kids about his war experiences. He held it from them, believing it was for their own best interest. He didn't talk much to anyone else about it either. As we spent more and more time together, just he and myself, he began to open up and reveal the horrors of patching up wounded men and seeing some that he couldn't save because of the severity of the damage to their mangled and broken bodies. Of all the things that my friend Bob had revealed to me over time, the three experiences had the most impact upon my mind and made me realize the heartache he suffered as a combat medic and infantryman.

BEING LONELY IN A CROWD

HIS MEDIC TRAINING HAD TAUGHT HIM TO EXCLUDE himself from getting close to anyone in his unit. He could not afford to let personal feelings come between himself and those he might have to attend to on the battlefield. Consequently, he didn't allow himself to even eat with his comrades; he would remove himself a few yards away and eat by himself, finding himself alone in a crowd. But he understood the reason why and complied and stuck to his training. Talking about it, I could tell the effect that it had, had upon his thoughts and feelings back then, which remained with him yet at the present time. It would begin to bring tears running down his face and put a distant, empty look in his eyes. He would choke up and be unable to go on.

LEARNING WHEN TO SPEAK, AND WHEN NOT TOO

Bob talked about having to kill enemy Chinese soldiers with his army-issue .45 automatic pistol to attend to a wounded comrade. At one time, he had to kill an enemy soldier with his bare hands to save a fellow soldier. I valued those moments of being close enough in mind, body, and soul to exchange our battlefield experiences with each other. He had learned to keep them all to himself, where they lay entrenched in his mind and out of reach of others. Those that may be sitting as a group at a table in a restaurant, when such things as are being discussed, they tend to slowly get up from the group and head for the nearest door. In body language, it says one of two things to me concerning someone who is attempting to get some awful things off his chest.

A SINCERE MAN SPEAKS OUT ABOUT SELF

The person doing that may be someone the same age as yourself, who somehow avoided any military service; and to them, it is an embarrassment that they feel guilty about. Just the other day, I was having a good conversation with my banker, a really nice guy and a good conversationalist with a great sense of humor. He thanked me for my service to our country, as I thanked him for doing it, asking if he had been in the military as well, so I could thank him in return. He told me no, but that it was the biggest regret in his life. If he had it to do it over again, he said it would be the first thing he would do; it had always lain heavy on his mind and thought process. The distant gaze in his eyes caused me to believe he meant what he had said.

LINGERING MEMORIES THAT LIVE ON

To those never being in the battlefield position of kill or be killed, and being expose to all the mind-numbing sights and sounds of dying mangled men, women, and children, both comrades and enemies alike, military and local civilians whose last dying screams of pain and anguish stay embedded in your mind, heart, and ears for the rest of your life, I still at this moment feel compelled to mention again how at times I still see the pitiful, anguished, and fearful eyes of a little Korean girl running after me with outstretched arms and tears of hopelessness and despair. I had showed her a few minutes of love and kindness; she was running now behind the truck that had picked me up, crying out, "Daddy, Daddy, Daddy." To some this can, and no doubt will, sound like a made-up story to disregard, but it is the truth of God. It happened to me.

REACHING ONE'S LIMITS

My friend Bob, after much time spent together, just him and myself alone, revealed his innermost act of what it is like in the day-after-day total misery, heartache, despair, and the mind-bending and obscene insanity of the never-ending pain and misery of having to live on, becoming more and more like a rabid, wild animal that kills and eats its own young. Killing, maiming, destroying, and doing away with others made in the image and likeness of God, who in their turn are hell-bent on doing the same thing to us. Bob confessed to me that he had, had his .45 automatic caliber pistol cocked and loaded at his head on four different occasions while serving in the Korean War hellhole on earth.

He had reached his limits at least four different times but somehow was able to jerk himself back together and survive one more day. Bob no longer has to suffer on in old memories that torment and torture the mind, his spirit now having returned to God who had given it to him at birth. I lost a dear friend with whom I had experienced many of the same things together but in differing places. The Veterans Administration who had promised to take care of his many combat-related mental and physical ailments were true to form and the last ones to break those promises and to let him down. We could talk about these things and get them off our chest. I miss Bob a lot. I am happy for him now, knowing he has reached a place where suffering ends.

The value of the Veterans Administration to address these problems and to deal with us on an individual basis is beginning to pay dividends for some of us. I was attending a group VA meeting for PTSD (posttraumatic stress disorder) in Traverse City, Michigan. We got Bob into our group to attend as well. It was beginning to help him to open up and unload some of the massive amount of combat garbage we all have inside from our experiences during the wartime. It is a safe place to say things that you cannot say to others without having gone through these same things. Some of these things are just too outlandish to accept and to believe by many others.

PROMISES GIVEN BY OUR NATION, THEN RENEGED UPON

Even the VA finally let Bob down big-time on his request for compensation for posttraumatic stress disorder, as well as for other war-related mental, emotional, physical, and spiritual wounds hidden inside his whole being. He went to his grave knowing well that the VA did not and would not authorize compensation for him that many others had been receiving for many years, having not gone through anything at all like he had experienced, or all that he had endured. I, however, was able to identify with the inner anger that was eating him up alive on the inside, from my own being denied again and again by the VA, because I had learned it well through the years.

Still, I am personally free from any guilt feelings myself for not being able to help him receive more help in getting that which was owed to him. He had earned it and had it coming to him, because I had done all that I knew to do in my attempts to help my close friend and buddy in his attempt at negotiating the often complex and double-standard reasoning that the VA uses to determine the eligibility of a veteran. Sometimes I personally believe it is simply brownnosing individuals sitting at their comfortable desks making their decisions to save government money to look good in the eyes of their superiors, in the hope of having it recognized that it feathers their own nest. Then they reach across their cluttered desk filled with the papers of other veterans needing the rubber stamp that announces, "Claim Denied."

EVERYONE WANTS PEACE; A FEW AT THE TOP WANT TO DICTATE THE TERMS

The VA denial in his own mind meant to him that they were calling him a liar. Oh well! Wars will continue on as mankind attempts to rule themselves in this Babylonian system that has been developed and put into place during biblical times. The high and mighty elite, movers and shakers that rule over us little people will sit in their cozy and warm war rooms, eating steak and drinking their champagne, waiting for the dancing girls to come on in for their private and personal entertainment. As they stick their territorial pins into the map to go to war, where they decide they will spend the lives of the next batch of military personnel, to suffer and die in or after they come back home as a vegetable, all shot to hell in body, mind, and soul, to have the VA turn their backs on them.

SOME HAD GONE INSANE

I am reminded of my own trip back to the good old USA. We left the army hospital in Osaka, Japan, and they loaded dozens of wounded military men from the different services in the Korean War. Army, Navy, Air Force, Marines, Coast Guard, and the Seabees. A stream of wounded men with every kind of wound imaginable, some walking, many being carried, some in wheelchairs, many in casts, one pilot in a full body cast (the only part of him visible was part of his face). Inside the cast, he was rotting, and the smell was overwhelming, especially so whenever they would have to move him. One pitiful sight after another of these young men all mangled and blown to pieces that could never be put back together again and made whole. Some have lost their minds from being overloaded beyond what a human mind is capable of receiving and still remaining sane.

WAREHOUSED AND FORGOTTEN VETERANS

It is a shame that for the procession of wounded men, and now women too, that are sent to places all over this world to secure our freedom in the most ungodly conditions known to mankind, or that exist here on planet Earth, there is not more transparency and the taking of actual photographic documentation when they do come back home barely alive and all shot to hell. Some more dead than alive, a mere mangled shell of a weakened, quivering humanity that a few months, weeks, or days ago stood strong and tall, paying their own bloody sacrifices for our freedom. Many, as I have already mentioned, will no doubt spend the rest of their lives warehoused out of sight and out of mind in the back rooms of some VA hospital.

BEING SPIT UPON AND CALLED BABY KILLERS

More people have become used to griping, complaining, judging, and condemning our government and military personnel that have what it takes to step up when asked and when needed. Those having been trained to do the dirty work of getting blood on their hands while others sit comfortably at home in their La-Z-Boy chairs, eating from the table of plenty and enjoying all that freedom has to offer that others have paid for, waiting for those to come home that paid the cost, of extracting an eye for an eye, a tooth for a tooth, or a life for a life. Coming home then to deal with never-ending nightmares that will not ever allow them to sleep. And then having to hide in the shadows and destroy their uniforms to keep from being spit upon or called baby killers. *(Thanks in part to Hanoi Jane.)*

LEAVING KOREA WAS THE HAPPIEST DAY OF MY LIFE

On March 9, 1951, two days after being relieved of my combat duty from the frontline battlefield, I was being carried onto a C-47 plane out of Wonju, Korea, to a hospital in Osaka, Japan. To this day, it is by far the happiest day of my life. I think I know pretty well how a condemned-to-death prison inmate must feel after getting a stay of execution and then being set free. I had not expected to survive Korea, and now things were really looking good. I held my breath until the plane had gotten in the air. I couldn't believe it was happening. Here I was now—my sentence was being commuted. I would live another day.

I THOUGHT I HAD FINALLY GOTTEN RID OF THE SNOW AND THE COLD

IN THE HOSPITAL IN OSAKA, JAPAN, IT WAS like being yanked out of a certain, never-ending hell, and here I was now, being waited on hand and foot by pretty little Japanese nurses and attendants. Getting everything good to eat imaginable and all that I wanted to go along with it. It was as though I had died and gone straight to heaven in that moment of time. It looked like I was going to live after all. A few weeks later, after gaining back some weight and strength, I got my orders to be going back home to recuperate. I remember on the flight out of Japan the plane had set down on Wake Island to refuel. I looked out the windows as we were landing, and all I could see was pure white snow. It gave me a sinking feeling, but the doors of the plane opened up, and we got an immediate blast of hot air. I had not known that Wake Island was solid white coral built up from the sea. I took in a big sigh of relief.

Leaving the Army Hospital in Osaka, Japan, I was loaded into a large double-deck plane known, I believe, as a C-124. A Globemaster that had been made by the Douglas Corporation. These giant planes were big enough to carry an armored vehicle, two big buses, or two hundred fully armed troops. It was a two-deck plane with four 3,500 horsepower engines, and passengers entered it by a nose ramp. The cost of the plane was about $1.8 million. The thought of going home was beginning to feel as though we wouldn't have to die on some frozen mountaintop or in one of their stinking rice paddies, being fertilized with human dung, after all. Once we got in the air, I breathed a sigh of relief. But the reality of war had not ended that soon or that easy.

ALL WERE NOW GOING HOME

THE PLANE WAS PACKED TO THE MAXIMUM WITH the horribly wounded who had been treated and kept alive in army hospitals in Japan. As bad as the cries of anguish and pain coming from those being attended would be at times, and as bad as it smelled on the plane from those badly wounded with casts enclosing their rotting flesh wounds inside, still there was a joy and a happiness being expressed as badly wounded men knew that they were now on their way home. Every heart, mind, and soul on that plane had to be silently thanking God that the Korean War, with all its horrors was over for them. They were homeward bound with some kind of a future to experience and look forward to. It is a time that I really enjoy looking back on, and I imagine all the rest of those on the plane to home, family, freedom, and plenty do too.

WHERE IS HE NOW?

A KID SAT BESIDE ME THAT DIDN'T APPEAR to be over fifteen or sixteen years old. He had, had his jaw blown or shot off, and all he wanted to do was to laugh or to talk. He was so anxious to be going home that he had to let it all out. I couldn't understand anything at all that he was saying, that came gurgling out of a hole in his neck where his mouth used to be. I listened the best I could and was happy for him, just like I was for myself. We had dodged the bullet and our time wasn't up yet. I stop and reflect back upon how excited he was about going home. All I could do was to wonder how his girlfriend or family would react when they got their first look at him. He was extremely grotesque and hard to look at. But we were going home. I still do wonder about how he was received by family and friends.

A young red-haired boy sat all trussed up in a straitjacket in the aisle of the plane. He had lost any resemblance of a normal human being and looked and acted more like a wild animal in a cage. He was never, as far as I know, taken out of the straitjacket to be given a break or to stretch his legs. He would snarl and try to bite anyone who would come close to him. He had obviously lost his mind; his handlers had to be careful in moving or attempting to feed him. The war had left its mark on him, and while it was over for him literally, I still wonder if he ever regained any real sanity, or is he still symbolically at war in his mind? Or was his mind so damaged that it was past any functioning at all?

Another person, a pilot, also lay in the aisle of the plane encased almost completely in a plaster cast. The only opening was a small part of his face and an opening to eliminate waste in the rear. He was three or foot away from where I was sitting. I could only try to imagine how mangled up on the inside of the cast he would have been. With him being in such close proximity and many others on the plane in casts as well, with all of that rotting flesh and blood puddled from within their casts, it smelled so awful and bad at times it would have gagged a maggot off a gut wagon. Still their morale and spirits stayed high, because everyone was contemplating going home to live in peace, being in comfort, and seeing their loved ones. And try to forget they had ever heard of a place called Korea.

HUNT DOWN AND KILL THE MAD DOGS

I came home fresh out of combat that required us to kill the enemies of our nation on a regular, daily basis, to kill, maim, and destroy individuals that we knew nothing about except that they were ordered to do the same thing to all of us. Then to put it all out of our mind, hearts, and reasoning and be able, prepared, and ready to do the same thing again tomorrow. It then seemed a reasonable thing to do—kill others that are intent upon killing you. Get them before they get you. Rid the earth of those not fit to live. My Uncle Sam had spent a lot of time in training me and programming my mind to accept it and to become a government hunter. My goal had become, *Hunt them down and kill them like the mad dogs that they were.*

BEWARE OF DRUNKEN COUSINS

I had not been home long, until one evening, at about dusk, a drunken female cousin of mine drove frantically into our yard, blowing the car horn. I went out to see what the problem was. A friend of ours had buried their little boy that day who had gotten into his mother's purse and taken a whole bottle of aspirin, which had killed him. My drunken cousin said, "Quick, you've got to come with me. Someone is over at the cemetery, and they are trying to dig up little Dougie." My brother happened to be visiting at the time, and we jumped into my car and followed her to the cemetery. It had gotten quite dark by then, and she stopped at the road going into the cemetery and blinked her lights a couple times.

THANKS FOR THE SIGNAL

This was a dead giveaway to both my brother and me that something strange was going on. She was giving a signal of some sort to someone. I didn't go into the cemetery; instead, I went straight to the grandfather of the little boy, who was our best friend. I told him what had happened, in case someone was attempting to set me up for something. He sent his older son out the next morning to look around the cemetery to see if things didn't look right. He learned that a few yards away from the new gravesite, the weeds had all been trampled down, and the area was strewn with beer bottles and cigarette butts. It became obvious to us that a couple of people had been lying in wait for me, supposing I would be alone. The blinking lights probably told them I had company with me.

CAUSING FOLKS TO RUN SCARED

I wasted no time at all in finding out who the culprits were. One was a neighbor I went to school with, a couple years older than myself. I knew him and his brother very well since their early childhood. The oldest one was a mean, backstabbing, drunken thug who was one of the most treacherous individuals I have ever known. He had been drafted during the Korean War, and when he got orders to go to Korea, he took his father's .30-30 Winchester and shot himself in the foot, reasoning, I suppose, that it was better to be a live coward than a dead hero. He and his brother had threatened to burn down a business in town for not serving them alcohol. The owners, old people afraid of the threats, sold out and left town. They had folks in our community intimidated and filled with fear because of how they were able to manipulate and intimidate others.

IRONHEADED GANGSTERS

They were both barred from every beer joint, tavern, dance hall, or anywhere else booze was sold or used. They spread the fear of reprisal throughout our community. I do not have to list their names down here, and no one will have to guess who it is that I am identifying here. Anyone reading this from my area would instantly know who I am speaking of during the 1950–1965/1970 time frame. They relished talking about their exploits of terrorism and the fear that they spread in our area. One state cop carried a five-cell flashlight as a conversational piece that he had bent over the head of the big one, which didn't even faze him, while attempting to break up a ruckus in a local bar.

NOT WANTING TO BE LIVE COWARDS, THEY BECAME DEAD ONES

I have a reason for explaining this to you. I had run around with both of these guys when they were kids and on into adulthood. I knew exactly how explosive and damaging they could be: both of them lived only to fight; they neither one could dance a lick, but they did go to all the honky-tonk joints in our area, to see who they could pick a fight with. The big one was about six feet two inches and with shoulders over two feet across, the smaller but way more treacherous one was about five feet eight or nine inches tall *(both dead now)*. They worked together like a wolf pack. If they met with someone they didn't think they could whip alone, they found a way to gang up on their victim.

OOPS, WRONG ONE HITS THE DECK

I HAD HAD A PROBLEM WITH THE TREACHEROUS one while I was playing in a band in the Taffle Town bar and dance hall over on Highway 66 north of Lake City, Michigan. He had tried to sic one of their half-drunk patrons on me that night by lying to him and telling him something he knew that would make him mad at me. Something that I supposedly had said about him. I had taken a break from playing the guitar with my buddy who was playing the accordion on the bandstand and was headed for the bathroom. The guy that he got all stirred up over me was so anxious to get a hold of me that he accidentally bumped into someone else and had almost knocked him down. That was when the shit hit the fan. The guy he had bumped into turned around and decked him in the middle of the crowd. So things from there cooled down that particular night.

ALL THE TALKING IS DONE

I KNEW THAT THE TREACHEROUS ONE WOULD NOT be thwarted forever on getting his pound of flesh, that he reasoned he had coming from my hide. Neither he nor his brother alone could whip me, because they had already tried several times, and failed to do so. I reasoned that as soon as they both got together and would get a snootful, my name would come up and give them cause to look me up and take care of business. One late fall day, I had gone into town to shop for something. I ran into them both in the store that they had run the old folks out of town from. Where they had not as yet been denied the right to buy booze, and that was what they were in the process of doing. Since neither one was very friendly, I decided the time had come to settle the score. They would most likely come looking for me.

THE GAME IS ON

THERE HAD BEEN A PRETTY GOOD SKIFF OF snow that had fallen the night before, and I had decided it was time to relieve folks in our area of having to look over their shoulders in anxious anticipation every time these two drunken hoodlums came to town looking for who they would terrorize this day. I went home and told Nancy to get the kids ready—we were going hunting. I loaded up my double-barrel 12-gauge shotgun with double-aught buckshot and took along a couple of slugs. I left a really easy trail in a skiff of snow that had fallen that night for them to follow down a back road where we live that had not been traveled that day. They knew the area as well as I did and had hunted it many times themselves. I went to a secluded spot where I had hunted before and built a fire to keep us warm. There would have been only one reason why those two brothers would have come back there looking for me, and I knew it.

GOD IS IN CONTROL OF ALL THINGS, AND ALL THE TIME

I HAD TAKEN NANCY AND THE KIDS WITH me because I didn't know what they might have done to them if I had left them home. I had every intention of ending the decades-long crime spree of those two that I felt had earned it, had it coming, and was long overdue. Having been trained to exercise my craft against young kids of another nation, involved in doing what they had been trained to do to us as well. Those who had not been guilty of doing anything to me personally. Any real justice seemed pretty clear in my mind and heart. I felt I had earned the right now, after protecting another nation and a people that I didn't even know, by shooting and killing their enemies to keep them safe from annihilation. Here I am now, facing two real enemies of my own family who were out to do me harm. This was something up close and personal to me.

I THANK GOD EVERY DAY THAT THEY DIDN'T COME

IF THEY HAD COME OUT AS I HAD expected them to do that day, the authorities would have most likely found their rotting bodies in the spring. I had every intention of killing them both. I say these things so that those reading this paper will be able to more fully understand what can, and often does, happen to a mind and heart that has been trained and programmed to kill and destroy its enemies. I have taken the time to explain this isolated incident that happened in my life, that others should realize that the exact same ability and possibility may for the most part lay dormant within each one of us carnal human-beings, that in a heart-beat if met with a certain set of the right circumstances, and the situation that one finds themselves in. It could trigger any one to react in a similar fashion. Especially so, if we factor in what has gone on in the background of the individual. To think or to believe otherwise is to call God a liar. He tells us in Proverbs, that it is not in man that walks to guide his own steps. Just as Christ could do nothing of and by Himself, He could do only that which He had seen His Father doing. We can do nothing of ourselves either, it is Christ in us that has accepted all responsibility for the actions of mankind. He will bring every last one of us up to His level of immortal, spirit life at the resurrections. When God's judgments are in the earth, all of the people will learn righteousness. I thank God every day that those two brothers did not come out looking for me that day so long ago. They both died young a long time ago now because of their drunken lifestyle.

I believe in my heart of hearts that God had been intimately involved in my life so much more than I could ever imagine. Long before I began to recognize that He was calling me into His service, and looking back upon my life, lifestyle, and my anti-God approach to things that I didn't understand, I can see where He must have sent His angels to keep me from destroying myself through unbelief, anarchy, stubbornness, stupidity, and self-centeredness. That is to name a few things that come to mind. Since God has known us all in our mother's womb, He also knows the end from the beginning and everything in between. Why then, should we not believe and accept it as actual fact, that the Almighty God of all that is, either seen or unseen, works in the lives of all his family of children? That means me and you and all of mankind.

Let me give you a little thumbnail sketch of managing my own life as I saw fit, and where it led me to. I have been revealing a lot of that to you here in this book that I am writing. To boil it down and condense it, it took me from birth to about age thirty-five or so before I began to recognize what part God should play in my everyday life. I began seriously in getting my life in order, that all of our work and spent effort not end up being taken away from us through stupidity and stubbornness. My first goal was to get completely out of debt, and I began in earnest to get that done and behind us. It all happened by the time I was forty years old. With obedience to the Word and way of God as best that I knew how to apply it, we had become totally debt free.

We no longer yet today pay even one penny of interest out to others to make them rich. We now collect interest; we have used the Discover card now for twenty-five years without paying a red cent of interest. Discover now pays us for using their card for all of our needs, wants, and desires. They have paid us several thousand dollars back over the years for always keeping our monthly balance paid off. And it is no big mystery how to go about doing that yourself, to get out from under the heavy burden of debt interest. Pay cash or do without, until you can take advantage of using a credit card to your own advantage.

In the Bible, Egypt is being symbolized as sin; in this way, I came to believe that I had spent most of my adult years in Egypt (sin) or wandering in the wilderness for forty years as the children of Israel had been guilty of doing by not following the Word and way of God, before being rescued and brought out of Egypt, or out of sin, by the strong arm of God. Why did Israel wander in the desert for forty years? This was considered a grave sin by God. Corresponding to the forty days that the spies toured the land, their God decreed that the Israelites would wander in the wilderness for forty years as a result of their unwillingness to take the land. For forty years, the Israelites wandered in the wilderness, eating quail and manna.

So I count a part of my forty-year segment of life before the calling and influence of the Spirit of God, as being led by the spirit that dwells in this world, the god of this world, the devil and Satan, as witnessed in 2 Corinthians. *"In whom the god of this world hath blinded the minds of them which believe not, lest the light of the glorious gospel of Christ, who is the image of God, should shine unto them."* God had caused me to have spent a total of forty years symbolically wandering in the wilderness, being, as it were, symbolic of my ancestors, the children of God, spending forty years wandering in the wilderness, until God did allow them to enter the promised land, symbolic also of the beginning journey on into immortal, spirit life in the coming kingdom of God.

At age forty, God had, unknown by me, been working with me on His potter's wheel for about eight years already. Smashing me down, knocking off rough edges, and remolding me into a more usable piece of clay. I had gotten my life in a good starting place to move on. I was learning how to maintain order and systematically bring about a change in my life and lifestyle. It's called repenting. We had learned to pay cash for things we needed until we could rightly manage using credit cards and borrowing money to our own advantage. I had come to accept and believe the Word and way of God and His Son Jesus Christ.

At that time, as time went on, I had determined that God was who He claimed He was, and He deserved and required to be worshipped beyond all other things, including my own family. God became first in my life as I began to slowly grow and develop into a more and more sincere and mature believer. I do not say I am a Christian on purpose, because I believe that Christianity as we see and hear it now being taught as the truth of God all around the world is a deceptive teaching. They definitely do not accept, believe, or teach anywhere even close to the gospel truth that Jesus Christ taught mankind to accept and to believe as the truth of God. I go forward now in the teaching of what I accept and believe is His actual truth. I recognize myself as a follower of God and His Word. Not as a Christian per their teaching of today.

In Malachi 3:10, we are told that God will pour out his blessing upon His people, to the point that the storehouse couldn't even hold them all. I feel that is exactly what God has done for me and my family, once I began to accept and to believe His truth being expounded upon and explained to me through the pages of the Bible, and through other dedicated individuals who have obeyed the Word of God in Revelation 18:4, where He commands us to come out of this world's counterfeit Christianity, the religion of custom, ritual, and traditions of men. Many of these followers of God and Jesus Christ have websites that have helped me along with understanding the truth of God. Let me wrap this segment up here by revealing a portion of how God has and still is blessing myself and my family.

I had grown in my understanding of life and its consequences for good or bad decisions. There would be blessings for obedience to the Word and way of God, and there would be curses for disobedience. I had learned from other businesspeople how to make better decisions and bring them to a successful conclusion, by sticking with the decisions made, working however you needed to, to bring them to fruition. *"A quitter never wins, and a winner never quits."* I knew well that my previous way of life fell way short of being acceptable to God. I determined to turn and go another way, a way that would be acceptable to God. I had worked jobs where I gained a wealth of information and common sense on good business practices. I decided it was time to keep the money I was working for instead of increasing someone else's wealth. Instead of letting someone else determine what I was worth in working for them, it was now time to tell them what I charged for my service *to them.*

I became what I identified as a *cleaning and restoration specialist.* Once I became a professional carpet cleaning agent, a professional hard surface floor technician, doing water, smoke, and vandalism damage and restoration, along with a host of other carpentry and handyman-type services, or most anything else that required two healthy arms and hands at the end of them, not afraid to get them dirty, and then adding a pretty healthy initiative to succeed, God began to bless our family in great abundance while leaving us plenty of time to enjoy life and not be worked to death for a little pittance that someone else thinks I am worth. I kept my overhead at a bare minimum, and that kept our expenses to a minimum too. One of the first things I did was to approach the shop I had worked for in Kalkaska, Michigan, that had determined I was worth a dollar and thirty-five cents per hour when they had hired me a few years earlier, and it was a job I appreciated at the time as well.

I went in to see the housekeeping authority and negotiated a dry carpet cleaning maintenance plan to take care of their facility on a yearly basic scheduling plan. Being dry didn't cause any wet, ruined carpeting or worker cessations or shut downs that a wet system would require. Consequently, as I explained to them the positives involved, we entered into a contract that lasted for several years. I bid the job at a competitive rate on a square footage basis. Every time, I would keep my appointed time to maintain their carpeting. I would average, after all expenses and overhead had been paid out, including wages for six workers, over two hundred and fifty dollars per hour, for the business, which was myself. Now that may seem like highway robbery at first glance, but everyone was happy and satisfied and pleased with the final job, and my philosophy is, "If it ain't broke, don't fix it."

I had based the cost of my services on what my competition was charging, and on a story I had heard down through the years about a high-level machine repairman who serviced large industrial plants. It taught me the concept of zeroing in on and specializing in a specific area unique to the area you live in, that everyone else is making a good living doing it in another way. On this certain day, one of this machine repairman's customers that I mention above had called him about a machine that was down and had idled the whole plant. He had immediately jumped into his service truck and was on his way to solve their problem, as they were losing big money every minute the shop was idle.

He arrived at the location, grabbed his toolbox, and soon was examining the problem machine. Taking out his stethoscope and listening carefully in a specific spot, he had determined the problem and reached for his toolbox and pulled out a little hammer. He reexamined the machine closely, and then, taking his little hammer and striking it down sharply on the specific spot he had determined the problem to be, the machine, without hesitation, began to start up, whirl, and run perfectly. The plant was back to work; everyone was happy.

The technician put his little hammer back in his toolbox, closed it up, and put it back in his truck as he reached into the glove compartment to get the paperwork to submit his invoice for services rendered. He handed the bill to the owner, who quickly looked it over with shock and surprise when his eyes fell on the amount of the service charge the machine repairman had given him. He had given him a bill for five thousand dollars.

As one might expect, the man was really upset as he turned to the repairman, asking him why he had charged so much for such a little amount of service, in just hitting the machine with his little hammer. The man came back with the answer that I used for motivation in keeping my prices up to a point that I could make a good living, and be around to do it tomorrow, next week, next month, and for many years to come. He said, "Oh, I didn't charge you anything for hitting the machine with my hammer. I gave that to you for free. I only charged you for knowing where to hit it."

And that, my friends, are one of the keys to success—to know what your service is worth and never be shy in charging for it. We can always help folks out and give them a lift up at times, free of any charge. That is one thing, and it is a good thing. But by always trying to undercut the other guys price, by cutting corners or using inferior materials will catch up with a person in due time. It is fun and enjoyable to watch an experienced person who knows how to perform well within his trade, in whatever trade it might be.

The more a person learns about life and how things operate, the more of a value they become to themselves and to anyone looking to use their service. The human mind is said to be the greatest agency in the universe: whatever we can see in our mind, we can create it with our hands. We have been given a helping part of God within us by His Holy Spirit. We need not that any man teaches us; the Holy Spirit will lead us into all truth. The person that does not read has no advantage over those that cannot read.

One more example: The Detroit Michigan area automobile tycoon Henry Ford ate in his own cafeteria at the plant where he operated out of, but he was very fussy about what he ate and who cooked it. He mostly lived on hamburger sandwiches, and even there, was only prepared by a specific cook. After a long and productive career of doing his job well, the cook finally retired to be with his family during his old age. A friend knowing the arrangement the cook had had with Henry Ford in not allowing anyone else to fix his hamburger for him asked why that was. The cook told him it was simple, that he had always planned in advance for Ford to order his hamburger by grinding up a porterhouse steak to use. Now that's what we would call understanding job security by one smart cook.

I would hope that no one would bother to brand me with the greed iron, using the time-worn argument that money is the root of all evil. Reasoning that I may be too tied up with seeking money. Because the Bible does not say that, as many deceived ministers of Satan will quote it as saying. *"For the LOVE of money is the root of all evil: which while some coveted after, they have erred from the faith, and pierced themselves through with many sorrows"* (1 Timothy 6:10, KJV). There is nothing at all wrong with money and wealth—it is the *love of money* that that is the root of all evil.

So it is the *love* of money that is the root of all evil. The will, desire, hope, and even the expectation, of God is that we all will prosper in our endeavor to use the awesome mind and reasoning power and strength that He has created within each one of us to put to good use. No one is intended to be a fly-on-the-wall observer, spectator, or onlooker; we have all been designed to be active participants in life, learning to go beyond our self-interests, doing things for our own well-being only. Christ tells us that He works and His Father works for the well-being of all. We need to be doing that same thing. God has blessed many sincere, honest, God-fearing, God-following, and decent, hardworking people with more money, material goods, fine homes, land,

and holdings almost beyond what their barns and banks can hold, because that is His nature. He loves all of us.

We all need to be using the talents that God has given us if we have any desire at all to please Him. To do otherwise is a disappointment to God, which He doesn't like and makes him give out correction to those who fail to do so with the talents He has created within us all. We are not intended to sit on our hands and long for a better life without supplying some action. We are not intended to head down to the casino to gamble away what little substance we do have, wishing and wanting to get rich the easy way, without supplying any energy to go along with it. The backbone will out produce the wishbone every time. We are, if and when possible, expected to get up off the couch, go out the door, and be involved in meaningful work. Look below in both the book of Matthew 25 and Luke 19 to find out the perspective of God on this issue.

Beginning in Matthew 25:13. "Therefore stay alert, because you do not know the day or the hour." For it is like a man going on a journey, who summoned his slaves and entrusted his property to them. To one he gave five talents, to another two, and to another one, each according to his ability. Then he went on his journey. The one who had received five talents went off right away and put his money to work and gained five more. In the same way, the one who had two gained two more. But the one who had received one talent went out and dug a hole in the ground and hid his master's money in it. After a long time, the master of those slaves came and settled his accounts with them.

The one who had received the five talents came and brought five more, saying, "Sir, you entrusted me with five talents. See, I have gained five more." His master answered, "Well done, good and faithful slave! You have been faithful in a few things. I will put you in charge of many things. Enter into the joy of your master."

The one with the two talents also came and said, "Sir, you entrusted two talents to me. See, I have gained two more." His master answered, "Well done, good and faithful slave! You have been faithful with a few things. I will put you in charge of many things. Enter into the joy of your master."

Then the one who had received the one talent came and said, "Sir, I knew that you were a hard man, harvesting where you did not sow and gathering where you did not scatter seed, so I was afraid, and I went and hid your talent in the ground. See, you have what is yours."

But his master answered, "Evil and lazy slave! So you knew that I harvest where I didn't sow and gather where I didn't scatter? Then you should have deposited my money with the bankers, and on my return, I would have received my money back with interest! Therefore, take the talent from him and give it to the one who has ten. For the one who has will be given more, and he will have more than enough. But the one who does not have, even what he has will be taken from him. And throw that worthless slave into the outer darkness, where there will be weeping and gnashing of teeth" *(Matthew 25:13–30; also Luke 19:12–28)*.

Now at age eighty-six years old, I have forty-five years of evidence to support and personally experience how following after the Word and ways of God and Jesus Christ has had a positive effect on my overall life and lifestyle and that of my family's. It has paid great dividends to our family. You have already read about some of my less-than-stellar exploits that have caused myself and my family much pain, suffering, and grief. Unbeknownst to me, God was using it all for my personal benefit. He had taken the time to beat me down and throw me on His potter's wheel again and again to cause me to eventually be a useful tool in His hands, to eventually become as His firstborn Son Jesus Christ now is. "For whom he did foreknow, he also did predestinate to be conformed to the image of his Son, that he might be the firstborn among many brethren" (Romans 8:29).

I have always worked and kept a pretty good-paying job for the most part. But it all seemed to be squandered and began slipping through my fingers, without having a lot to show for it. Because of my prior lifestyle, we lost completely everything we had worked for and owned three different times. Having to come crawling home like a spanked puppy dog. And barely staying out of some court procedure that some irate recipient was filing against me, and that I had brought upon myself. Still, being a glutton for punishment, I continued on, putting one foot in front of the other, one at a time, in self-medication and having some bar owner putting his hand on my back at closing time and pushing me out the door after 2:00 a.m.

As I began to acknowledge God in the equation as my Lord and Savior who loved me unconditionally and was on my side and had the desire to help me to achieve, and also that there was a future that I could look forward to beyond the here and now, and I was going to belong in it. Life took on an altogether different and wonderful meaning. Now I could anticipate God keeping His promise of reconciling all of creation back to Himself through His Son Jesus Christ. Talk and thinking about a revelation of such massive blessings for all of mankind made me want to take off all of my clothing, rub ashes all over my body, and run naked into the sunset. Well! *Maybe not*, but it certainly is the best news that mankind will ever hear.

What a wonderful and exciting thing I found it to be as God began to reveal it to me. We were not going to be wafted off to heaven to gaze upon the face of God for all eternity or be lying back in our spiritual La-Z-Boy chairs, being fanned, fed grapes, and caressed by eighteen virgins that meet us on the other side. Neither are we going to be drinking cool lemonade while drifting around on pink clouds in the sky. I was learning the truth of God, and at the same time I was trying to unlearn the endless number of the all-out lies, distortions, deceptions, and anti-God slop being taught, accepted, believed, and followed by the so-called Christian church. While their congregations wait in vain to hear some of the awesome truth of God.

Christ is going to return to earth this time as the King of Kings and Lord of Lords in exactly the way He tells us He is going to in His Word. He, along with His elect, will rule with a rod of iron in the government of God right here on earth until all of mankind learns to respect, recognize, accept, believe, and follow the One who has always claimed to be the Savior of all of mankind without one exception, which the counterfeit Christian church refuses to accept and believe as His spoken truth. They rejoice, sing, dance, have visions of sugar plums dancing around in their heads and are happy that they think they will be saved, but balk and smart like having a nest of fire ants way deep down in their bones in even thinking that God is going to save us all.

We are going to be here on earth with our older brother Jesus Christ, with our Almighty God and Father of all that exists, and it is going to last forever, and we are always going to have meaningful, interesting, inspiring, and God-oriented work to do. It is all going to be happening right here on earth, where God is going to be. He will be in us as we will also be in him. God is going to *be all, in all.* To believe otherwise and to teach others to believe otherwise is calling God a liar. It is a putrid sin that stinks to high heaven in the nostrils of our God and Father.

"One God and Father of all, who is over all and through all and in all"

(Ephesians 4:6, NIV).

"For 'God has put everything under His feet.' Now when it says that everything has been put under Him, this clearly does not include the One who put everything under Him. And when all things have been subjected to Him, then the Son Himself will be made subject to Him who put all things under Him, so that God may be <u>all</u> in <u>all</u>. If these things are not so, what will those do who are baptized for the dead? If the dead are not raised at all, why are people baptized for them"

(1 Corinthians 15:27–29).

None of my family, friends, or acquaintances will ever have to spend even one nanosecond in the literal flames of a Christian-contrived hell, in pain and suffering being so severe as to be beyond the imaginations of men. And neither will any of your loved ones either. Simply because it is being taught and accepted as truth by a counterfeit Christianity that deals with falsehoods, customs, rituals, and traditions of men doesn't make it true. It is a bald-faced satanic lie of pure ignorance and ungodly deception.

Taught throughout the world by the counterfeit Christian churches that circle the globe. Those known as the Babylon of confusion, those talked about in Revelation 18:4, where God commands His people to come out of *her, (this worlds Christian religion as it is being taught today)* as He addresses them all as *His people.* If we claim to be His people, there is no way to squirm out of disobeying His command, without blatantly separating ourselves from obedience to His truth, and in so doing, we call Him a liar and make a mockery out of His omnipotence, power, and mighty majesty.

My mother, father, brothers and sisters, friends, and acquaintances will all be accounted for to live out through all eternity. The false preaching and teaching of a counterfeit Christianity will have been taken apart and dismantled forever. We will all have an immortal spirit body just like our Father God and His Son Jesus Christ. One that not only will never die, but *cannot* die. Death will already have been destroyed forever. Do we have even a small glimmer of what this means to all of us eventually?

With this little introduction into my first forty years of life, I will fairly quickly bring the last forty-five years into a conclusion. We arrive here in our declining years after learning the value of following the Word and ways of God, which has brought us up and out of the way I had become accustomed to following after. One of the first things I noticed was the fact that God had given me the initiative to quit working for others who had been skimming the top layer off for themselves, and I got that leftover amount that they deemed that I was worth to them. People have told me that I have been lucky, but to me luck has nothing at all to do with it. If we are able to prepare ourselves properly for the hard knocks of life, along with the ability to overcome them, let me say one more time, "The harder and smarter I work, the luckier I seem to get." But the real force behind it all is God's blessings for obedience.

As I have mentioned a few paragraphs back, I had gone to work at a little shop in Kalkaska, Michigan, that I did very much appreciate at the time, because I needed to work and take care of my family. They had determined that I was worth one dollar and thirty-five cents per hour. And it helped me feed my family, along with another job of ten dollars a night playing guitar on the weekends in a beer joint, which also decided I was worth ten dollars in helping them sell booze.

Along about that time, I had the opportunity to buy a house and forty acres of land as an investment, for seven hundred dollars, within a mile of where I was living. I wanted it the worst kind of way as a rock-solid investment but had to pass it up because it was taking all I was making to survive, keep a roof over our heads, and pay the mortgage on the house we were building. I couldn't borrow any money because I had shortly before filed for bankruptcy, brought on by me medicating myself with alcohol and playing smashmouth in some honky-tonk joint.

I worked in that little shop for a while until I quit and went to work as a plumber with a friend of mine. The friend and I played music in the beer joints, dance halls, and for special occasions. I went on from there and got a good-paying job as a delivery driver salesman, first of bread and other food stuffs, and then moved on to running a laundry route. A few years went by, and I had developed myself in different areas that would help me strike out on my own. I was meeting and getting acquainted with a lot of businesspeople, learning why some were successful and some were going belly up. I finally had had enough of being yanked around by people and organizations that were intent on only feathering their own nest. Paying you just enough to get by on but not any extra where you could look for a better-paying job.

I quit my job cold turkey and decided to work for myself. I had been aware of a carpet cleaning system that used a dry-cleaning method that I had tried and thought I could sell my services to others that had gotten tired of having wet carpets to deal with that often had picked up new dirt by the time they were dry and looked just as bad as they did before being cleaned. I had also heard folks in different business settings complaining about having their carpets ruined by inexperienced technicians using steam cleaning that caused their carpets to delaminate, fade, and become a sagging rag flopping around on the floor, or losing money waiting for their carpets to dry after being steam cleaned. With the information I had collected on these things, I decided to take the plunge.

I called the big gun, the head honcho of a dry-cleaning concern that sold their equipment and cleaning supplies to carpet-cleaning businesses all around the world. Their headquarters was in Racine, Wisconsin, and I had made an appointment to come over to their location for a two-day seminar on how to use their product and machinery properly. I was impressed and had been prepared to invest in machinery and cleaning supplies if things would materialize that would allow me to invest in it. I had done some little research on them and reasoned that I might be able to negotiate a dealership with them in order to sell their systems and supplies to other potential customers. It would be another source of income to help me get started.

I had borrowed fifteen hundred dollars and was able to cut a deal with them to buy two used machines and a decent amount of their cleaning supplies under the conditions that they make me a distributor of their system in lower and upper Michigan, to which they had agreed to. With little more than a mop and a pail and the courage to step out in faith, I became a professional janitor and carpet cleaner. I knew basically how I would operate; it would be on a cash basis, with no extended credit to anyone. I had been stuck too many times with other promises to pay me next week.

Along with that, I wouldn't get into a price war by undercutting my competition, where no one makes any money. To ensure that I would not be sweet-talked or intimidated into a lower price by anybody, my mother was my first customer, and I charged her the going rate that I had decided upon. To make myself keep from cutting prices to get business, I developed the attitude and business philosophy that I felt would cause me, in my own mind at least, to be successful. If I will not give my mother a lesser charge for cleaning her carpets, what chance do you think you have of making me work for less than my service is worth?

Then I had expanded quickly as folks began asking me to do other types of maintenance for them. It soon included hard-surface floors, overstuffed furniture, drapery, and smoke, vandalism, and water damage control. If anyone asked for something I didn't do, or didn't have the equipment for, I would call a competitor and pick his mind on how to go about doing it, how to charge and such. Any specific problems or drawbacks I needed to know about. Spending the right amount of time in picking the right people's minds to ensure I would be prepared enough to be able to succeed.

The next day after, that I would become a professional in that field and be able and qualified to do the job. I studied the going rate in the area and charged likewise, sometimes a little more. I had watched small business practices for a long time while I had been a delivery person over the years in food stuffs and laundry things of a rental nature as a driver salesman. I had developed a philosophy to not start undercutting anyone's prices. Too soon, no one is making any money, and I had seen several business places go belly up over the years doing it.

At one point in time, a large concern with money to burn had gotten in touch with me through a professional designer. The lady designer called me and asked me about using a fabric guard on a large handmade pure white sectional that had just been delivered to this mansion in Traverse City, Michigan. We met at the location where the sectional was. She was questioning me constantly about my qualifications. My wife, Nancy, was with me, and I had insisted we wear our dazzling white coverall uniforms with our name and logo on the back. We operated under the DBA (doing business as) name of American Carpet Cleaning Service. I had never used the product we were going to use on the super-expensive furniture, drapery, and oriental rugs that she wanted treated too. But I had talked to a distributor of the product at great lengths, and he was adamant that it would work on any material.

When we had agreed upon the price and had arrived to do the job, the designer and the owner both were there too. I tried to take my time getting set up, in hopes one or both of them would leave. Nancy and I were spreading white sheets all around this big white sectional, to absorb any overspray onto their expensive hardwood floors and to create a professional touch. I stalled as long as I could and finally realized they wanted to watch the operation. I finally got my sprayer all filled and ready to go, and both Nancy and the designer were as nervous as a cat on a hot tin roof.

I looked for them both to start to hyperventilate at any moment; I think maybe they already had. I wasn't looking forward to giving any mouth-to-mouth resuscitation to either one of them. So I pulled the trigger on the sprayer and started along the top of the sectional, and I almost fainted myself. It was turning it yellow. I knew better than to get all bug-eyed and quit spraying the fabric protector, or to even show any concern at all. I just smiled at them on the outside and kept on spraying. I didn't want Nancy to know it, but on the inside, I was beginning to think, *"Lawsuit."*

There was nothing in the world that I could do now but keep spraying the sectional. The now-white-as-a-ghost designer anxiously tapped me on the shoulder, saying, "It's turning it yellow." My heart was pounding like it was going to jump right out of my chest. But I maintained an outward appearance of being calm, composed, and together, just long enough to tell her it was the way it was supposed to work, that it would all cure out just as it was before. She breathed a sigh of relief as I continued on spraying the fabric coating on the sectional. When we had finished the job and had loaded our gear back in the van, Nancy's first question was, "What if it doesn't cure out white again, what's going to happen then?"

I told her, "We are going to know how it feels to buy a really expensive piece of furniture."

We came back the next day, and it was just as pure white as it could be. Decisions like this have to be made on a regular, almost-daily basis; but the difference is being made up for by being paid enough on every job, that if things do go sour, you have the monetary means to take care of the problem. A good lesson to learn: be competitive, but keep your service charges high enough that you will still be there tomorrow to serve your customers. Then you won't have to fold up your tent, go broke, and be back working for a dollar and thirty-five cents an hour.

Another way of putting it is this: I want to know when this old fat boy gets off the couch, loads up all of my equipment and supplies, and gets out in the middle of a tough job that is being difficult to deal with. It is all going to be well worth my time and effort, and any extra frustrations I am apt to encounter in doing the job that my customers whom I do appreciate, will be happy and satisfied with the finished product; and it will at the same time be compensating me for my spent energy, sweat, and the weight of being responsible and in authority. I can remind myself I was getting well paid for it, and no one was skimming anything off the top.

There is a lot to be said for owning and operating your own business. You are the one responsible and have to make some tough decisions; but in the long run, it is a terrific asset for any person wanting to become a leader that must step up and make decisions that can often be awkward to deal with. But I believe that is what God would like us all to be doing. We have the opportunity in this way to put what we've learned by His Word into practice. Positions of leadership have never been easy for me, and I have always tried to avoid them. However, knowing that God has a purpose and a plan for us all in the future in His Kingdom, I think we should all be learning to accept the amount of responsibility we are able to handle here and now on this earth.

Education is a wonderful thing. I wish I'd had more. Wisdom, knowledge, and understanding are right up near the top on the list of things to cause one to succeed in life. The more a person knows, academically as well as what life along the way can teach us, the more likely we are to have a decent income on which to marry, raise a family, support our communities, and be able to become successful in life. Success means different things to different people. To some, it is the acquiring of assets and money in great and massive amounts. No matter who you may have had to walk over and stomp down in the dust to get there.

Knowing that it equates with having power and control over others. Money and power corrupt, the greater massing of money and power that one can lay up for themselves, the greater possibility exists as well of the greater corruption along the way to get there. I have noticed in life that those with great power, quite often are those with great weaknesses too. It can usually mean that during their journey of acquiring, they have had to step on a lot of toes, been involved in shady deals, backstabbing, lying, stealing, and cheating that has caused them to become successful but also corrupted.

I very much value academic education and the ability of one to be able to talk, write, and communicate correctly in accordance to our English language, and I wish that I had the capability to do it properly too. To help me to more properly be able to communicate in proper English, in sentence structure, spelling and punctuation, which words to capitalize to reach the mind and heart of others, with the true message of God that is now, has been, and will continue to be polluted, distorted, and made of no effect by the counterfeit Christian church, who accepts, believes, and teaches a totally false gospel to their gullible flocks.

Flocks being interested only in a brick-and-mortar church that they can feel a connection to through their sight, thinking, feeling, and their herdlike instincts for a connection with others of like mind and feelings. A visible sign that identifies it as being a church. Accepting, believing, and teaching the customs, rituals, and the traditions of men, as opposed to the truth of God. Soon the church itself crowds out the teaching of God from being first in our lives. It will have become a part of our empirical self as God gets put in His place on a back burner. A church that accepts, believes, and teaches one hundred and eighty degrees opposite of the Word and way of God. One with a pagan cross on its roof, a pagan steeple to adorn it too, with ministers of Satan masquerading as angels of light and apostles of Christ. Do they ever wonder what God has to say about it?

> *"For such men are false apostles, deceitful workers, masquerading as apostles of Christ. And no wonder, for Satan himself masquerades as an angel of light. It is not surprising, then, if his servants masquerade as servants of righteousness. Their end will correspond to their actions"*
>
> (2 Corinthians 11:13–15).

I cannot offer any impressive college-earned letters after or before my name. I do not claim, and never have claimed, that I am the sharpest tool in the shed. But I can offer something of much greater importance and of far greater value that can, and does by far, outweigh many theology professors in the understanding and teaching of the Word of God. As Jesus Christ has been my mentor and teacher now for over a half century, He has been shining a light upon the Word of God and has given me an understanding now, beyond that of most every so-called Christian church or theologian around this world in which we live. We need to remember that the disciples of Christ were unlearned men themselves. So I am not making such an outlandish claim as it might seem at first glance.

> *"When they saw the courage of Peter and John and realized that they were unschooled, ordinary men, they were astonished and they took note that these men had been with Jesus"*
>
> (Acts 4:13).

If God had not called me those fiftysome years ago as He did, to teach me His truth, I would be just as mixed up, misinformed, and confused as the counterfeit Christian church, known too as the Babylon of confusion, find themselves today. You shouldn't believe me just because I tell you this to be true, but you should believe it when God has left it recorded for you, myself, and all of mankind to accept, believe, and to follow. If one is not being called today, we all will be at the time that God determines it should happen.

> *"'Stop grumbling among yourselves,' Jesus answered. 'No one can come to me unless the Father who sent me draws them, and I will raise them up at the last day. It is written in the Prophets: 'They will all be taught by God.' Everyone who has heard the Father and learned from him comes to me"*
>
> (John 6:43–45).

Please notice, that God affirms that we will all be taught by Himself. He has been tutoring and teaching me now for at least the past fifty-four years. Now I have come to accept and believe that it might well be ever since my birth and before I was even born. There came a time when I sensed that God was obviously sending me signals and telling me that He had mentored me long enough—I now needed to get off the Pablum baby food of His Word and begin teaching others by adding some real and strong meat to it.

As this book illustrates the fact that I have accepted the leading of His Holy Spirit and am now involving myself in teaching His awesome Good News about the coming of His Kingdom that will within the appointed time and season of His will soon begin when Christ returns to establish the Kingdom of God upon this sin-sick world. We have all been admonished by our brother Jesus Christ to pray thusly.

> *"So then, this is how you should pray: 'Our Father in heaven, hallowed be Your name, Your kingdom come, Your will be done, on earth as it is in heaven'"*
>
> (Matthew 6:9–10)

> *"May your Kingdom come soon. May your will be done on earth, as it is in heaven"*
>
> (Matthew 6:10, NLT).

Much of my education came about in a way different than many others. I had had enough of academic education. I wanted to get on with life and see the world and the things that it held for me to learn from. I quit school after completing the ninth grade and joined the army in 1949. I spent three and a half years in my education of hard knocks. I was discharged in 1952, got married to my sweetheart, and soon began to raise two little kids. The three of them were the light of my life. I soon ended up driving truck cross country. One day I was headed to Minnesota with a load of speedboats. I was stopped by a state police trooper for being loaded too high. It was during a time they were trying to recruit more troopers. He noticed on my driver's license that I qualified physically and tried to recruit me.

I told him I had not graduated high school. He told me it wasn't a problem and told me where to go to get a GED test for a high school equivalency diploma, to see if I could qualify. I had gone down to the Rackham Building in Ann Arbor, Michigan, and took the test. I had gotten the results within a few days, which indicated an education level of two years of college. It qualified me for the state police, but being an over-the-road trucker, I had gotten too many speeding tickets to allow me to be a trooper.

But it was not all for naught. I had learned for myself that in the school of hard knocks that God had put me through while putting me on His potter's wheel and working with this difficult lump of clay that I was, He was also smashing me down and reworking me until I began to meet His specifications. It had paid great dividends. God has given me a thirst for knowledge, and with the knowledge explosion available nowadays on the Internet, I spend much time seeking and searching for answers to satisfy my questioning mind. Without the knowledge of God, we would all be left without a focal point from which to start learning the truth.

THE MASTER PLAN OF GOD

As far-fetched as it might sound to a mind to which God has not yet revealed His master plan of the redemption and salvation of all mankind to, it is closing in on this world and coming to its God planned conclusion. Let us once more consider the size, scope, magnitude, and endless reaches of this universe in which we live, and which is still expanding at the speed of light. Light that travels at 186,000 miles per second. At that speed it takes light four years to reach the nearest star.

The light reflected from the surface of the moon takes only a second to reach Earth. The sun is more than eight light-minutes away. And so, if the light from the nearest star (Alpha Centauri) takes more than four years to reach us, we're seeing that star four years in the past. Take a little time thinking on this and how it might fit into our eventual immortal and spirit life. When God has brought us all up to maturity, to have life as He and His Son Jesus Christ have life. What an absolutely amazing future we have to anticipate and to look forward to. Space beyond measure that we as immortal spirit beings will have before us to develop and create in forever, without any end.

The plan of God is something that the brightest minds and most respected scholars are unable to grasp or explain with any concrete degree of absolute certainty. It is being revealed to a few in basic terms, that we as yet in the juvenile stage can begin to understand. Given to a small number of people today, known as the elect of God. If God does not reveal it to us, we cannot understand it. And yet, it is all being explained for us in the Word of God. We read right on past it looking for His truth when we are seeing it with our own eyes and holding it in our own hands.

I am reminded of the story of a man, his wife, and little kids who had a little homestead out west, with a stream running through it. More than anything else, the man wanted to be rich, as he panned for gold every day in that little creek, and the only thing he ever found in the creek was a big old rock he had to move out of the way to pan for gold beneath it. He had taken it into the house and was using it for a doorstop. He was barely able to feed his family, as he had given up working his little homestead. He finally had had enough of toil and strife and through his hands up in disgust and despair. He left his wife and little kids to fend for themselves and went out to the California gold fields to become rich and successful.

Years had gone by, and he finally had died a pauper, a sad and lonely old man without a penny to his name. His family had now grown up, and his son had become a successful geologist, and the whole family was being cared for in good fashion now. Visiting the old homestead of years back to settle the final estate, the son noticed for the first time the big old rock doorstop. He now knew at first glance that it possessed great value. Having it assayed, he found it worth many hundreds of thousands of dollars. How often do we go through life looking for riches somewhere else as this old man did, only to find out it was right in our midst all along?

It is no longer any mystery for those whose minds God has opened to His understanding. Strange things are happening here on planet Earth that defy the ability of man to grasp and to understand them without the revelation of God, the creator of all. Listen carefully to me here, my brothers, sisters, and friends. Because it is the aforeplanned destiny of all creation that God put into effect before the world began. None of us have to leave and go anywhere to find the great unsearchable riches beyond our imaginations. This is where we have been planted; this is where we need to grow. Jesus Christ, the greatest hidden treasure ever known, is in our midst at all times. He will never ever leave nor forsake us. He is hiding in plain sight in the Bible on our nightstand. Pick it up, dust it off, read it, accept what it says, believe it ask God to open your mind and come out of the Babylon of confusion (Revelation 18:4).

The strangest thing of all, has been put right before our eyes in His Word, but most fail to accept the truth and to believe God and His Son Jesus Christ. Get ready to be shocked out of your socks. This great and wonderful orb that we all call Earth and home has been chosen and put into the exact location that God handpicked to be the center of all future activity. A gigantic, awesome, and most powerful kingdom that will forever exist, to cover and govern the entire universe. And all of us are going to be a part of it. Out from our Father God came our older brother Jesus Christ. Then out from Jesus Christ came all that exists everywhere.

"In whom we have redemption, the forgiveness of sins. The Son is the image of the invisible God, the firstborn over all creation. For in Him all things were created, things in heaven and on earth, visible and invisible, whether thrones or dominions or rulers or authorities. All things were created through Him and for Him" (Colossians 1:14–16).

CROSS REFERENCES

"Also, I will make him my firstborn, higher than the kings of the earth"

(Psalm 89:27).

No one has ever seen God, but the one and only Son, who is himself God and is in closest relationship with the Father, has made him known"

(John 1:18, NIV).

"Jesus answered: 'Don't you know me, Philip, even after I have been among you such a long time? Anyone who has seen me has seen the Father. How can you say, 'Show us the Father'"

(John 14:9).

"For those whom He foreknew [and loved and chose beforehand], *He also predestined to be conformed to the image of His Son* [and ultimately share in His complete sanctification], *so that He would be the firstborn* [the most beloved and honored] *among many believers"*

(Romans 8:29).

"The god of this age (Satan) *has blinded the minds of unbelievers so they cannot see the light of the gospel of the glory of Christ, who is the image of God"*

(2 Corinthians 4:4).

Now to the King eternal, immortal, and invisible, the only God, be honor and glory forever and ever. Amen"

(1 Timothy 1:17).

By faith Moses left Egypt, not fearing the king's anger; he persevered because he saw Him who is invisible"

(Hebrews 11:27).

Collusions 1:13-15 (KJV) *Who hath delivered us from the power of darkness, and hath translated us into the kingdom of his dear Son: In whom we have redemption through his blood, even the forgiveness of sins: Who is the image of the invisible God, the firstborn of every creature:*

Now I ask you, should we sit in the front-row seat in any of or all the counterfeit Christian churches around the world and add our "Amen" to the preacher at the podium who week after week, month after month, and year after year continues to preach and teach a contrary message of customs, rituals, and traditions to the congregation instead of the actual and real truth of God? Well, my friends, neighbors, acquaintances, and family members, as much as any of us might desire to know and understand the truth of God. I pray that God will open the mind up to receive His truth that I write about here today, that it might strike a chord in you the individual, the reader. I ask God that He might allow this truth to take root and grow into a lifelong passion for even more truth. I ask it now in the name of Jesus Christ. Amen!

If we accept and believe His truth alone, it is a virtual impossibility for us to ever believe and accept the wisdom and teaching coming out of the Babylon of confusion. Unless or until God calls them and opens their mind to receive it, and then they begin teaching it. Understanding the truth of God cannot and will not happen according to Jesus Christ, by any amount of work and energy spent in their attempt at coming to Jesus Christ on their own terms. *"No man can come to me (Christ), except the Father which hath sent me draw him: and I will raise him up at the last day"* (John 6:44).

The Spirit gives life; the flesh counts for nothing. The words I have spoken to you, "they are full of the Spirit and life. Yet there are some of you who do not believe" For Jesus had known from the beginning which of them did not believe and who would betray him. He went on to say, "This is why I told you that no one can come to me unless the Father has enabled them." From this time many of his disciples turned back and no longer followed him. "You do not want to leave too, do you?" Jesus asked the

Twelve. Simon Peter answered him, "Lord, to whom shall we go? You have the words of eternal life. We have come to believe and to know that you are the Holy One of God."

(John 6:63–69)

We can see by the words that Christ has spoken in the above scripture of the cause of people leaving and reconnecting themselves to the false teachings of their day, and the exact same thing is happening all around the world today. Counterfeit Christianity continues on building their massive brick-and-mortar churches, their megachurches that impress the minds of their naïve Satan-influenced followers. Supposing that the rich and opulent objects they worship in place of God in the church building itself, such as their gold or jewel-covered ornaments, their multiple thousand-dollar diamond chandeliers, or the solid gold crosses they enjoy having on display, to bow down to secretly in their heart of hearts. All being paid for and sustained by the poor and less fortunate within our society.

They sit in their pews every week sucking up swill from the table of demons who have them locked into the custom, ritual and traditions of men, while turning their collective backs upon the true Word of God. They make good-sounding sermons for and about things for the ears of the ones they have already confused, and where they want to keep those confused that are void of any truth at all. Void because they have settled for the customs, rituals, and the traditions of men instead of believing the true Word of God. They are no doubt at all the people of God, because that is how He has identified them in the book of Revelation, where He has this to say to them all. *"Come out of her MY PEOPLE"* (Revelation 18:4). A command to come out of the Babylon of confusion, this world's Christian religion around the world.

There is no shortage in their talking about God and His Son Jesus Christ, but they refuse to accept and to believe that Christ is who He claims to be, the Savior of all mankind. Setting themselves up at the return of Christ to hear him declare the following:

Not everyone that saith unto me, Lord, Lord, shall enter into the kingdom of heaven; but he that doeth the will of my Father which is in heaven. Many will say to me in that day, Lord, Lord, have we not prophesied in thy name? and in thy name have cast out devils? and in thy name done many wonderful works? And then will I profess unto them, I never knew you: depart from me, ye that work iniquity.

(Matthew 7:21–23)

God in His creating Jesus Christ first, calling Him the first fruit, is reproducing Himself, first in Christ, then in all of mankind. We have the absolute and certain good reason to literally call Him our Father, because we are part of Him, and He is part of us. He really is our Father, and Christ is our older brother. We are in Them, they are in us, we have the DNA of God pulsating in, around, and throughout our existing being; and afterward our brother Jesus Christ reconciles all things back into God the Father, and then submits Himself back under the rule and authority of God the Father.

Death will have been destroyed and will no longer exist. At that point, we all will have life as God and Christ have life. We will all have immortal spirit life that can never die. God will be all in all, the purpose and plan of God will have come to maturity. I know I am repeating myself as we go along here, but if the Word of God is in any way important to you who read these words, perhaps some of it will stick in your mind long enough that you will exercise the mind that God has given you and, like the Bereans, study to show yourselves to be approved.

Throughout this book, I have suggested that I am or will be one of the elect of God. Called, chosen, and set aside to rule with Jesus Christ at His return. While I have reason to believe that I indeed might be, I have no way of knowing for certain. The scripture tells us that many are called but few will be chosen. Most of those familiar with the Word of God believe the number of the elect to be one hundred and forty-four thousand to be chosen, twelve thousand from each tribe of Israel, from all the way back to Adam and Eve. I realize that for me to think that I will belong in that number is against the astronomical odds. Only God knows who will be in that number. With that being said, I must say that while I never have had the proclivity, aptitude, or the desire to lead others, I at least can see now why I should be developing the ability to do so. I will continue to do the best that I can now to make myself ready to fill that position of responsibility if Christ calls upon me to do so.

Be that as it may be, though, I do not wish to be where I do not belong and where God has not called me to be, and I am certain that God will not put me where I do not belong. We will all be placed and belong exactly where God decides we fit within His Kingdom, within His purpose and plan for us. I anxiously await and look forward to that day and time when God will reveal to each of us our individual position in His Kingdom. While I pray for His Kingdom to come, His will to be done on earth as it is in heaven, asking that he speed that day to its conclusion. To put a stop to the evil, anti-God direction that the god of this world *(Satan)* has been leading us into. This all I give thanks for and ask in the name of His Son Jesus Christ. Amen!

I believe that God used my military experience of some of the most ungodly sights, sounds, and misery beyond the imaginations of men, to cause me to be pliable in His hands. If you are finding out things in this book that strike a chord in your heart and mind as to being the actual truth of God, God may be also calling you for a position of responsibility in His soon-coming kingdom also. He has softened me up to become a usable tool that He will be able to use within His purpose and plan for the redemption, reconciliation, and the salvation of all of mankind without even one exception. Not only my wartime experiences alone, but from life from my mother's womb, until my death.

I do not believe that I am alone in this, nor are any or all of my experiences. It is just the way that God works in bringing His children that He loves unconditionally, into His awesome and Almighty plan for all eternity. That applies to all who read these words here as well. God uses our great weaknesses eventually for His purpose of bringing us all up to the god level of existence, to be as He and His Son Jesus Christ now are. To have immortal, spirit life, to have life as God and Jesus Christ have life.

So, my friends, my brothers and sisters in the Lord and Savior Jesus Christ, and to all my military comrades, whether dead or alive. To all who have ever lived, who live now or ever will live, be of good cheer. Your salvation is certain. Jesus Christ has paid the total cost for all sins for all time. Our lives all began in God our Father, and that is where we will remain forever. We are in God, He is in us; and after death has been destroyed, God will *be all in all*.

> *"For He* (Christ) *must reign until He has put all His enemies under His feet. The last enemy to be destroyed s death. For 'God has put everything under His feet.' Now when it says that everything has been put under Him, this clearly does not include the One who put everything under Him. When he has done this, then the Son himself will be made subject to him who put everything under him, so that God may be all in all"*
>
> (1 Corinthians 15:25–28)

We are able to discern here by the true word of God, beyond any shadow of a doubt that God the Father and Jesus Christ are not coequals, as the Babylon of confusion believes, teaches, and accepts as the truth of God. Calling our Almighty God, a triune god, a three-in-one god, a supposed closed trinity of God the Father, Jesus Christ, and the Holy Spirit. That is absolute Satanism 101, no truth at all. God, instead of being a closed-off Trinity, is instead bringing all the god-kind made like Himself and his firstborn Son Jesus Christ, into the God Family. God the Father is over all else through the entire universe and beyond. Is now, always has been, and always will be. All things have been brought into existence to serve His good purpose and plan from before the beginning of time.

"CHRIST CAME HERE TO BE LIKE US, THAT WE ALL WILL BE AS HE IS"

IN THIS BOOK, I HAVE TRIED TO SHOW by my personal experiences in life and in the kill-or-be-killed situation a person finds themselves in, in a war zone, and especially so in frontline combat where it becomes your job and your obligation to kill and destroy others made in the image and likeness of God as we human beings all find ourselves in. Life under the normal everyday circumstances can in itself be tough and demanding for most all of us. Adding to that the shock and awe of one being shoved into being a government hunter involved in either running down and killing our enemies or having them in return doing the same thing to us, adds another element that has the potential to cause many different problems in the spirit, mind, heart, soul, and emotional makeup of a person.

I have documented some of those things for you to consider throughout this book. Whether good, bad, or indifferent, which changes any individual into having a different mind-set, you become a different person in many differing ways. Each of us within our makeup and back ground would likely be affected in differing degrees by having gone through a similar experience. Take, for instance, the boy who sat beside me on the hospital plane that brought us back home to the United States of America. The kid that had his jaw shot or blown off in the battlefields of Korea and talked through a hole in his neck where his mouth used to be will never be the same person again no matter how long he lives. He looked at the world around him in an altogether different way than he did when he left home. Much of the change in him may have been caused by how others were looking at him.

Or the redheaded boy who sat all trussed up in a straitjacket in the aisle of the plane like an animal after losing his mind in seeing too much of the warring of humanity against itself, while being in the blood and gore of combat. Not being allowed to be loosed for even a second, for fear he would damage himself or other badly wounded men on the plane loaded to the max with every wound known to mankind. All he was able to do was to growl and snap like a dog at anyone who came close to him. Or like the marine pilot also lying in the aisle in a full body cast with only part of his face exposed. In absolute and total dependence on others to care for his well-being. Then adding to that the multiple thousands upon thousands of others going home with mangled bodies, broken spirits, depressed minds, and a mixed-up thought process that is still trying to cope with this new life that has been thrust upon them.

All these thousands of damaged human beings would have at some point in life have to make a conscious decision. A decision in the direction he or she would choose to go in. Would they allow it to become a giant stumbling block to grind themselves down even more, or would they resolve to rise above their damaged condition and use the change in their looks, in their mental state and perception, in their physical condition, in their emotional change, in their spiritual and personal life to move on and overcome everything standing in their pathway, to become all that God has put us here for and expects of us? We know the answer to this from past accomplishments of many who have been there and done that, such as these five who come immediately to mind in John McCain, Bob Dole, JFK, Daniel Krauthammer, and Christopher Reeve. Google up Krauthammer and Reeve to understand how they both overcame impossible odds in accidents that had left them both quadriplegic. They both went on to attain great wealth and status during their life after being paralyzed.

So then, my friends, whoever we are, wherever we live, and no matter what afflictions befall us in our life's journey here on planet Earth, it is all in the grand design that God has put into place to reproduce Himself in all of mankind without one exception. We are all designed to become as He and His Son Jesus Christ now are, to become immortal spirit beings, and to have life everlasting as He and Christ have life. It is all in perfect accordance with the purpose and plan of God from before the beginning of the world. God works all things out through the power, might, authority, and purpose of His own will.

This is truth that only a select few of His people accept as the truth, believe, and teach unto others who cannot yet grasp it. Check it out here in Ephesians. In whom also we have obtained an inheritance, being predestinated according to the purpose of him who worketh *all things* after the counsel of *his own will*" (Ephesians 1:11). What part, then, is there for us wormlike human beings in comparison to God, left to do to secure our own salvation? One must decide on whom to follow and whom to worship and whom to believe. Will it be your deceived Christian church and its ministers of Satan masquerading as an angel of light?

Will it be scientific theories that are the most reliable, rigorous, and comprehensive form of scientific knowledge in contrast to the more common uses of the word *theory* that imply that something is unproven or speculative, which in formal terms is better characterized by the word *hypothesis*, or will it be the Almighty God of all heaven and earth? We must learn to determine and test the source of the words being used: are they from God, or are they from the world? There are two kinds of wisdom, knowledge, and understanding. One is acquired knowledge from the world of trial and error. The other is revealed knowledge that comes to us by the true Word of God.

We must learn the true word of God.

And the only place it is available is in the Word of God. We cannot learn it unless or until God reveals it to us, and even then, He *(Christ)* will give us only what we can bear to hear at any time.

(John 16:12)

As you know already, I do not claim to be anything beyond an ambassador of God and Jesus Christ. I have been called by God to represent Him and teach His truth. My citizenship is not of this world—it is in and of the kingdom of God to be administered right here on earth where the administrative government of God will go forth all around the world and in fact and in truth throughout the universe. It is the reason that God has admonished us to pray thusly. "Thy kingdom *come*, thy *will* be done *on earth* as it is in heaven."

The Word of God tells us this in 1 John 2:27, "But the anointing which ye have received of him abideth in you, and *ye need not that any man teach you*: but as the same anointing teacheth you of all things, and is truth, and is no lie, and even as it hath taught you, ye shall abide in him."

"The Spirit of truth. The world cannot receive Him, because it neither sees Him nor knows Him. But you do know Him, for He abides with you and will be in you"

(John 14:17).

"But the Advocate, the Holy Spirit, whom the Father will send in My name, will teach you all things and will remind you of everything I have told you"

(John 14:26).

"I still have much to tell you, but you cannot yet bear to hear it"

(John 16:12).

So go ahead and go to the church of your choice if you are willing to exercise the Berean policy of checking up on your teachers to see what truth is and what is not truth. I can tell you ahead of time, all you will be getting is a heavy dose of customs, rituals, and traditions with another heavy dose of paganism and idolatry. To eventually be hearing this from God at the resurrection: "Depart from me you that work iniquity, I know you not."

"But he will say, ?I tell you, I don't know you or where you're from. Get away from me, all you evildoers!"

(Luke 13:27)

"Then I will tell them plainly, 'I never knew you; depart from Me, you workers of lawlessness'"

(Matthew 7:23)

That is at the first resurrection where only the elect of God are going to be saved and brought into their immortal, spirit image to serve with Jesus Christ for a thousand years. At the great white throne of judgment, also known as the second resurrection, all of mankind who have ever lived, the great masses of mankind will be brought into the kingdom of God by way of the symbolic fire—not literal fire of God that He tells us He is in.

(Hebrews 12:29)

Our God is a consuming fire. The fire of God that purifies and makes righteous all of mankind. It is the fire of God that saves and makes righteous; all else will be burned up and destroyed.

"If any man's work shall be burned, he shall suffer loss: but he himself shall be saved; yet so as by fire"

(1 Corinthians 1:15)

A good portion of my book deals with war and its consequences, but to me it becomes difficult to talk about life on any level and leave God out of the equation. Somehow it doesn't make for a complete understanding on any matter to leave the Creator and God of all things not being addressed in the scheme of things. Especially if we consider where we are all going to end up in our service, worship, and interacting with God and all of our spiritual counterparts of immortal substance made in the image and likeness of God. Having attained the ultimate then in becoming full-fledged gods ourselves to conquer, explore, develop, and create throughout the vastness of the universe as we all have been designed to be able to do. It is exactly what we have been created to do for all of eternity.

But it is not something you will be hearing in your church, because they refuse to believe it and accept it as the truth of God themselves. God has not revealed it to them yet. That is why it is of paramount importance that we invite God into our lives, that

His Holy Spirit dwell in us and lead us into all truth as His Word tells us. I feel that God is actually using me, a high school dropout with a ninth-grade education, as a proof of His ability to raise up stones if need be as children of Abraham to rule with Christ. Christ corrects the mind-set of His people for claiming that Abraham was their father. He knew Abraham was their father while going contrary to His Word and His way. *"And do not presume to say to yourselves, 'We have Abraham as our father.' For I tell you that out of these stones God can raise up children for Abraham"* (Matthew 3:9). I am a stone, then, being raised up to be a part of the foundation of the kingdom of God.

To bring His truth to many who otherwise would not or could not ever come to His wonderful understanding. Here He is telling His people in John 8:37, *"I know you are Abraham's descendants, but you are trying to kill Me because My word has no place within you."* Nothing has changed since that time; His own people refuse to believe Him and accept His Word as truth yet to this day. Hate is the spirit of murder, and His message is still being hated by His people. They do not want to hear it. I am telling you that truth right here, and you do not believe it or want to hear it now any more than His people that crucified Him two thousand years ago wanted to hear it.

War is hell on earth, my friends, as I have documented it, laid out, and exposed some of the things that have happened in my life on the battlefields of Korea. And yet as everything else that happens to us, that can cause untold negative trauma, personal tribulations, sleepless night terrors, a constant troubled mind, and so many other maladies too numerous to mention. In reality, every cloud, no matter how dark, seems to have a silver lining of a positive nature as well. I count all that I have gone through in life, including my wartime experience in Korea, as a great and wonderful blessing of untold value. I do hope that I have gleaned enough from it all not to have to go through it again.

A priceless pearl, a rare jewel beyond any monetary amount in all of heaven and earth, an irrevocable gift of God that can never be outdone or taken away. Like others before me, I had been driven to my knees and found myself back on the potter's wheel of God, again and again, to be pummeled around and beaten down into a workable piece of clay in the hands of the potter, to finally be used by God the Master Potter. I have gone through the fire of God that He tells us He is in *Hebrews 12:29*. *"For our God is a consuming fire."* Not a literal fire, lest it cause confusion in your mind to accept the Christian hell myth as truth, but a symbolic fire that is destroying all unrighteousness.

> Therefore, this gift of truth that God has given me is by far the greatest gift that I will ever get, either in this life or in the life to come. Christ is giving this truth to me in amounts that I can bear. He tells me that I cannot bear to get it all at once, that He has

much more to reveal to me. *"I have yet many things to say unto you, but ye cannot bear them now. Howbeit when he, the Spirit of truth, is come, he will guide you into all truth: for he shall not speak of himself; but whatsoever he shall hear, that shall he speak: and he will shew you things to come. He shall glorify me: for he shall receive of mine and shall shew it unto you"*

(John 16:12–14, KJV).

The often-repeated quote that tells us that what God will bring us to, He will also bring us through, has been true to me in my case many different times in different places and for different reasons. I have been attacked by a knife-wielding madman at least three different times and only getting hurt by one of them. I have had two cocked and loaded .45-caliber government-issue pistols aimed at my head with the promise to shoot me, and neither one did. I was lured into a cemetery to be waylaid by the husband of my drunken cousin and another drunk living in our area, and their plot was foiled.

I rolled a loaded propane tanker over with ten thousand gallons of volatile product inside on Easter Sunday 1977 with no injuries at all, while the truck I was driving at the time was being torn apart. I have had two other roll-over accidents with different cars without any injuries. While closing in on the enemy, I was sitting down on the skyline of a hill in Korea eating a can of C-ration beans and franks in plain sight of our Chinese enemies a hundred yards or so away when they began shooting at me. A comrade grabbed me and dragged me out of sight cursing me out for being brain dead and not knowing they were shooting at me, but I didn't get hit.

I had been in combat directly in front of an incoming Burp gun fire in the hands of multiple Chinese soldiers that carried them in the first wave in their bonsai attacks against us. They filled the air with an immense and overwhelming amount of hot lead, and yet I was never hit myself. I saw others drop dead around me, without getting a scratch myself. I came close many times in my life, narrowly escaping death by the skin of my teeth, by a split second here and an inch or two there. I know there are many others that have experienced these things too and feel guilty about having their life being spared to live on another day, while others around them have to die. And especially so if it be in frontline combat. I have never felt guilty about it, just extremely thankful to God.

I know He created me and accepts all responsibility for me, as He does for you too. We do not have to suffer and agonize about going to hell or being done away with altogether. God has a purpose and plan for every last person who has ever lived on this earth. He accepts all responsibility upon Himself to see to it that He bring us all up to His own level of immortal, spirit life. To have life just the same as His Son and Himself have life. We are not required to jump through any spiritual hoops to get there either. The sacrifice of Jesus Christ paid the God required price for all sin and for all time.

For whatever reason that I may never know, it has of late come to mind that He has had a use for that which He has mentored and trained me for the past fiftysome years and more. I have been tutored by God through a speaking club patterned after Toastmasters International several different times. Tutored to think, act, and speak on my feet and to be able to write and to articulate my thoughts and beliefs in simple-to-understand words that others can understand and identify with. In short, I acknowledge, accept, and recognize that God is using me to confound the mighty. See how His Word explains it below in 1 Corinthians 1:18–28.

> For the preaching of the cross is to them that perish foolishness; *[they will likely not ever in this lifetime accept and believe the truth of God, however at the great white throne judgment they will all accept and believe His truth]* but unto us which are saved it is the power of God. For it is written, I will destroy the wisdom of the wise *[the so called brilliant seminary taught theology professors and their holier than thou crowd]* and will bring to nothing the understanding of the prudent. Where is the wise? where is the scribe? where is the disputer of this world? hath not God made foolish the wisdom of this world? *[those made up of His people written about in Revelation 18:4, where God commands us all to come out of her, this world wide false Christian teaching]* For after that in the wisdom of God the *(the counterfeit Christian)* world by wisdom *knew not God*, it pleased God by the foolishness of preaching to save them that believe. For the Jews require a sign, and the Greeks seek after wisdom: But we preach Christ crucified, unto the Jews a stumbling block, and unto the Greeks foolishness; But unto them which are called, both Jews and Greeks, Christ the power of God, and the wisdom of God. *(it behooves us to accept and to believe His truth, yet very few Christians actually do, being happier and more content in following after custom, ritual and traditions of men instead of the Word and way of God, as they remain joined at the hip with paganism and idolatry)* Because the foolishness of God is wiser than men; and the weakness of God is stronger than men. For ye see your calling, brethren, how that *not many wise men* after the flesh, not *many mighty*, not *many noble*, are called: *[I don't claim to be any of these, any wisdom and understanding I have, God has given it to me]* But God hath chosen *(me and others like me)* the *foolish things* of the world to confound the wise; and God hath chosen the weak things of the world *[like me and others]* to confound the things which are mighty; And base things of the world, and things which are despised, hath God chosen, yea, and things which are not, to bring to nought things that are: That no flesh should glory in his presence. But of him are ye in Christ Jesus, who of God is made unto us wisdom, and righteousness, and sanctification, and redemption: That, according as it is written, He that glorieth, let him glory in the Lord.

This book was intended to be mostly about my military action in a war zone and my frontline experience of being in combat against others made in the image and likeness of God. When my hand starts toward the letters on my computer keyboard, they just instinctively seem to go where my spirit, heart, and mind mostly dwell upon, and that happens to be the Word of God—the only real truth available throughout the universe. Our Almighty God works in mysterious ways, His ways are unfathomable, He customarily turns bad things into good things to encourage, to uplift and bless His children, who we all are. Every time I look into His Word, I find another scripture that becomes my favorite. Here is one recorded below in Genesis.

> *"As for you, you meant evil against me, but God meant it for good, to bring it about that many people should be kept alive, as they are today"*
>
> (Genesis 50:20*)*

What a great thing it is to know, realize, and understand the unadulterated truth of God, that the world that surrounds us is being filled with all kinds of evil and sinister folks looking to take advantage of us at every turn in the road when we let our guard down and put our trust and confidence in people instead of God. People who are always on the lookout for an unsuspecting new pigeon to pluck and take things from them that they have worked hard all of their lives for. Yet God, as the scripture declares, tells us that they meant it as evil against us, but God meant it for our good. We worship and serve a God of unbounded wisdom, understanding, and power to achieve His purpose and plan for all of us, His children. Not a single one to be denied salvation, becoming as God and Christ now are—immortal spirit entities.

Christians around the world have been afflicted with a terribly contagious disease, the more time they spend in their church that has now become a part of their empirical self. The more inclined they are to come down with this nearly incurable disease, while God takes a back seat in their spiritual lives. The disease of which I speak is their almost-universal acceptance and belief etched in granite on their hearts, minds, and psyches. They believe that God is going to save them, of that there is no question; but they one and all stick to the false teaching brought to them by a confused and counterfeit Christian teaching that most all others are to be annihilated and done away with altogether.

Or the other alternative for them would require that they be relegated to spend all of eternity, trillions upon trillions of years of torment and torture, alive in the raging flames of hell. Being quite happy and smug themselves, in their lofty holier-than-thou mind-set, certain of their own salvation but in denial of the Word of God plainly telling us that He will save all. They quite simply do not want to believe that Jesus Christ is who He claims to be, the Savior of all of mankind without exception. The way to diagnose their malady by name is to recognize it as it really is—*self-righteousness*. They do not want to even entertain or think about the possibility that God would save those they consider so far beneath themselves.

I have tried to give the reader of this book a thumbnail sketch of what happens on the battlefields where wars are being fought on a regular basis. Along with that, as the title reflects, I want folks to understand some of the aftereffects on the human heart, mind, spirit, emotions, and the direction that it drives different folks into after the war. In my case, I feel God has used it all to steer me into a positive direction to be useful to Himself and to give me the means, passion, and desire to write about and support His Word and the way that He admonishes each one of us in the proper direction we must go in accordance with His perfect instructions.

God is not a respecter of persons. I do not believe I have a direct and special line or connection to God any more than anyone else does. What He has done for one, He will do for all. He continues to help me with my war demons and all other aspects of life, just the same as He does for all His children whom He loves unconditionally. Believe me, my brothers and sisters and friends, we all have a magnificent and wonderful life to look forward to. Our great, omnipotent, loving God has put into motion, and still is expanding, our universe at the rate of the speed of light, at 186,000 miles per second.

What we all have to look forward to is so far above and beyond our ability to grasp it in this physical, wormlike body in comparison to the immortal spirit bodies of God and His Son Jesus Christ, or the new immortal one God will give us all at the resurrection. My advice to all of you is to get excited. There is never ever, ever going to be anything comparable to what lies ahead for us all once we have attained full sonship of our Father God. To have life like God and Christ have life. Immortal spirit life that will never end, never to be tarnished or taken away from us, for God's gifts are irrevocable. Below is the promise of God.

ALL OF MANKIND TO BE SAVED

> "As far as the gospel is concerned, they are enemies for your sake; but as far as election is concerned, they are loved on account of the patriarchs for God's gifts and his call are *irrevocable*. Just as you who were at one time disobedient to God have now received mercy as a result of their disobedience"
>
> (Romans 11:28–30, NIV).

Do not allow your church or deceived minister of Satan masquerading as an angel of light to continue on in feeding you lies from the table of demons, telling you that you worship and serve a god lacking the power and authority to save every last man, woman, and child that has ever been born on this earth.

Unless that really is the god you want to worship and serve. But in doing so, you will be worshipping the god of this world, which is the devil and Satan according to 2 Corinthians 4:4. The god of this age *[Satan]* has blinded the minds of unbelievers, *[so-called Christians denying and being in unbelief of the true word of God]* so that they cannot see the light of the gospel that displays the glory of Christ, who is the image of God.

But as for me, I will worship and serve the God who has the know-how, power, and authority and has given us His promise to save all of creation. A God who does not shy away from letting us know the truth of that throughout His Word.

May the God of all heaven and earth bless us all with a tender, pliable heart and an open mind to receive truth with. In the name of His Son Jesus Christ, we pray and ask it here now. Amen!

A SHOT ACROSS THE BOWS, TO ALL UNPATRIOTIC COWARDS

Written by Leith Lyman Cunningham for the 4th of July 2019

WHEN I SEE OUR FLAG; I STAND IN awe of what could have been, or what could have happened down through the pages of time, up until today, if our enemies had succeeded in their attempts at bringing us down on our knees and paying tribute to them as our masters during the 20th century. It would have been a brutal blood bath unlike anything we had ever imagined before, it would have been getting even time for the Germans, to rub our noses in the dirt for defeating their so-called master race. It would have involved the taking over of our peoples to do as they pleased with, I shudder to think about it after serving time in the Korean War and being a first-hand witness, having a front row seat, to some of the most atrocious happenings beyond the imaginations of mankind, being shoved down the throats of everyone under the authority of their conqueror. There would have been no end to the suffering heaped upon our families of that time segment. The old and infirmed, the young and innocent, rape and lawlessness against the vulnerable would have become common place that would have had no option but to take it and pray to God that it would someday have an end to it.

Had the enemy defeated us in WW1 and WW2, the warring Germans by nature would have put into place some of the most stringent, evil and harsh punishment that mankind could have come up with at the time, had they prevailed and conquered us as they have tried to do before. They no doubt at all in my mind would have forced us into slavery. What the Germans couldn't think of bad enough to have been cruel and animalistic enough to suit the tortured orientated Japanese, they would have stepped in and made certain the job was being done right. Where our raw materials, produce, machinery, food stuffs of every nature and the cream of the crop of the great minds we have brought into existence here in the good old USA, would have been shipped off to Germany or Japan. Where we have been given the right and the obligation to use our American expertise for the God given purpose that is being documented throughout the pages of the Word of God, to do good, it would all have gone toward world domination and the slavery of the inhabitants of the conquered nations.

But for the ultimate purpose and plan of God from the beginning, it could all have been squandered away by the German nation and their cohorts bringing the world under their own domination, to pay all of our substance gained by our own hard work, they would have demanded from us all, that we could produce, to the bulging coffers of the Father-Land! Where we would then have had the opportunity to experience for ourselves how the Germans treated the Jews in their concentration camps. Certainly, no reader is so naive as to accept and believe the lie that The Holocaust never happened.

History Speaks: The Holocaust, also known as the Shoah, was the World War II genocide of the European Jews. Between 1941 and 1945, across German-occupied Europe, Nazi Germany and its collaborators systematically murdered some six million Jews, around two-thirds of Europe's Jewish population

Will we learn that lesson before it becomes a reality, or will we continue to set in a pan of warm water like a frog and be boiled to death first, while the movers and shakers of socialism lull us to sleep? That system that has already destroyed every other nation that has ever tried it? The Nazi *(National Socialists)* party under Hitler got so bad with inflation that the story about a guy that was walking down the street and came upon a wheel borrow filled to over flowing with money. Had dumped the money out and stole the wheel borrow.

But for the grace of God, we could all now be speaking the German language and bowing down yet to the past image of Schicklgruber. (Schicklgruber is a surname. Notable people with the surname includes: Alois Schicklgruber, better known as Alois Hitler, Austrian civil servant and the father of Adolf Hitler. Josef Schicklgruber (born 1967), Austrian footballer. Maria Schicklgruber (1795–1847), the paternal grandmother of Adolf Hitler). We could have been spending our days and nights working in stalag 13. *In Germany, stalag was a term used for prisoner-of-war camps. Stalag is a contraction of "Stammlager", itself short for Kriegsgefangenen-Mannschafts-Stammlager.* We would probably still be making sauerkraut and wienerschnitzel to peddle free of charge to the now German elite that would not have to bother working anymore after proving beyond any shadow of doubt, that they really were and are the master race.

I write this piece about our awesome, wonderful and colorful American flag and the symbolism that it conjures up within the minds and hearts of real honest hard-working loyal Americans that love our flag and our country and that staunchly and firmly stand behind and with Donald J. Trump, the President and highly honored leader of the great nation that we all live in. It is for you that have learned to respect authority as opposed to anarchy that I want to thank for your steadfastness in the face of the anti-God and anti-American liberal segment of our society such as the biased news media against all that is right and good for our nation, that spout their poisonous lies and half truths out against our president and our nation on a regular daily, hourly and minute by minute effort to reach their naive and gullible audience to program their ignorant hearts, minds and whole being. In that way they have succeeded in doing so. Anyone being missed by their broadcasts; the Hollywood elite and the left-wing socialist democrats jump right in and take up the slack. May the God of all that is, help us all to sort out fact from fiction. In the name of Jesus Christ, I pray to God and ask that He bring it about. Amen!

If we here in this great country do not make a giant course correction, and soon, we stand an almost absolute and certainty of being over thrown and relegated to slavery to some other country or group of countries. While you may question what I am saying, we all would do well to hear the word of God on this matter. Mark 3:24-25 If a kingdom is divided against itself, **it cannot stand.** <u>If a house is divided against itself,</u> **it cannot stand.** Is there one single thinking soul anywhere in our country so willingly ignorant as not to recognize how deep, wide and long the gap between the ruling classes of our nation has drifted apart since the election for a president in 2016? Will they all have to wait until we have lost our power as a nation and end up bowing down low to those who have taken us over and dictate our every action and move, before we look across the page wire fence enclosure, from the pen that has become our home, before it is too late to negotiate in good faith for the so badly needed solutions that have to be made in order for us all to remain free? But where do we start?

Abraham Lincoln said, "He has a right to criticize, who has the heart to help". Having the heart to help, I have taken it upon myself to seek out the existing laws that are already on the books of our country that govern how we treat our national symbol, the American flag. In my opinion it is not even close to being tough enough on the unpatriotic haters of our country, but that stay here to suck up all they can use for self-aggrandizement, self-interests, money by the truck load, and in opposing and thumbing their ungrateful noses at those in authority. To lazy and to uninterested lawmakers and law enforcement officials to bother doing anything about it. How long is it going to take for our law enforcement agency to step up and do the job that they are being paid and expected to do? The law is already there and is being spelled out so a child will be able to understand it. How long would it take to put a stop to this insanity of anarchy that allows this to happen on a regular basis? And if the existing laws are not strong enough to get the job done, write more stringent ones with double the penalty until they do the required job. But of course, that would mean waking up and getting someone in authority off their donkey and enforcing them.

18 U.S. Code § 700.Desecration of the flag of the United States; penalties

- U.S. Code
- Notes

(a)

(1)

Whoever knowingly mutilates, defaces, physically defiles, burns, maintains on the floor or ground, or tramples upon any <u>flag of the United States shall be fined under this title or imprisoned for not more than one year, or both.</u>

(2)

This subsection does not prohibit any conduct consisting of the disposal of a flag when it has become worn or soiled.

(b)

As used in this section, the term "<u>flag of the United States</u>" <u>means any flag of the United States, or any part thereof, made of any substance, of any size, in a form that is commonly displayed.</u>

(c)

Nothing in this section shall be construed as indicating an intent on the part of Congress to deprive any<u> State, territory, possession, or the Commonwealth of Puerto Rico of</u>

jurisdiction over any offense over which it would have jurisdiction in the absence of this section.

(d)

(1)

An appeal may be taken directly to the Supreme Court of the United States from any interlocutory or final judgment, decree, or order issued by a United States district court ruling upon the constitutionality of subsection (a).

(2)

The Supreme Court shall, if it has not previously ruled on the question, accept jurisdiction over the appeal and advance on the docket and expedite to the greatest extent possible.

(Added Pub. L. 90–381, § 1, July 5, 1968, 82 Stat. 291; amended Pub. L. 101–131, §§ 2, 3, Oct. 28, 1989, 103 Stat. 777.)

When I see our flag; it reminds me first of the great nation that God has made and is allowing and causing us to live in; in the degree of freedom, safety and plenty we have fought for during our past, present and the willingness to continue doing so in our future. May the awesome Almighty God of all that is continue to bless our nation and return a thankful and grateful mindset to all that have been given so much through the lives lost in deadly and brutal combat on some out of the way battlefield on the other side of this orb we call home.

When I see our flag; I recall going to a one room school house across the road from where we have lived for the past 58 years. It was during the 2nd world war and it was the job of us boys to take the flag out and pull it up into the shy. What it represented back then would bring tears to my eyes at times because my oldest brother Teddy was in the US Army serving in 101st Airborne at Normandy. The teacher would lead us in pledging allegiance to our beautiful flag. We would often follow up by all of us singing the song about Pearl Harbor where the Japanese sneak attack had wreaked havoc on our Naval Forces anchored there and were caught totally off guard. Where the Japanese naval forces with their bombing and strafing with 50 caliber machine guns had sunk so many ships and killed so many sailors. The USS Arizona is still there under water as a perpetual memorial for the devastation against our nation.

A total of **1,177 men** died on board, the greatest death toll ever on a US warship. Only 229 bodies were recovered. The rest remain entombed in the wreckage. A visit to the USS Arizona Memorial begins on shore in the open-air lobby of the visitor center, where each person receives a numbered ticket.

My comment; To all of you malcontents that hate our flag and are intent on destroying our nation with your vile tongue that constantly and continually drips the venom of slop and disease out of that big slit under your nose. You do not have to wait until you are entombed on the earth by a nuclear device turned loose inadvertently by a nervous hand and shaky fingers like rocket boy or anybody else, in a knee jerk movement on this earth where you live at opposing everything our president is doing to keep us from it. If perchance you are a flag hater and our country cannot do anything to please you and you are looking for a way to solve the problem that you think you have to live with and in, I have the answer. Quit your crying, sniveling and whining like a spoiled child, as you throw your unhinged snot filled, sad eyed temper tantrums, and get up off your always seeking and searching for a free meal, free medication, free love, free everything, pick up your free blankie, fold it up nice and neat and go find a giant sized toilet, jump in it and pull the chain as you wave good-by to all that is wrong with this most awesome and wonderful United States of America, compared to anywhere else on earth. If that will make you happy, but do not expect any tears from me, and our country will be better off without that which you bring to the table.

Author: Leith Lyman Cunningham, a Korean War survivor

When I see our flag; It reminds me of so many of my military comrades and buddies that fought and died in the Korean War, and yet God brought me home alive. I see the faces and remember the uniqueness of their character traits, each one of them. I can hear them laugh and see the happy smiles on their faces. I can recall when I may have gone too far in jesting them at certain times, then had to listen to them rake me over the coals. Most all of my good buddies spent a lot of time trying to get even with me, they never did, at least in my estimation, they didn't. But maybe Ernie did after all, when I stop and think about it. I had come up this slope and over a ridge in the middle of a Burp Gun attack by the swarming Chinese soldiers. A medic had Ernie propped up against a tree trying to administer first aid. When Ernie seen me, the grimace came off his face as he replaced it with a forced out laugh and said, **"ha ha you son of a bitch, I'm getting out of here before you"**. I never knew whether he lived or died.

When I see our flag; And especially so at home where I have them all over our home and property area, waving and snapping in the wind. I always remember my two best army buddies, Ernie Lee and Billy Magee. Amidst all of the flags and other decorations I built a nice memorial for them both that has been mounted on the end of our garage that faces the road. It cannot really be seen very good from the road, but the important thing is, that I know it is there, and they will not be forgotten in my lifetime. They both at different times were a big part of my life and good memories. I will include a picture of that memorial here for everyone to see and that I can assure you without any question at all, how well that I know, that both of these guys had your back on the brutal and bloody battlefields of Korea.

The memorial of granite picture I attached earlier in the veteran's park in Traverse City, Michigan that lists the battle causalities of the Korean War who gave up all of their tomorrows, that we at home would be able to enjoy all of our own today's. Billy Magee's name is on it with many others. It always helps me to remember my good buddy and best friend that joined the army together with me. His serial number was one Dijet before mine. Billy never really got a chance to live a regular life that he had to pay for in his own blood in the stinking rice paddies that so many others had to suffer and die in as they breathed their last breath of life as well. This a current picture of myself below, The author of this book. Leith Cunningham

When I see our flag; a feeling of thankfulness, gratefulness and gratitude wells up inside me as it passes by in a parade or I witness it in all of its majesty and proud waving in the breeze hanging from the flagpole in honor of all whom cherish it; how fortunate we all are that our God continues to bless us in a fashion almost beyond our capacity to receive it all. May it continue to wave proudly over the land of the free, because of the brave men and women who have stepped up and made themselves available and willing to die for it in the past, present and future. And may all of those who disrespect and dishonor it to live long enough to have their freedom taken from them.

When I see our flag; passing by in a parade It causes me to stand tall with a feeling of national pride within. It brings goose bumps up my spine and a desire to stand and salute it with respect and honor. Our red white and blue flag with its field of navy blue covered with fifty beautiful white stars that represent our United States of America, reflects the special status that our God has given us, His people, to wave as a symbol, as we acknowledge Him as our Lord and Savior of all creation.

When I see our flag; I give thanks personally that I was fortunate enough to have been born and raised up in this great nation.

When I see our flag; I am reminded again and again of all that have given their own last measure of life in all wars, giving up all of their tomorrows, that the rest of us have the privilege of enjoying all of our today's together with our family.

When I see our flag; I am reminded of all of my friends, buddies and comrades that had to die in some horrible, grotesque and brutal fashion at the hands of our enemies that we engaged in combat on the battlefields of Korea, and all other wars being fought for the freedom of their occupants, to cherish, love and be thankful for.

When I see our flag; I remember Billy Magee, my good friend and buddy that I joined the U.S. Army and went through basic training together with at Fort Riley, Kansas. He was butchered by the brutal North Korean enemy before he was old enough to drink a legal beer, get married, raise a family or to even vote. I see him yet in my mind's eye and visit his grave often over in Garfield cemetery. He will not be forgotten by me in my lifetime. My flag display all around my home and property brings back remembrance and honor of those that were killed in combat on the battlefields of Korea beside me. As well as all others that left their homes in all wars; to return again to their loved ones in a flag draped coffin.

When I see our flag; I remember Ernie Lee, my closest buddy on the frontline during the battle of Wonju, Korea. We were in the middle of an all-out assault against the attacking Communist Chinese Army. We were being swarmed over by Chinese soldiers carrying Russian Burp Guns. They can fire 900 rounds a minute, they have the capability of filling the air with a lot of hot lead. And especially so if they are coming at you while using a half dozen or so Burp Guns at once. It is a sound that gets your attention and brings cold chills up your spine and will raise the hair up on the back of your neck. I came over this ridge and looking off to my left, a medic had Ernie propped up against a tree and was ripping off his upper body clothing, he had been hit with a burst from a Russian Burp Gun. The snow covered ground was covered with

Ernie's blood. I had to keep moving, the blood saturated drifted snow reminding me of when my father would butcher a hog during the winter months back home. I never seen or heard anything about Ernie after that, I didn't know if he lived or died, but the support and comradery of my only good buddy left in combat was gone and life on the frontlines became even harder after that.

When I see our flag; I have vivid recall of comrades fighting by my side that I didn't even know their name. Being shot stone cold dead and dropping in their tracks or being badly wounded and needing help, or blown all to hell. Then feeling guilty because I was glad it was them and not me. Thinking and reasoning that maybe the god of war had taken his quota for the day and I would live to see another tomorrow.

When I see our flag; I still see the last haunting look in an enemy's eyes as he dies by my feet or the steam rising out of his spent dead and mangled body. Another human being made in the image and likeness of God as same as myself. Doing for his country the exact same thing that is being required of each one of us.

When I see our flag; I remember my father telling of his combat service against Germany in trench warfare somewhere in France, during the first world war. He had also been wounded in action by shrapnel and suffered from being exposed to mustard gas, for which he received the Purple Heart. He was unable to smell or taste anything for the rest of his life.

When I see our flag; I am reminded of myself and three other brothers serving in the military to insure peace and freedom. Myself and brother Ted in frontline combat. Ted died last July as the last man alive having served in the 101st Glider Infantry during WW11.

When I see our flag; I remember my uncles, cousin's other relatives and friends serving in WW11 when I was growing up. I remember parents displaying stars in their windows to indicate how many of their family members were serving to protect our freedom at that time.

When I see our flag; I remember the double deck plane load of horribly wounded; mangled and broken bodies evacuated back to our great nation with me during March of 1951.

When I see our flag; I specifically have vivid recall of the boy that sat next to me on the plane. He had, had his jaw blown off and was missing part of his face. He was happy to be going home and all he wanted to do was talk; but I couldn't understand a word he was saying, that came gurgling out of a hole in his neck. I wonder still about how he was received by a wife, a girlfriend or society that might be unable to accept the horribly disfigured face of the boy that left to go to war whole; and the different one that would come back home.

When I see our flag; I remember too, on that same plane loaded to maximum with mangled human flesh of every nature and description. A pilot lay in the isle in a full body cast. Only part of his face was visible as he quietly lay there in sedation. In total dependence of his care givers. The smell of rotting flesh inside his cast along with that of other badly wounded men on the plane, was nearly unbearable at times, still everyone was happy; we were going home.

When I see our flag; I remember another young red haired boy that sat in the isle of the plane also. He was trussed up in a strait jacket to keep him from hurting himself or others. His mind had completely lost any human function or resemblance, he would snarl and snap at anyone near him, as his face would become twisted and demonic in appearance, he seemed more like an animal as opposed to human.

When I see our flag; I remember the whole plane was loaded with cases just like this and worse. There were many plane loads before us and many more to follow. There were 103,284 wounded and another 8,196 of our men missing in action during the Korean war.

When I see our flag; I remember well and have a vivid recall of being evacuated out of combat, off the Korean battlefield on March 7th 1951 for frost bitten feet. Then two days later on March 9th being loaded on a C-47 and flown to an Army hospital in Osaka, Japan. It was the happiest day of my life. The kill or be killed 24/7 duty in below zero weather without proper food or clothing was over for me, only the memory continues to cling and fasten itself inside my mind and heart. Wars my brothers, sisters, and friends are absolute insanity. Every ounce of everything inside causing life inside you to keep going will be taken out, leaving an empty and hollow shell of emaciated boys in uniform in their teens to struggle and freeze or starve to death because some old men in a room thousands of miles away sticking pins in maps inside their cozy war rooms, eating steak and drinking champagne while waiting on the exotic dancing girls to come in and entertain them, decide to make war while the young have to die in them. I weighed barely over one hundred pounds when I arrived in the hospital in Osaka, Japan.

When I see our flag; I have grateful and thankful recall of spending most all of the next year recovering in Percy Jones Army Hospital in Battle Creek, Michigan. Seeing first-hand the effects of war on human bodies and minds that are being in the process of being put back together again the best that can be done and making do with whatever is left of the one being dealt with. Many to live out the rest of their lives being warehoused in the back room of some VA hospital or other facility.

When I see our flag; It means a lot to me to know I had a part in making history and being a part of keeping the nation where God has placed me, a land of freedom and plenty. Even though in reality I consider myself to be an ambassador for Jesus Christ and the kingdom of God. In essence I swear allegiance to God and His kingdom first, while doing the best that I can living here and abiding by our nations laws that do not go contrary to the laws of God as I understand them. Our flag reminds me of the blessings of God on myself and my family. Our flag encourages and inspires me and has a special place in my heart and mind.

When I see our flag; in the evening after everything has been done, when the shadows are growing longer as we sit outside, Nancy and myself sitting in the cool gentle breeze, drinking cool water together and recounting our blessings of sixty-seven years of marriage, enjoying the many flags surrounding us, on flag poles and everywhere else we can find a place for one more to be displayed in as a memorial to those that died for freedom. The sight and sounds of flags as they unfurl, whip and snap in the early night air and the fragrant smell of God's creation becomes even more pronounced and pungent. The sound of the breeze as it blows through the big white pine trees in our yard, along with its distinct odor. I begin to imagine being a kid at home again before all of the kill or be killed savagery and never-ending blood and gore of war began to shape my life. I imagine hearing a lone distant coyote yip and howl down in the swamp back of our home or the comforting song of the whippoorwills as they keep busy flitting here and there filling their bellies with insects. Then chasing after the lightening bugs that were always a fascination to my brother and myself. Then to imagine hearing someone playing the lonely bugle taps out there in the distance against the disappearing sun, for all that have paid the ultimate cost for freedom. My eyes get moist as these thoughts run through my mind and stay lodged in my heart, in honor and remembrance of all who have paid the ultimate price for freedom.

When I see our flag; it gives me a personal determination to make sure I never take freedom for granted. That I be filled with grateful and enduring thankfulness for all of those before me who gave their lives up for freedom, all that served with me in Korea and in all other wars that died on foreign soil and all who will step up in the future when needed, to fight and to die if necessary to provide a place on this earth where kids of our future generations will also be able to live in peace and freedom. May God bless our nation, and may we be deserving of it. Until such time as He talks about in His Word when He sends Jesus Christ back to usher in His Kingdom on earth. Mankind will no longer make war, one with another. Peace and freedom will exist forever after. We all should be praying; Thy kingdom come, thy will be done, on earth as it is in heaven. But in our present state of never-ending wars, I will leave you with this.

When I see our flag; I thank God that He has given us a president in Donald J. Trump who is keeping his word to make America great again in every way possible, even though the opposing branch of government are obstructing his loyal efforts at every turn in the road, yet he has prevailed. President Trump is a true patriot that loves our country and everything he does and says points in that direction. President Trump has done more to promote, uplift and raise awareness of our beautiful red, white and blue flag and what it stands for then any other person in my lifetime. May our Almighty God of all that is, give us another four years of leadership from a dedicate American that has worked for and earned the honor due a leader of his stature and resolve to keep America great, in the work he has begun in that direction.

On this 4th day of July 2019; I want to dedicate all of the many American flags that are being displayed here at our home and all around our yard, as a memorial with my personal thankfulness for all veterans of all military branches of services. All of those having served in war or in peacetime. Thank you for your service to our country and to each one of us personally. May God bless our nation by His steady hand from above. I pray that your will be done on earth as it is in heaven, that your kingdom come quickly to replace this present evil age with your righteous rule that will never end. In Christ' name I pray. Amen!

I have decided to close this segment of the book out with a true story that I was told by a waitress at the restaurant we have breakfast at every morning. I think it fits well with malcontents and haters of our flag and country. Mary, the waitress had noticed my cowboy hat which announced my service in the Korean War. She noticed the guy sitting in front of us also wearing a cap with words on it, being a social person that likes to compliment folks, she asked him if he had been in the service too? He told her no, that he had, had back problems that kept him out of the military. She then asked him what problem he had with his back? He told her that he had a yellow streak going all the way down it. With that I rest my case.

WAR: And The After Effects On Those Doing The Dirty Work Of Killing

-A part of war that those at home do not have to bother thinking much about-

A frontline combat soldier being comforted by another, during the Korean War. He may have witnessed a buddy being blown all to pieces, it could have been his first killing of another human being made in the image of God, maybe a kid, a little boy or innocent little girl, in the wrong place at the wrong time. Or the gut wrenching mental and emotional pain and trauma of just seeing and being too much a part of the death and dismemberment of comrades and enemy alike, just a normal and ongoing buildup of the insanity of war that overloads the mind. This soldiers war will follow him to his grave if he survived Korea. His mind-numbing war experiences will have moved inside and out of sight and out of reach of family and friends that have noticed he had gone away a certain kind of person, and came back an altogether different one. Yet, for the most part he is left to deal with it alone, and behind closed doors.

For some, death can be a sought after and desired relief. Those that did make it home, often had to hide their uniforms and blend into a society that treated them like rabid mad dog killers that were not good enough to bother spitting on. The never Trumpers and flag haters of today may someday cry bitter tears of remorse, if the socialist movement brings to power the likes of what we see on television today in their attempt at turning our country into a total welfare state where everything is free. While we will be going headlong down the tube like so many socialist nations have gone before us. Remembering things as they are today will not seem all that bad when they who conquer and defeat us cram you into boxcars and send you out to work the farms. To late you will have awakened out of your sleepy-eyed condition of stupidity and gullibility. The only thing left will be to remind folks around you picking cotton from morning unto darkness, to be sent to Germany or some other nation to make more military uniforms for the elite master race, of how good things used to be. But oh well! What do I know?

www.ingramcontent.com/pod-product-compliance
Lightning Source LLC
LaVergne TN
LVHW060152080526
838202LV00052B/4139